CRACKNELL'S STATUTES

Contract, Tort and Remedies

Fourth Edition

D G CRACKNELL
LLB, of the Middle Temple, Barrister

D1354322

OLD BAILEY PRESS

OLD BAILEY PRESS
at Holborn College, Woolwich Road,
Charlton, London, SE7 8LN

First published 1997
Fourth edition 2005

ISBN 1 85836 583 X

British Library Cataloguing-in-Publication Data

A catalogue record for this book is available from the
British Library.

Printed and bound in Great Britain

CONTENTS

Contents

Contents

PREFACE

THIS book sets out the text of those statutory provisions a knowledge of which is essential for the purpose of most Contract and Torts examinations. Whenever a statutory provision is here included, the text incorporates any repeals, amendments or substitutions made (and in force) on or before 1 January 2005. A note at the end of the Act or statutory instrument indicates the source of any changes.

Many changes have been made in this edition. The new material includes the liability provisions of the Countryside and Rights of Way Act 2000 (which came into force on 19 September 2004) and the addition to the Highways Act 1980 made by the Railways and Transport Safety Act 2003 concerning a highway authority's duty in relation to snow and ice.

Important changes have been made to the Damages Act 1996 by the Courts Act 2003, but since the relevant provisions were not in force on 1 January 2005, they have been included in the Appendix and reference is made to them in appropriate places in the main text. The Appendix also includes, for the same reason, provisions of the Health and Social Care (Community Health and Standards) Act 2003 relating to the recovery of NHS charges.

Suggestions as to statutes or statutory instruments, or provisions of them, which could helpfully be included in future editions would always be most gratefully received.

ALPHABETICAL TABLE OF STATUTES AND REGULATIONS

STATUTE OF FRAUDS 1677
(29 Car 2 c 3)

4   No action upon a special promise unless agreement, etc, be in writing, and signed

No action shall be brought whereby to charge the defendant upon any special promise to answer for the debt default or miscarriages of another person unless the agreement upon which such action shall be brought or some memorandum or note thereof shall be in writing and signed by the party to be charged therewith or some other person thereunto by him lawfully authorised.

As amended by the Statute Law Revision Act 1883; Law of Property Act 1925, s207, Schedule 7; Statute Law Revision Act 1948; the Law Reform (Enforcement of Contracts) Act 1954, s1.

GAMING ACT 1710
(9 Anne c 19)

1 Security given for money, etc, won by gaming or for repayment of money lent for gaming void

All notes bills bonds judgments mortgages or other securities or conveyances whatsoever given granted drawn or entered into or executed by any person or persons whatsoever where the whole or any part of the consideration of such conveyances or securities shall be for any money or other valuable thing whatsoever won by gaming or playing at cards dice tables tennis bowles or other game or games whatsoever or by betting on the sides or hands of such as do game at any of the games aforesaid or for the reimbursing or repaying any money knowingly lent or advanced for such gaming or betting as aforesaid or lent or advanced at the time and place of such play to any person or persons so gaming or betting as aforesaid or that shall during such play, so play or bett shall be utterly void frustrate and of none effect to all intents and purposes whatsoever any statute law or usage to the contrary thereof in any wise notwithstanding.

As amended by the Gaming Act 1835, s3.

FIRES PREVENTION (METROPOLIS) ACT 1774
(14 Geo 3 c 78)

86   No action to lie against a person where the fire accidentally begins

And no action, suit or process whatever shall be had, maintained or prosecuted against any person in whose house, chamber, stable, barn or other building, or on whose estate any fire shall accidentally begin, nor shall any recompense be made by such person for any damage suffered thereby, any law, usage or custom to the contrary notwithstanding provided that no contract or agreement made between landlord and tenant shall be hereby defeated or made void.

As amended by the Statute Law Revision Acts 1861, 1888, 1948 and 1958.

LIBEL ACT 1792
(32 Geo 3 c 60)

Whereas doubts have arisen whether on the trial of an indictment or information for the making or publishing any libel, where an issue or issues are joined between the King and the defendant or defendants, on the plea of not guilty pleaded, it be competent to the jury impanelled to try the same to give their verdict upon the whole matter in issue:

1   On the trial of an indictment for a libel the jury may give a general verdict upon the whole matter put in issue

On every such trial the jury sworn to try the issue may give a general verdict of guilty or not guilty upon the whole matter out in issue upon such indictment or information, and shall not be required or directed by the court or judge before whom such indictment or information shall be tried to find the defendant or defendants guilty merely on the proof of the publication by such defendant or defendants of the paper charged to be a libel, and of the sense ascribed to the same in such indictment or information.

2   The court shall give their opinion and directions

Provided always, that on every such trial the court or judge before whom such indictment or information shall be tried shall, according to their or his discretion, give their or his opinion and directions to the jury on the matter in issue between the King and the defendant or defendants, in like manner as in other criminal cases.

STATUTE OF FRAUDS
AMENDMENT ACT 1828
(9 Geo 4 c 14)

6 Action not maintainable on representations of character, etc, unless they be in writing signed by the party chargeable

No action shall be brought whereby to charge any person upon or by reason of any representation or assurance made or given concerning or relating to the character, conduct, credit, ability, trade, or dealings of any other person, to the intent or purpose that such other person may obtain credit, money, or goods upon, unless such representation or assurance be made in writing, signed by the party to be charged therewith.

GAMING ACT 1835
(5 & 6 Will 4 c 41)

1   Securities given for considerations arising out of illegal transactions not to be void, but to be deemed to have been given for an illegal consideration

Every note bill or mortgage which if this Act had not been passed would, by virtue of the said several lastly herein-before mentioned Acts [including the Gaming Act 1710] or any of them, have been absolutely void, shall be deemed and taken to have been made, drawn, accepted, given or executed for an illegal consideration; and the said several Acts shall have the same force and effect which they would respectively have had, if, instead of enacting that any such note, bill, or mortgage should be absolutely void, such Acts had respectively provided that every such note, bill or mortgage should be deemed and taken to have been made, drawn, accepted, given, or executed for an illegal consideration: Provided always, that nothing herein contained shall prejudice or affect any note, bill, or mortgage which would have been good and valid if this Act had not been passed.

As amended by the Statute Law Revision Act 1874; Statute Law Revision (No 2) Act 1890.

JUDGMENTS ACT 1838
(1 & 2 Vict c 110)

17   Judgment debts to carry interest

(1) Every judgment debt shall carry interest at the rate of 8 per cent per annum from such time as shall be prescribed by rules of court until the same shall be satisfied, and such interest may be levied under a writ of execution on such judgment.

(2) Rules of court may provide for the court to disallow all or part of any interest otherwise payable under subsection (1).

As amended by the Procedure Acts Repeal Act 1879, s2, Schedule, Pt I; Statute Law Revision (No 2) Act 1888; Judgment Debts (Rate of Interest) Order 1993; Civil Procedure (Modification of Enactments) Order 1998, art 3.

PARLIAMENTARY PAPERS ACT 1840
(3 & 4 Vict c 9)

1   Proceedings, criminal or civil, against persons for publication of papers printed by order of Parliament, to be stayed upon delivery of a certificate and affidavit to the effect that such publication is by order of either House of Parliament

It shall and may be lawful for any person or persons who now is or are, or hereafter shall be, a defendant or defendants in any civil or criminal proceeding commenced or prosecuted in any manner soever, for or on account or in respect of the publication of any such report, paper, votes, or proceedings by such person or persons, or by his, her, or their servant or servants, by or under the authority of either House of Parliament, to bring before the court in which such proceeding shall have been or shall be so commenced or prosecuted, or before any judge of the same (if one of the superior courts at Westminster), first giving twenty-four hours' notice of his intention so to do to the prosecutor or plaintiff in such proceeding, a certificate under the hand of the lord high chancellor of Great Britain, or the lord keeper of the great seal, or of the speaker of the House of Lords, for the time being, or of the clerk of the Parliaments, or of the speaker of the House of Commons, or of the clerk of the same house, stating that the report, paper, votes, or proceedings, as the case may be, in respect whereof such civil or criminal proceeding shall have been commended or prosecuted, was published by such person or persons, or by his, her, or their servant or servants, by order or under the authority of the House of Lords or of the House of Commons, as the case may be, together with an affidavit verifying such certificate, and such court or judge shall thereupon immediately stay such civil or criminal proceeding; and the same, and every writ or process issued therein, shall be deemed and taken to be finally put an end to, determined, and superseded by virtue of this Act.

2   Proceedings to be stayed when commenced in respect of a copy of an authenticated report, etc

In case of any civil or criminal proceeding hereafter to be commenced or prosecuted for or on account or in respect of the publication of any copy of such report, paper, votes, or proceedings, it shall be lawful for the defendant or defendants at any stage of the proceedings to lay before the court or judge such report, paper, votes, or proceedings, and such copy, with an affidavit verifying such report, paper, votes or proceedings, and the correctness of such copy, and the court or judge shall immediately stay such civil or criminal proceeding; and the same, and every writ or process issued therein, shall be and shall be deemed and taken to be finally put an end to, determined and superseded by virtue of this Act.

3   In proceedings for printing any extract or abstract of a paper, it may be shewn that such extract was bona fide made

It shall be lawful in any civil or criminal proceeding to be commenced or prosecuted for printing any extract from or abstract of such report, paper, votes, or proceedings, to give in evidence such report, paper, votes or proceedings, and to show that such extract or abstract was published bona fide and without malice; and if such shall be the opinion of the jury, a verdict of not guilty shall be entered for the defendant or defendants.

4   Act not to affect the privileges of Parliament

Provided always that nothing herein contained shall be deemed or taken, or held or construed, directly or indirectly, by implication or otherwise, to affect the privileges of Parliament in any manner whatsoever.

As amended by the Statute Law Revision (No 2) Acts 1888 and 1890; Statute Law Revision Act 1958.

LIBEL ACT 1843
(6 & 7 Vict c 96)

1 Offer of an apology admissible in evidence in mitigation of damages in action for defamation

In any action for defamation it shall be lawful for the defendant (after notice in writing of his intention so to do, duly given to the plaintiff at the time of filing or delivering the plea in such action,) to give evidence, in mitigation of damages, that he made or offered an apology to the plaintiff for such defamation before the commencement of the action, or as soon afterwards as he had an opportunity of doing so, in case the action shall have been commenced before there was an opportunity of making or offering such apology.

2 In an action against a newspaper for libel, the defendant may plead that it was inserted without malice and without negligence, and that he has published or offered to publish an apology

In an action for libel contained in any public newspaper or other periodical publication it shall be competent to the defendant to plead that such libel was inserted in such newspaper or other periodical publication without actual malice, and without gross negligence, and that before the commencement of the action, or at the earliest opportunity afterwards, he inserted in such newspaper or other periodical publication a full apology for the said libel, or, if the newspaper or periodical publication in which the said libel appeared should be ordinarily published at intervals exceeding one week, had offered to publish the said apology in any newspaper or periodical publication to be selected by the plaintiff in such action; and to such plea to such action it shall be competent to the plaintiff to reply generally, denying the whole of such plea.

As amended by the Statute Law Revision Acts 1891 and 1892.

LIBEL ACT 1845
(8 & 9 Vict c 75)

2   Defendant not to plead matters allowed by the Libel Act 1843 without payment into court

It shall not be competent to any defendant in such action, whether in England or Ireland, to file any such plea, without at the same time making a payment of money into court by way of amends but every such plea so filed without payment of money into court shall be deemed a nullity, and may be treated as such by the plaintiff in the action.

As amended by the Statute Law Revision Act 1891.

GAMING ACT 1845
(8 & 9 Vict c 109)

18 Contracts by way of gaming to be void, and wagers or sums deposited with stakeholders not to be recoverable at law – Saving for subscriptions for prizes

All contracts or agreements, whether by parole or in writing, by way of gaming or wagering, shall be null and void; and no suit shall be brought or maintained in any court of law and equity for recovering any sum of money or valuable thing alleged to have been won upon any wager, or which shall have been deposited in the hands of any person to abide the event on which any wager shall have been made: Provided always, that this enactment shall not be deemed to apply to any subscription or contribution, or agreement to subscribe or contribute, for or towards any plate, prize, or sum of money to be awarded to the winner or winners of any lawful game, sport, pastime, or exercise.

As amended by the Statute Law Revision Act 1891.

BILLS OF EXCHANGE ACT 1882
(45 & 46 Vict c 61)

3   Bills of exchange defined

(1) A bill of exchange is an unconditional order in writing, addressed by one person to another, signed by the person giving it, requiring the person to whom it is addressed to pay on demand or at a fixed or determinable future time a sum certain in money to or to the order of a specified person, or to bearer.

(2) An instrument which does not comply with these conditions, or which orders any act to be done in addition to the payment of money, is not a bill of exchange.

(3) An order to pay out of a particular fund is not unconditional within the meaning of this section; but an unqualified order to pay, coupled with (a) an indication of a particular fund out of which the drawee is to re-imburse himself or a particular account to be debited with the amount, or (b) a statement of the transaction which gives rise to the bill, is unconditional.

(4) A bill is not invalid by reason –

    (a) That it is not dated;

    (b) That it does not specify the value given, or that any value has been given therefor;

    (c) That it does not specify the place where it is drawn or the place where it is payable.

17   Definition and requisites of acceptance

(1) The acceptance of a bill is the signification by the drawee of his assent to the order of the drawer.

(2) An acceptance is invalid unless it complies with the following conditions, namely:

    (a) It must be written on the bill and be signed by the drawee. The mere signature of the drawee without additional works is sufficient.

    (b) It must not express that the drawee will perform his promise by any other means than the payment of money.

26   Person signing as agent or in representative capacity

(1) Where a person signs a bill as a drawer, indorser, or acceptor, and adds words

to his signature, indicating that he signs for or on behalf of a principal, or in a representative character, he is not personally liable thereon; but the mere addition to his signature of words describing him as an agent, or as filling a representative character, does not exempt him from personal liability.

(2) In determining whether a signature on a bill is that of the principal or that of the agent by whose hand it is written, the construction most favourable to the validity of the instrument shall be adopted.

27   Value and holder for value

(1) Valuable consideration for a bill may be constituted by, –

    (a) Any consideration sufficient to support a simple contract;

    (b) An antecedent debt or liability. Such a debt or liability is deemed valuable consideration whether the bill is payable on demand or at a future time.

(2) Where value has at any time been given for a bill the holder is deemed to be a holder for value as regards the acceptor and all parties to the bill who became parties prior to such time.

73   Cheque defined

A cheque is a bill of exchange drawn on a banker payable on demand.

Except as otherwise provided in this Part, the provisions of this Act applicable to a bill of exchange payable on demand apply to a cheque.

83   Promissory note defined

(1) A promissory note is an unconditional promise in writing made by one person to another signed by the maker, engaging to pay, on demand or at a fixed or determinable future time, a sum certain in money, to, or to the order of, a specified person or to bearer.

(2) An instrument in the form of a note payable to maker's order is not a note within the meaning of this section unless and until it is indorsed by the maker.

(3) A note is not invalid by reason only that it contains also a pledge of collateral security with authority to sell or dispose thereof.

(4) A note which is, or on the face of it purports to be, both made and payable within the British Islands is an inland note. Any other note is a foreign one.

LAW OF LIBEL AMENDMENT ACT 1888
(51 & 52 Vict c 64)

1   Interpretation

In the construction of this Act the word 'newspaper' shall have the same meaning as in the Newspaper Libel and Registration Act 1881.

5   Consolidation of actions

It shall be competent for a judge or the court, upon an application by or on behalf of two or more defendants in actions in respect to the same, or substantially the same, libel brought by one and the same person, to make an order for the consolidation of such actions, so that they shall be tried together; and after such order has been made, and before the trial of the said actions, the defendants in any new actions instituted in respect to the same, or substantially the same, libel shall also be entitled to be joined in a common action upon a joint application being made by such new defendants and the defendants in the actions already consolidated. In a consolidated action under this section the jury shall assess the whole amount of the damages (if any) in one sum, but a separate verdict shall be taken for or against each defendant in the same way as if the actions consolidated had been tried separately; and if the jury shall have found a verdict against the defendant or defendants in more than one of the actions so consolidated, they shall proceed to apportion the amount of damages which they shall have so found between and against the said last-mentioned defendants; and the judge at the trial, if he awards to the plaintiff the costs of the action, shall thereupon make such order as he shall deem just for the apportionment of such costs between and against such defendants.

NB The 1881 Act provides that the word 'newspaper' means 'any paper containing public news, intelligence, or occurrences, or any remarks or observations therein printed for sale, and published in England or Ireland periodically, or in parts or numbers at intervals not exceeding twenty-six days between the publication of any two such papers, parts, or numbers. Also any paper printed in order to be dispersed, and made public weekly or oftener, or at intervals not exceeding twenty-six days, containing only or principally advertisements.'

FACTORS ACT 1889
(52 & 53 Vict c 45)

1 Definitions

For the purposes of this Act:

(1) The expression 'mercantile agent' shall mean a mercantile agent having in the customary course of his business as such agent authority either to sell goods, or to consign goods for the purpose of sale, or to buy goods, or to raise money on the security of goods;

(2) A person shall be deemed to be in possession of goods or of the documents of title to goods, where the goods or documents are in his actual custody or are held by any other person subject to his control or for him or on his behalf;

(3) The expression 'goods' shall include wares and merchandise;

(4) The expression 'document of title' shall include any bill of lading, dock warrant, warehouse-keeper's certificate, and warrant or order for the delivery of goods, and any other document used in the ordinary course of business as proof of the possession or control of goods, or authorising or purporting to authorise, either by endorsement or by delivery, the possessor of the document to transfer or receive goods thereby represented;

(5) The expression 'pledge' shall include any contract pledging, or giving a lien or security on, goods, whether in consideration of an original advance or of any further or continuing advance or of any pecuniary liability;

(6) The expression 'person' shall include any body of persons corporate or unincorporate.

2 Powers of mercantile agent with respect to disposition of goods

(1) Where a mercantile agent is, with the consent of the owner, in possession of goods or of the document of title to goods, any sale, pledge, or other disposition of the goods, made by him when acting in the ordinary course of business of a mercantile agent, shall, subject to the provisions of this Act, be as valid as if he were expressly authorised by the owner of the goods to make the same; provided that the person taking under the disposition acts in good faith, and has not at the time of the disposition notice that the person making the disposition has not authority to make the same.

(2) Where a mercantile agent has, with the consent of the owner, been in possession of goods or of the documents of title to goods, any sale, pledge, or other disposition, which would have been valid if the consent had continued, shall be valid notwithstanding the determination of the consent: provided that the person taking under the disposition has not at the time thereof notice that the consent has been determined.

(3) Where a mercantile agent has obtained possession of any documents of title to goods by reason of his being or having been, with the consent of the owner, in possession of the goods represented thereby, or of any other documents of title to the goods, his possession of the first-mentioned documents shall, for the purposes of this Act, be deemed to be with the consent of the owner.

(4) For the purposes of this Act the consent of the owner shall be presumed in the absence of evidence to the contrary.

3   Effect of pledges of documents of title

A pledge of the documents of title to goods shall be deemed to be a pledge of the goods.

4   Pledge for antecedent debt

Where a mercantile agent pledges goods as security for a debt or liability due from the pledgor to the pledgee before the time of the pledge, the pledgee shall acquire no further right to the goods than could have been enforced by the pledgor at the time of the pledge.

5   Rights acquired by exchange of goods or documents

The consideration necessary for the validity of a sale, pledge, or other disposition, of goods, in pursuance of this Act, may be either a payment in cash, or the delivery or transfer of other goods, or of a document of title to goods, or of a negotiable security, or any other valuable consideration; but where goods are pledged by a mercantile agent in consideration of the delivery or transfer of other goods, or of a document of title to goods, or of a negotiable security, the pledgee shall acquire no right or interest in the goods so pledged in excess of the value of the goods, documents, or security when so delivered or transferred in exchange.

6   Agreements through clerks, etc

For the purposes of this Act an agreement made with a mercantile agent through a clerk or other person authorised in the ordinary course of business to make contracts of sale or pledge on his behalf shall be deemed to be an agreement with the agent.

7   Provisions as to consignors and consignees

(1) Where the owner of goods has given possession of the goods to another person for

the purpose of consignment or sale, or has shipped the goods in the name of another person, and the consignee of the goods has not had notice that such person is not the owner of the goods, the consignee shall, in respect of advances made to or for the use of such person, have the same lien on the goods as if such person were the owner of the goods, and may transfer any such lien to another person.

(2) Nothing in this section shall limit or affect the validity of any sale, pledge, or disposition, by a mercantile agent.

PARTNERSHIP ACT 1890
(53 & 54 Vict c 39)

1 Definition of partnership

(1) Partnership is the relation which subsists between persons carrying on a business in common with a view of profit.

(2) But the relation between members of any company or association which is –

(a) registered as a company under the Companies Act 1862 or any other Acts of Parliament for the time being in force and relating to the registration of joint stock companies; or

(b) formed or incorporated by or in pursuance of any other Act of Parliament or letters patent, or Royal Charter;

is not a partnership within the meaning of this Act.

4 Meaning of firm

(1) Persons who have entered into partnership with one another are for the purposes of this Act called collectively a firm, and the name under which their business is carried on is called the firm-name. ...

5 Power of partner to bind the firm

Every partner is an agent of the firm and his other partners for the purpose of the business of the partnership; and the acts of every partner who does any act for carrying on in the usual way business of the kind carried on by the firm of which he is a member bind the firm and his partners, unless the partner so acting has in fact no authority to act for the firm in the particular matter, and the person with whom he is dealing either knows that he has no authority, or does not know or believe him to be a partner.

6 Partners bound by acts on behalf of firm

An act or instrument relating to the business of the firm done or executed in the firm-name, or in any other manner showing an intention to bind the firm, by any person thereto authorised, whether a partner or not, is binding on the firm and all the partners. Provided that this section shall not affect any general rule of law relating to the execution of deeds or negotiable instruments.

7   Partner using credit of firm for private purposes

Where one partner pledges the credit of the firm for a purpose apparently not connected with the firm's ordinary course of business, the firm is not bound, unless he is in fact specially authorised by the other partners; but this section does not affect any personal liability incurred by an individual partner.

8   Effect of notice that firm will not be bound by acts of partner

If it has been agreed between the partners that any restriction shall be placed on the power of any one or more of them to bind the firm, no act done in contravention of the agreement is binding on the firm with respect to persons having notice of the agreement.

9   Liability of partners

Every partner in a firm is liable jointly with the other partners, and in Scotland severally also, for all debts and obligations of the firm incurred while he is a partner; and after his death his estate is also severally liable in a due course of administration for such debts and obligations, so far as they remain unsatisfied, but subject in England or Ireland to the prior payment of his separate debts.

10   Liability of the firm for wrongs

Where, by any wrongful act or omission of any partner acting in the ordinary course of the business of the firm, or with the authority of his co-partners, loss or injury is caused to any person not being a partner in the firm, or any penalty is incurred, the firm is liable therefore to the same extent as the partner so acting or omitting to act.

11   Misapplication of money or property received for or in custody of the firm

In the following cases; namely –

(a) Where one partner acting within the scope of his apparent authority receives the money or property of a third person and misapplies it; and

(b) Where a firm in the course of its business receives money or property of a third person, and the money or property so received is misapplied by one or more of the partners while it is in the custody of the firm;

the firm is liable to make good the loss.

12   Liability for wrongs joint and several

Every partner is liable jointly with his co-partners and also severally for everything for which the firm while he is a partner therein becomes liable under either of the two last preceding sections.

45   Definition [of ...] 'business'

In this Act, unless the contrary intention appears, – ...

The expression 'business' includes every trade occupation or profession.

As amended by the Statute Law (Repeals) Act 1998.

SLANDER OF WOMEN ACT 1891
(54 & 55 Vict c 51)

1   Amendment of law

Words spoken and published which impute unchastity or adultery to any woman or girl shall not require special damage to render them actionable. Provided always, that in any action for words spoken and made actionable by this Act, a plaintiff shall not recover more costs than damages, unless the judge shall certify that there was reasonable ground for bringing the action.

As amended by the Statute Law Revision Act 1908.

GAMING ACT 1892
(55 & 56 Vict c 9)

1 Promises to repay sums paid under contracts void by the Gaming Act 1845 to be null and void

Any promise, express or implied, to pay any person any sum of money paid by him under or in respect of any contract or agreement rendered null and void by the Gaming Act 1845, or to pay any sum of money by way of commission, fee, reward, or otherwise in respect of any such contract, or of any services in relation thereto or in connexion therewith, shall be null and void, and no action shall be brought or maintained to recover any such sum of money.

RAILWAY FIRES ACT 1905
(5 Edw 7 c 11)

1   Liability of railway companies to make good damage to crops by their engines

(1) When, after this Act comes into operation, damage is caused to agricultural land or to agricultural crops, as in this Act defined, by fire arising from sparks or cinders emitted from any locomotive engine used on a railway, the fact that the engine was used under statutory powers shall not affect liability in an action for such damage.

(2) Where any such damage has been caused through the use of an engine by one company on a railway worked by another company, either company shall be liable in such an action; but, if the action is brought against the company working the railway, that company shall be entitled to be indemnified in respect of their liability by the company by whom the engine was used. ...

(3) This section shall not apply in the case of any action for damage unless the claim for damage in the action does not exceed £3,000 or such greater sum as may for the time being be prescribed by order made by the Secretary of State.

(3A) An order under subsection (3) above shall be made by statutory instrument which shall be subject to annulment in pursuance of a resolution of either House of Parliament. ...

4   Definitions and application

In this Act –

The expression 'agricultural land' includes arable and meadow land and ground used for pastoral purposes or for market or nursery gardens, and plantations and woods and orchards, and also includes any fences on such land, but does not include any moorland or buildings;

The expression 'agricultural crops' includes any crops on agricultural land, whether growing or severed, which are not led or stacked;

The expression 'railway' includes any light railway and any tramway worked by steam power. ...

This Act shall apply to agricultural land under the management of the Commissioners of Woods, and to agricultural crops thereon.

As amended by s38(1) of the Transport Act 1981.

MARINE INSURANCE ACT 1906
(6 Edw 7 c 41)

1   Marine insurance defined

A contract of marine insurance is a contract whereby the insurer undertakes to indemnify the assured, in manner and to the extent thereby agreed, against marine losses, that is to say, the losses incident to marine adventure.

3   Marine adventure and maritime perils defined

(1) Subject to the provisions of this Act, every lawful marine adventure may be the subject of a contract of marine insurance.

(2) In particular there is a marine adventure where –

(a) Any ship goods or other moveables are exposed to maritime perils. Such property is in this Act referred to as 'insurable property';

(b) The earning or acquisition of any freight, passage money, commission, profit, or other pecuniary benefit, or the security for any advances, loan or disbursements, is endangered by the exposure of insurable property to maritime perils;

(c) Any liability to a third party may be incurred by the owner of, or other person interested in or responsible for, insurable property, by reason of maritime perils.

'Maritime perils' means the perils consequent on, or incidental to, the navigation of the sea, that is to say, perils of the seas, fire, war perils, pirates, rovers, thieves, captures, seisures, restraints, and detainments of princes and peoples, jettisons, barratry, and any other perils, either of the like kind or which may be designated by the policy.

4   Avoidance of wagering or gaming contracts

(1) Every contract or marine insurance by way of gaming or wagering is void.

(2) A contract of marine insurance is deemed to be a gaming or wagering contract –

(a) Where the assured has not an insurable interest as defined by this Act, and the contract is entered into with no expectation of acquiring such an interest; or

(b) Where the policy is made 'interest or no interest', or 'without further proof of interest than the policy itself', or 'without benefit of salvage to the insurer', or subject to any other like term:

Provided that, where there is no possibility of salvage, a policy may be effected without benefit of salvage to the insurer.

5 Insurable interest defined

(1) Subject to the provisions of this Act, every person has an insurable interest who is interested in a marine adventure.

(2) In particular a person is interested in a marine adventure where he stands in any legal or equitable relation to the adventure or to any insurable property at risk therein, in consequence of which he may benefit by the safety or due arrival of insurable property, or may be prejudiced by its loss, or damage thereto, or by the detention thereof, or may incur liability in respect thereof.

17 Insurance is uberrimae fidei

A contract of marine insurance is a contract based upon the utmost good faith, and, if the utmost good faith be not observed by either party, the contract may be avoided by the other party.

18 Disclosure by assured

(1) Subject to the provisions of this section, the assured must disclose to the insurer, before the contract is concluded, every material circumstance which is known to the assured, and the assured is deemed to know every circumstance which, in the ordinary course of business, ought to be known by him. If the assured fails to make such disclosure, the insurer may avoid the contract.

(2) Every circumstance is material which would influence the judgment of a prudent insurer in fixing the premium, or determining whether he will take the risk.

(3) In the absence of inquiry the following circumstances need not be disclosed, namely: –

> (a) Any circumstance which diminishes the risk;
>
> (b) Any circumstance which is known or presumed to be known to the insurer. The insurer is presumed to know matters of common notoriety or knowledge, and matters which an insurer in the ordinary course of his business, as such, ought to know;
>
> (c) Any circumstance as to which information is waived by the insurer;
>
> (d) Any circumstance which it is superfluous to disclose by reason of any express or implied warranty.

(4) Whether any particular circumstance, which is not disclosed, be material or not is, in each case, a question of fact.

(5) The term 'circumstance' includes any communication made to, or information received by, the assured.

19   Disclosure by agent effecting insurance

Subject to the provisions of the preceding section as to circumstances which need not be disclosed, where an insurance is effected for the assured by an agent, the agent must disclose to the insurer –

(a) Every material circumstance which is known to himself, and an agent to insure is deemed to know every circumstance which in the ordinary course of business ought to be known by, or to have been communicated to, him; and

(b) Every material circumstance which the assured is bound to disclose, unless it come to his knowledge too late to communicate it to the agent.

20   Representations pending negotiation of contract

(1) Every material representation made by the assured or his agent to the insurer during the negotiations for the contract, and before the contract is concluded, must be true. If it be untrue the insurer may avoid the contract.

(2) A representation is material which would influence the judgment of a prudent insurer in fixing the premium, or determining whether he will take the risk.

(3) A representation may be either a representation as to a matter of fact, or as to a matter of expectation or belief.

(4) A representation as to a matter of fact is true, if it be substantially correct, that is to say, if the difference between what is represented and what is actually correct would not be considered material by a prudent insurer.

(5) A representation as to a matter of expectation or belief is true if it be made in good faith.

(6) A representation may be withdrawn or corrected before the contract is concluded.

(7) Whether a particular representation be material or not is, in each case, a question of fact.

21   When contract is deemed to be concluded

A contract of marine insurance is deemed to be concluded when the proposal of the assured is accepted by the insurer, whether the policy be then issued or not; and, for the purpose of showing when the proposal was accepted, reference may be made to the slip or covering note or other customary memorandum of the contract.

33   Nature of warranty

(1) A warranty, in the following sections relating to warranties, means a promissory warranty, that is to say, a warranty by which the assured undertakes that some particular thing shall or shall not be done, or that some condition shall be fulfilled, or whereby he affirms or negatives the existence of a particular state of facts.

(2) A warranty may be express or implied.

(3) A warranty, as above defined, is a condition which must be exactly complied with, whether it be material to the risk or not. If it be not so complied with, then, subject to any express provision in the policy, the insurer is discharged from liability as from the date of the breach of warranty, but without prejudice to any liability incurred by him before that date.

34   When breach of warranty excused

(1) Non-compliance with a warranty is excused when, by reason of a change of circumstances, the warranty ceases to be applicable to the circumstances of the contract, or when compliance with the warranty is rendered unlawful by any subsequent law.

(2) Where a warranty is broken, the assured cannot avail himself of the defence that the breach has been remedied, and the warranty complied with, before loss.

(3) A breach of warranty may be waived by the insurer.

35   Express warranties

(1) An express warranty may be in any form of words from which the intention to warrant is to be inferred.

(2) An express warranty must be included in, or written upon, the policy, or must be contained in some document incorporated by reference into the policy.

(3) An express warranty does not exclude an implied warranty, unless it be inconsistent therewith.

36   Warranty of neutrality

(1) Where insurable property, whether ship or goods, is expressly warranted neutral, there is an implied condition that the property shall have a neutral character at the commencement of the risk, and that, so far as the assured can control the matter, its neutral character shall be preserved during the risk.

(2) Where a ship is expressly warranted 'neutral' there is also an implied condition that, so far as the assured can control the matter, she shall be properly documented, that is to say, that she shall carry the necessary papers to establish her neutrality, and that she shall not falsify or suppress her papers, or use simulated papers. If any loss occurs through breach of this condition, the insurer may avoid the contract.

37   No implied warranty of nationality

There is no implied warranty as to the nationality of a ship, or that her nationality shall not be changed during the risk.

38   Warranty of good safety

Where the subject-matter insured is warranted 'well' or 'in good safety' on a particular day, it is sufficient if it be safe at any time during that day.

39 Warranty of seaworthiness of ship

(1) In a voyage policy there is an implied warranty that at the commencement of the voyage the ship shall be seaworthy for the purpose of the particular adventure insured.

(2) Where the policy attaches while the ship is in port, there is also an implied warranty that she shall, at the commencement of the risk, be reasonably fit to encounter the ordinary perils of the port.

(3) Where the policy relates to a voyage which is performed in different stages, during which the ship requires different kinds of or further preparation or equipment, there is an implied warranty that at the commencement of each stage the ship is seaworthy in respect of such preparation or equipment for the purposes of that stage.

(4) A ship is deemed to be seaworthy when she is reasonably fit in all respects to encounter the ordinary perils of the seas of the adventure insured.

(5) In a time policy there is no implied warranty that the ship shall be seaworthy at any stage of the adventure, but where, with the privity of the assured, the ship is sent to sea in an unseaworthy state, the insurer is not liable for any loss attributable to unseaworthiness.

40 No implied warranty that goods are seaworthy

(1) In a policy on goods or other moveables there is no implied warranty that the goods or moveables are seaworthy.

(2) In a voyage policy on goods or other moveables there is an implied warranty that at the commencement of the voyage the ship is not only seaworthy as a ship, but also that she is reasonably fit to carry the goods or other moveables to the destination contemplated by the policy.

41 Warranty of legality

There is an implied warranty that the adventure insured is a lawful one, and that, so far as the assured can control the matter, the adventure shall be carried out in a lawful manner.

42 Implied condition as to the commencement of risk

(1) Where the subject-matter is insured by a voyage policy 'at and from' or 'from' a particular place, it is not necessary that the ship should be at that place when the contract is concluded, but there is an implied condition that the adventure shall be commenced within a reasonable time, and that if the adventure be not so commenced the insurer may avoid the contract.

(2) The implied condition may be negatived by showing that the delay was caused by circumstances known to the insurer before the contract was concluded, or by showing that he waived the condition.

86   Ratification by assured

Where a contract of marine insurance is in good faith effected by one person on behalf of another, the person whose behalf if is effected may ratify the contract even after he is aware of a loss.

87   Implied obligations varied by agreement or usage

(1) Where any right, duty or liability would arise under a contract of marine insurance by implication of law, it may be negatived or varied by express agreement, or by usage, if the usage be such as to bind both parties to the contract.

(2) The provisions of this section extend to any right, duty or liability declared by this Act which may be lawfully modified by agreement.

88   Reasonable time, etc, a question of fact

Where by this Act any reference is made to reasonable time, reasonable premium, or reasonable diligence, the question what is reasonable is a question of fact.

91   Savings ...

(2) The rules of the common law including the law merchant, save in so far as they are inconsistent with the express provisions of this Act, shall continue to apply to contracts of marine insurance.

As amended by the Finance Act 1959, s37(5), Schedule 8, Pt II.

LIMITED PARTNERSHIPS ACT 1907
(7 Edw 7 c 24)

3   Interpretation of terms

In the construction of this Act the following words and expressions shall have the meanings respectively assigned to them in this section, unless there be something in the subject or context repugnant to such construction:

'firm', 'firm name' and 'business' have the same meanings as in the Partnership Act 1890:

'general partner' shall mean any partner who is not a limited partner as defined by this Act.

4   Definition and constitution of limited partnership

(1) Limited partnerships may be formed in the manner and subject to the conditions by this Act provided.

(2) A limited partnership must consist of one or more persons called general partners, who shall be liable for all debts and obligations of the firm, and one or more persons to be called limited partners, who shall at the time of entering into such partnership contribute thereto a sum or sums as capital or property valued at a stated amount, and who shall not be liable for the debts or obligations of the firm beyond the amount so contributed.

(3) A limited partner shall not during the continuance of the partnership, either directly or indirectly, draw out or receive back any part of his contribution, and if he does so draw out or receive back any such part shall be liable for the debts and obligations of the firm up to the amount so drawn out or received back

(4) A body corporate may be a limited partner.

6   Modifications of general law in case of limited partnerships

(1) A limited partner shall not take part in the management of the partnership business, and shall not have power to bind the firm: Provided that a limited partner may by himself or his agent at any time inspect the books of the firm and examine into the state and prospects of the partnership business, and may advise with the partners thereon. If a limited partner takes part in the management of the partnership business he shall be liable for all debts and obligations of the firm

incurred while he so takes part in the management as though he were a general partner.

(2) A limited partnership shall not be dissolved by the death of bankruptcy of a limited partner, and the lunacy of a limited partner shall not be a ground for dissolution of the partnership by the court unless the lunatic's share cannot be otherwise ascertained and realised.

(3) In the event of the dissolution of a limited partnership its affairs shall be wound up by the general partners unless the court otherwise orders.

(5) Subject to any agreement expressed or implied between the partners –

(a) Any difference arising as to ordinary matters connected with the partnership business may be decided by a majority of the general partners;

(b) A limited partner may, with the consent of the general partners, assign his share in the partnership, and upon such an assignment the assignee shall become a limited partner with all the rights of the assignor;

(c) The other partners shall not be entitled to dissolve the partnership by reason of any limited partner suffering his share to be charged for his separate debt;

(d) A person may be introduced as a partner without the consent of the existing limited partners;

(e) A limited partner shall not be entitled to dissolve the partnership by notice.

7 Law as to private partnerships to apply where not excluded by this Act

Subject to the provisions of this Act, the Partnership Act 1890 and the rules of equity and of common law applicable to partnerships, except so far as they are inconsistent with the express provisions of the last-mentioned Act, shall apply to limited partnerships.

As amended by the Companies (Consolidation) Act 1908, s286, Schedule 6, Pt I, Statute Law Revision Act 1927; Regulatory Reform (Removal of 20 Member Limit in Partnerships, etc), Order 2002, art 3.

LAW OF PROPERTY ACT 1925
(15 & 16 Geo 5 c 20)

41   Stipulations not of the essence of a contract

Stipulations in a contract, as to time or otherwise, which according to rules of equity are not deemed to be or to have become of the essence of the contract, are also construed and have effect at law in accordance with the same rules.

49   Applications to the court by vendor and purchaser

(1) A vendor or purchase of any interest in land, or their representatives respectively, may apply in a summary way to the court, in respect of any requisitions or objections, or any claim for compensation, or any other question arising out of or connected with the contract (not being a question affecting the existence or validity of the contract), and the court may make such order upon the application as to the court may appear just, and may order how and by whom all or any of the costs of and incident to the application are to be borne and paid.

(2) Where the court refuses to grant specific performance of a contract, or in any action for the return of a deposit, the court may, if it thinks fit, order the repayment of any deposit.

(3) This section applies to a contract for the sale or exchange of any interest in land.

(4) The county court has jurisdiction under this section where the land which is to be dealt with in the court does not exceed £30,000 in capital value.

52   Conveyances to be by deed

(1) All conveyances of land or of any interest therein are void for the purpose of conveying or creating a legal estate unless made by deed.

(2) This section does not apply to –

    (a) assents by a personal representative;

    (b) disclaimers made in accordance with sections 178 to 180 or sections 315 to 319 of the Insolvency Act 1986, or not required to be evidenced in writing;

    (c) surrenders by operation of law, including surrenders which may, by law, be effected without writing;

    (d) leases or tenancies or other assurances not required by law to be made in writing;

(e) receipts other than those falling within section 115 below [Reconveyances of mortgages by endorsed receipts];

(f) vesting orders of the court or other competent authority;

(g) conveyances taking effect by operation of law.

53   Instruments required to be in writing

(1) Subject to the provisions hereinafter contained with respect to the creation of interests in land by parol –

(a) no interest in land can be created or disposed of except by writing signed by the person creating or conveying the same, or by his agent thereunto lawfully authorised in writing, or by will, or by operation of law;

(b) a declaration of trust respecting any land or any interest therein must be manifested and proved by some writing signed by some person who is able to declare such trust or by his will;

(c) a disposition of an equitable interest or trust subsisting at the time of the disposition, must be in writing signed by the person disposing of the same, or by his agent, thereunto lawfully authorised in writing or by will.

(2) This section does not affect the creation or operation of resulting, implied or constructive trusts.

54   Creation of interests in land by parol

(1) All interests in land created by parol and not put in writing and signed by the persons so creating the same, or by their agents thereunto lawfully authorised in writing, have, notwithstanding any consideration having been given for the same, the force and effect of interest at will only.

(2) Nothing in the foregoing provisions of this Part of this Act shall affect the creation by parol of leases taking effect in possession for a term not exceeding three years (whether or not the lessee is given power to extend the term) at the best rent which can be reasonably obtained without taking a fine.

55   Savings in regard to last two sections

Nothing in the last two foregoing sections shall –

(a) invalidate dispositions by will; or

(b) affect any interest validly created before the commencement of this Act; or

(c) affect the right to acquire an interest in land by virtue of taking possession; or

(d) affect the operation of the law relating to part performance.

56   Persons taking who are not parties

(1) A person may take an immediate or other interest in land or other property, or

the benefit of any condition, right of entry, covenant or agreement over or respecting land or other property, although he may not be named as a party to the conveyance or other instrument.

(2) A deed between parties, to effect its objects, has the effect of an indenture though not indented or expressed to be an indenture.

205 General definitions

(1) In this Act unless the context otherwise requires, the following expressions have the meanings hereby assigned to them respectively, that is to say: ...

(ii) 'Conveyance' includes a mortgage, charge, lease, assent, vesting declaration, vesting instrument, disclaimer, release and every other assurance of property or of an instrument therein by any instrument, except a will; 'convey' has a corresponding meaning; and 'disposition' includes a conveyance and also a devise, bequest, or an appointment of property contained in a will; and 'dispose of' has a corresponding meaning; ...

(ix) 'Land' includes land of any tenure, and mines and minerals, whether or not held apart from the surface, buildings or parts of buildings (whether the division is horizontal, vertical or made in any other way) and other corporeal hereditaments; also a manor, an advowson, and a rent and other incorporeal hereditaments, and an easement, right, privilege, or benefit in, over, or derived from land; and 'mines and minerals' include any strata or seam of minerals or substances in or under any land, and powers of working and getting the same; and 'manor' includes a lordship, and reputed manor or lordship; and 'hereditament' means any real property which on an intestacy occurring before the commencement of this Act might have devolved upon an heir; ...

As amended by the County Courts Act 1984, s148(1), Schedule 2, Pt II, para 2(1), (3); Insolvency Act 1986, s439(2), Schedule 14; Law of Property (Miscellaneous Provisions) Act 1989, s1(8), Schedule 1, para 2; High Court and County Courts Jurisdiction Order 1991, art 2(8), Schedule; Trusts of Land and Appointment of Trustees Act 1996, s25(2), Schedule 4.

LAW REFORM (MISCELLANEOUS PROVISIONS) ACT 1934
(24 & 25 Geo 5 c 41)

1 Effect of death on certain causes of action

(1) Subject to the provisions of this section, on the death of any person after the commencement of this Act all causes of action subsisting against or vested in him shall survive against, or, as the case may be, for the benefit of, his estate. Provided that this subsection shall not apply to causes of action for defamation.

(1A) The right of a person to claim under section 1A of the Fatal Accidents Act 1976 (bereavement) shall not survive for the benefit of his estate on his death.

(2) Where a cause of action survives as aforesaid for the benefit of the estate of a deceased person, the damages recoverable for the benefit of the estate of that person –

(a) shall not include –

(i) any exemplary damages;

(ii) any damages for loss of income in respect of any period after that person's death;

(c) where the death of that person has been caused by the act or omission which gives rise to the cause of action, shall be calculated without reference to any loss or gain to his estate consequent on his death, except that a sum in respect of funeral expenses may be included.

(4) Where damage has been suffered by reason of any act or omission in respect of which a cause of action would have subsisted against any person if that person had not died before or at the same time as the damage was suffered, there shall be deemed, for the purposes of this Act, to have been subsisting against him before his death such cause of action in respect of that act or omission as would have subsisted if he had died after the damage was suffered.

(5) The rights conferred by this Act for the benefit of the estates of deceased persons shall be in addition to and not in derogation of any rights conferred on the dependants of deceased persons by the Fatal Accidents Act 1976, and so much of this Act as relates to causes of action against the estates of deceased persons shall apply in relation to causes of action under the said Acts as it applies in relation to other causes of action not expressly excepted from the operation of subsection (1) of this section.

(6) In the event of the insolvency of an estate against which proceedings are maintainable by virtue of this section, any liability in respect of the cause of action in respect of which the proceedings are maintainable shall be deemed to be a debt provable in the administration of the estate, notwithstanding that it is a demand in the nature of unliquidated damages arising otherwise than by a contract, promise or breach of trust.

As amended by the Statute Law Revision Act 1950; Carriage by Air Act 1961, s14(3), Schedule 2; Law Reform (Miscellaneous Provisions) Act 1970, s7, Schedule; Proceedings Against Estates Act 1970, s1; Administration of Justice Act 1982, ss4(1), (2), 75(1), Schedule 9.

LAW REFORM (MARRIED WOMEN AND TORTFEASORS) ACT 1935

(25 & 26 Geo 5 c 30)

PART I

CAPACITY, PROPERTY, AND LIABILITIES OF MARRIED WOMEN, AND LIABILITIES OF HUSBANDS

1   Capacity of married women

Subject to the provisions of this Part of this Act, a married woman shall –

(a) be capable of acquiring, holding, and disposing of, any property; and

(b) be capable of rendering herself, and being rendered, liable in respect of any tort, contract, debt, or obligation; and

(c) be capable of suing and being sued, either in tort or in contract or otherwise; and

(d) be subject to the law relating to bankruptcy and to the enforcement of judgments and orders.

in all respects as if she were a feme sole.

2   Property of married women

(1) Subject to the provisions of this Part of this Act all property which –

(a) immediately before the passing of this Act was the separate property of a married woman or held for her separate use in equity; or

(b) belongs at the time of her marriage to a woman married after the passing of this Act; or

(c) after the passing of this Act is acquired by or devolves upon a married woman,

shall belong to her in all respects as if she were a feme sole and may be disposed of accordingly.

3 Abolition of husband's liability for wife's torts and ante-nuptial contracts, debts and obligations

Subject to the provisions of this Part of this Act, the husband of a married woman shall not, by reason only of his being her husband, be liable –

(a) in respect of any tort committed by her whether before or after the marriage, or in respect of any contract entered into, or debt or obligation incurred, by her before the marriage; or

(b) to be sued, or made a party to any legal proceeding brought, in respect of any such tort, contract, debt, or obligation.

4 Savings

(1) Nothing in this Part of this Act shall –

(a) during converture which began before the first day of January eighteen hundred and eighty-three, affect any property to which the title (whether vested or contingent, and whether in possession, reversion, or remainder) of a married woman accrued before that date, except property held for her separate use in equity;

(b) affect any legal proceeding in respect of any tort if proceedings had been instituted in respect thereof before the passing of this Act;

(c) enable any judgment or order against a married woman in respect of a contract entered into, or debt or obligation incurred, before the passing of this Act, to be enforced in bankruptcy or to be enforced otherwise than against her property.

(2) For the avoidance of doubt it is hereby declared that nothing in this Part of this Act –

(a) renders the husband of a married woman liable in respect of any contract entered into, or debt or obligation incurred, by her after the marriage in respect of which he would not have been liable if this Act had not been passed;

(b) exempts the husband of a married woman from liability in respect of any contract entered into, or debt or obligation (not being a debt or obligation arising out of the commission of a tort) incurred by her after the marriage in respect of which he would have been liable if this Act had not been passed;

(c) prevents a husband and wife from acquiring, holding, and disposing of, any property jointly or as tenants in common, or from rendering themselves, or being rendered, jointly liable in respect of any tort, contract, debt or obligation, and of suing and being sued either in tort or in contract or otherwise, in like manner as if they were not married;

(d) prevents the exercise of any joint power given to a husband and wife.

As amended by the Married Women (Restraint upon Anticipation) Act 1949, s1(2), (4), Schedule 2; Law Reform (Husband and Wife) Act 1962, s3(2), Schedule.

LAW REFORM (FRUSTRATED CONTRACTS) ACT 1943
(6 & 7 Geo 6 c 40)

1   Adjustment of rights and liabilities of parties to frustrated contracts

(1) Where a contract governed by English law has become impossible of performance or been otherwise frustrated, and the parties thereto have for that reason been discharged from the further performance of the contract, the following provisions of this section shall, subject to the provisions of section two of this Act, have effect in relation thereto.

(2) All sums paid or payable to any party in pursuance of the contract before the time when the parties were so discharged (in this Act referred to as 'the time of discharge') shall, in the case of sums so paid, be recoverable from him as money received by him for the use of the party by whom the sums were paid, and, in the case of sums so payable, cease to be so payable:

Provided that, if the party to whom the sums were so paid or payable incurred expenses before the time of discharge in, or for the purpose of, the performance of the contract, the court may, if it considers it just to do so having regard to all the circumstances of the case, allow him to retain or, as the case may be, recover the whole or any part of the sums so paid or payable, not being an amount in excess of the expenses so incurred.

(3) Where any party to the contract has, by reason of anything done by any other party thereto in, or for the purpose of, the performance of the contract, obtained a valuable benefit (other than a payment of money to which the last foregoing subsection applies) before the time of discharge, there shall be recoverable from him by the said other party such sum (if any), not exceeding the value of the said benefit to the party obtaining it, as the court considers just, having regard to all the circumstances of the case and, in particular, –

    (a) the amount of any expenses incurred before the time of discharge by the benefited party in, or for the purpose of, the performance of the contract, including any sums paid or payable by him to any other party in pursuance of the contract and retained or recoverable by that party under the last foregoing subsection, and

    (b) the effect, in relation to the said benefit, of the circumstances giving rise to the frustration of the contract.

(4) In estimating, for the purposes of the foregoing provisions of this section, the amount of any expenses incurred by any party to the contract, the court may, without prejudice to the generality of the said provisions, include such sum as appears to be reasonable in respect of overhead expenses and in respect of any work or services performed personally by the said party.

(5) In considering whether any sum ought to be recovered or retained under the foregoing provisions of this section by any party to the contract, the court shall not take into account any sums which have, by reason of the circumstances giving rise to the frustration of the contract, become payable to that party under any contract of insurance unless there was an obligation to insure imposed by an express term of the frustrated contract or by or under any enactment.

(6) Where any person has assumed obligations under the contract in consideration of the conferring of a benefit by any other party to the contract upon any other person, whether a party to the contract or not, the court may, if in all the circumstances of the case it considers it just to do so, treat for the purposes of sub-section (3) of this section any benefit so conferred as a benefit obtained by the person who has assumed the obligations as aforesaid.

2   Provision as to application of this Act

(1) This Act shall apply to contracts, whether made before or after the commencement of this Act, as respects which the time of discharge is on or after the first day of July, nineteen hundred and forty-three, but not to contracts as respects which the time of discharge is before the said date.

(2) This Act shall apply to contracts to which the Crown is a party in like manner as to contracts between subjects.

(3) Where any contract to which this Act applies contains any provision which, upon the true construction of the contract, is intended to have effect in the event of circumstances arising which operate, or would but for the said provision operate, to frustrate the contract, or is intended to have effect whether such circumstances arise or not, the court shall give effect to the said provision and shall only give effect to the foregoing section of this Act to such extent, if any, as appears to the court to be consistent with the said provision.

(4) Where it appears to the court that a part of any contract to which this Act applies can properly be severed from the remainder of the contract, being a part wholly performed before the time of discharge, or so performed except for the payment in respect of that part of the contract of sums which are or can be ascertained under the contract, the court shall treat that part of the contract as if it were a separate contract and had not been frustrated and shall treat the foregoing section of this Act as only applicable to the remainder of that contract.

(5) This Act shall not apply –

    (a) to any charterparty, except a time charterparty or a charterparty by way of demise, or to any contract (other than a charterparty) for the carriage of goods by sea; or

(b) to any contract of insurance, save as is provided by subsection (5) of the foregoing section; or

(c) to any contract to which section 7 of the Sale of Goods Act 1979 (which avoids contracts for the sale of specific goods which perish before the risk has passed to the buyer) applies, or to any other contract for the sale, or for the sale and delivery, of specific goods, where the contract is frustrated by reason of the fact that the goods have perished.

3 Interpretation

(2) In this Act the expression 'court' means, in relation to any matter, the court or arbitrator by or before whom the matter falls to be determined.

As amended by the Sale of Goods Act 1979, s63, Schedule 2, para 2.

LAW REFORM (CONTRIBUTORY NEGLIGENCE) ACT 1945

(8 & 9 Geo 6 c 28)

1   Apportionment of liability in case of contributory negligence

(1) Where any person suffers damage as the result partly of his own fault and partly of the fault of any other person or persons, a claim in respect of that damage shall not be defeated by reason of the fault of the person suffering the damage, but the damages recoverable in respect thereof shall be reduced to such extent as the court thinks just and equitable having regard to the claimant's share in the responsibility for the damage:

Provided that –

    (a) this subsection shall not operate to defeat any defence arising under a contract;

    (b) where any contract or enactment providing for the limitation of liability is applicable to the claim, the amount of damages recoverable by the claimant by virtue of this subsection shall not exceed the maximum limit so applicable.

(2) Where damages are recoverable by any person by virtue of the foregoing subsection subject to such reduction as is therein mentioned, the court shall find and record the total damages which would have been recoverable if the claimant had not been at fault.

(5) Where, in any case to which subsection (1) of this section applies, one of the persons at fault avoids liability to any other such person or his personal representative by pleading the Limitation Act 1939, or any other enactment limiting the time within which proceedings may be taken, he shall not be entitled to recover any damages from that other person or representative by virtue of the said subsection.

(6) Where any case to which subsection (1) of this section applies is tried with a jury, the jury shall determine the total damages which would have been recoverable if the claimant had not been at fault and the extent to which those damages are to be reduced.

3   Saving for Maritime Conventions Act 1911 and past cases

(1) This Act shall not apply to any claim to which section one of the Maritime

Conventions Act 1911 applies and that Act shall have effect as if this Act had not passed.

(2) This Act shall not apply to any case where the acts or omissions giving rise to the claim occurred before the passing of this Act.

4   Interpretation

The following expressions have the meanings hereby respectively assigned to them, that is to say –

'court' means, in relation to any claim, the court or arbitrator by or before whom the claim falls to be determined;

'damage' includes loss of life and personal injury;

'fault' means negligence, breach of statutory duty or other act or omission which gives rise to a liability in tort or would, apart from this Act, give rise to the defence of contributory negligence.

As amended by the National Insurance (Industrial Injuries) Act 1946, s89(1), Schedule 9; Carriage by Air Act 1961, s14(3), Schedule 2; Fatal Accidents Act 1976, s6(2), Schedule 2; Civil Liability (Contribution) Act 1978, s9(2), Schedule 2.

CROWN PROCEEDINGS ACT 1947
(10 & 11 Geo 6 c 44)

PART I

SUBSTANTIVE LAW

1   Right to sue the Crown

Where any person has a claim against the Crown after the commencement of this Act, and, if this Act had not been passed, the claim might have been enforced, subject to the grant of His Majesty's fiat, by petition of right, or might have been enforced by a proceeding provided by any statutory provision repealed by this Act, then, subject to the provisions of this Act, the claim may be enforced as of right, and without the fiat of His Majesty, by proceedings taken against the Crown for that purpose in accordance with the provisions of this Act.

2   Liability of the Crown in tort

(1) Subject to the provisions of this Act, the Crown shall be subject to all those liabilities in tort to which, if it were a private person of full age and capacity, it would be subject –

(a) in respect of torts committed by its servants or agents;

(b) in respect of any breach of those duties which a person owes to his servants or agents at common law by reason of being their employer; and

(c) in respect of any breach of the duties attaching at common law to the ownership, occupation, possession or control of property:

Provided that no proceedings shall lie against the Crown by virtue of paragraph (a) of this subsection in respect of any act or omission of a servant or agent of the Crown unless the act or omission would apart from the provisions of this Act have given rise to a cause of action in tort against that servant or agent or his estate.

(2) Where the Crown is bound by a statutory duty which is binding also upon persons other than the Crown and its officers, then, subject to the provisions of this Act, the Crown shall, in respect of a failure to comply with that duty, be subject to all those liabilities in tort (if any) to which it would be so subject if it were a private person of full age and capacity.

(3) Where any functions are conferred or imposed upon an officer of the Crown as such either by any rule of the common law or by statute, and that officer commits

a tort while performing or purporting to perform those functions, the liabilities of the Crown in respect of the tort shall be such as they would have been if those functions had been conferred or imposed solely by virtue of instructions lawfully given by the Crown.

(4) Any enactment which negatives or limits the amount of the liability of any Government department, part of the Scottish administration or officer of the Crown in respect of any tort committed by that department, part or officer shall, in the case of proceedings against the Crown under this section in respect of a tort committed by that department, part or officer, apply in relation to the Crown as it would have applied in relation to that department, part or officer if the proceedings against the Crown had been proceedings against that department, part or officer.

(5) No proceedings shall lie against the Crown by virtue of this section in respect of anything done or omitted to be done by any person while discharging or purporting to discharge any responsibilities of a judicial nature vested in him, or any responsibilities which he has in connection with the execution of judicial process.

(6) No proceedings shall lie against the Crown by virtue of this section in respect of any act, neglect or default of any officer of the Crown, unless that officer has been directly or indirectly appointed by the Crown and was at the material time paid in respect of his duties as an officer of the Crown wholly out of the Consolidated Fund of the United Kingdom, moneys provided by Parliament, the Scottish Consolidation Fund or any other Fund certified by the Treasury for the purposes of this subsection or was at the material time holding an office in respect of which the Treasury certify that the holder thereof would normally be so paid.

4 Application of law as to indemnity, contribution, joint and several tortfeasors, and contributory negligence

(1) Where the Crown is subject to any liability by virtue of this Part of this Act, the law relating to indemnity and contribution shall be enforceable by or against the Crown in respect of the liability to which it is so subject as if the Crown were a private person of full age and capacity.

(3) Without prejudice to the general effect of section one of this Act, the Law Reform (Contributory Negligence) Act 1945 (which amends the law relating to contributory negligence) shall bind the Crown.

11 Saving in respect of acts done under prerogative and statutory power

(1) Nothing in Part I of this Act shall extinguish or abridge any powers or authorities which, if this Act had not been passed, would have been exercisable by virtue of the prerogative of the Crown, or any powers or authorities conferred on the Crown by any statute, and, in particular, nothing in the said Part I shall extinguish or abridge any powers or authorities exercisable by the Crown, whether in time of peace or of war, for the purpose of the defence of the realm or of training, or maintaining the efficiency of, any of the armed forces of the Crown.

(2) Where in any proceedings under this Act it is material to determine whether anything was properly done or omitted to be done in the exercise of the prerogative of the Crown, a Secretary of State may, if satisfied that the act or omission was necessary for any such purpose as is mentioned in the last preceding subsection, issue a certificate to the effect that the act or omission was necessary for that purpose; and the certificate shall, in those proceedings, be conclusive as to the matter so certified.

PART II

JURISDICTION AND PROCEDURE

21   Nature of relief

(1) In any civil proceedings by or against the Crown the court shall, subject to the provisions of this Act, have power to make all such orders as it has power to make in proceedings between subjects, and otherwise to give such appropriate relief as the case may require:

Provided that –

> (a) where in any proceedings against the Crown any such relief is sought as might in proceedings between subjects be granted by way of injunction or specific performance, the court shall not grant an injunction or make an order for specific performance, but may in lieu thereof make an order declaratory of the rights of the parties; and

> (b) in any proceedings against the Crown for the recovery of land or other property the court shall not make an order for the recovery of the land or the delivery of the property, but may in lieu thereof make an order declaring that the plaintiff is entitled as against the Crown to the land or property or to the possession thereof.

(2) The court shall not in any civil proceedings grant any injunction or make any order against an officer of the Crown if the effect of granting the injunction or making the order would be to give any relief against the Crown which could not have been obtained in proceedings against the Crown.

PART IV

MISCELLANEOUS AND SUPPLEMENTAL

38   Interpretation

(1) Any reference in this Act to the provisions of this Act shall, unless the context otherwise requires, include a reference to rules of court or county court rules made for the purposes of this Act.

(2) In this Act, except in so far as the context otherwise requires or it is otherwise expressly provided, the following expressions have the meanings hereby respectively assigned to them, that is to say –

'Agent', when used in relation to the Crown, includes an independent contractor employed by the Crown;

'Civil proceedings' includes proceedings in the High Court or the county court for the recovery of fines or penalties, but does not include proceedings on the Crown side of the King's Bench Division; ...

'Officer', in relation to the Crown, includes any servant of His Majesty, and accordingly (but without prejudice to the generality of the foregoing provision) includes a Minister of the Crown and a member of the Scottish Executive;

'Order' includes a judgment, decree, rule, award or declaration;

'Prescribed' means prescribed by rules of court or county court rules, as the case may be;

'Proceedings against the Crown' includes a claim by way of set-off or counter-claim raised in proceedings by the Crown;

'Ship' has the same meaning as in the Merchant Shipping Act 1995;

'Statutory duty' means any duty imposed by or under any Act of Parliament.

(3) Any reference in this Act to His Majesty in His private capacity shall be construed as including a reference to His Majesty in right of His Duchy of Lancaster and to the Duke of Cornwall.

(4) Any reference in Parts III or IV of this Act to civil proceedings by or against the Crown, or to civil proceedings to which the Crown is a party, shall be construed as including a reference to civil proceedings to which the Attorney-General, or any Governmental department, or any officer of the Crown as such is a party: Provided that the Crown shall not for the purposes of Parts III and IV of this Act be deemed to be a party to any proceedings by reason only that they are brought by the Attorney-General upon the relation of some other person. ...

40   Savings

(1) Nothing in this Act shall apply to proceedings by or against, or authorise proceedings in tort to be brought against, His Majesty in His private capacity. ...

As amended by the Civil Liability (Contribution) Act 1978, s9(2), Schedule 2; Statute Law (Repeals) Act 1981; Merchant Shipping Act 1995, s314(2), Schedule 13, para 21; Scotland Act 1998, s125(1), Schedule 8, para 7(1), (2)(c); Scotland Act 1998 (Consequential Modifications) (No 1) Order 1999, art 4, Schedule 2, Pt I, para 4(1), (2); Scotland Act 1998 (Consequential Modifications) (No 2) Order 1999, art 4, Schedule 2, Pt I, para 21.

LAW REFORM (PERSONAL INJURIES) ACT 1948
(11 & 12 Geo 6 c 41)

1   Common employment

(1) It shall not be a defence to an employer who is sued in respect of personal injuries caused by the negligence of a person employed by him, that that person was at the time the injuries were caused in common employment with the person injured. ...

(3) Any provision contained in a contract of service or apprenticeship, or in an agreement collateral thereto (including a contract or agreement entered into before the commencement of this Act) shall be void in so far as it would have the effect of excluding or limiting any liability of the employer in respect of personal injuries caused to the person employed or apprenticed by the negligence of persons in common employment with him.

2   Measure of damages

(4) In an action for damages for personal injuries (including any such action arising out of a contract), there shall be disregarded, in determining the reasonableness of any expenses, the possibility of avoiding these expenses or part of them by taking advantage of facilities available under the National Health Service Act 1977 ...

3   Definition of 'personal injury'

In this Act the expression 'personal injury' includes any disease and any impairment of a person's physical or mental condition, and the expression 'injured' shall be construed accordingly.

4   Application to Crown

This Act shall bind the Crown.

As amended by the Social Security (Consequential Provisions) Act 1975, s1(3), Schedule 2, para 8; National Health Service Act 1977, s129, Schedule 15, para 8; Social Security Act 1989, ss22, 31(2), Schedule 4, Pt IV, para 22, Schedule 9; Social Security Act 1990, s7, Schedule 1, para 7; Social Security (Consequential Provisions) Act 1992, s2, Schedule 2, para 2; Social Security (Recovery of Benefits) Act 1997, s33(1), (2), Schedule 3, para 1, Schedule 4.

DEFAMATION ACT 1952
(15 & 16 Geo & Eliz 2 c 66)

2   Slander affecting official, professional or business reputation

In an action for slander in respect of words calculated to disparage the plaintiff in any office, profession, calling, trade or business held or carried on by him at the time of the publication, it shall not be necessary to allege or prove special damage, whether or not the words are spoken of the plaintiff in the way of his office, profession, calling, trade or business.

3   Slander of title, etc

(1) In an action for slander of title, slander of goods or other malicious falsehood, it shall not be necessary to allege or prove special damage –

(a) if the words upon which the action is founded are calculated to cause pecuniary damage to the plaintiff and are published in writing or other permanent form; or

(b) if the said words are calculated to cause pecuniary damage to the plaintiff in respect of any office, profession, calling, trade or business held or carried on by him at the time of the publication. ...

5   Justification

In an action for libel or slander in respect of words containing two or more distinct charges against the plaintiff, a defence of justification shall not fail by reason only that the truth of every charge is not proved if the words not proved to be true do not materially injure the plaintiff's reputation having regard to the truth of the remaining charges.

6   Fair comment

In an action for libel or slander in respect of words consisting partly of allegations of fact and partly of expression of opinion, a defence of fair comment shall not fail by reason only that the truth of every allegation of fact is not proved if the expression of opinion is fair comment having regard to such of the facts alleged or referred to in the words complained of as are proved.

9 Extension of certain defences to broadcasting

(1) Section three of the Parliamentary Papers Act 1840 (which confers protection in respect of proceedings for printing extracts from or abstracts of parliamentary papers) shall have effect as if the reference to printing included a reference to broadcasting by means of wireless telegraphy.

10 Limitation on privilege at elections

A defamatory statement published by or on behalf of a candidate in any election to a local government authority, to the Scottish Parliament or to Parliament shall not be deemed to be published on a privileged occasion on the ground that it is material to a question in issue in the election, whether or not the person by whom it is published is qualified to vote at the election.

11 Agreements for indemnity

An agreement for indemnifying any person against civil liability for libel in respect of the publication of any matter shall not be lawful unless at the time of the publication that person knows that the matter is defamatory, and does not reasonably believe there is a good defence to any action brought upon it.

12 Evidence of other damages recovered by plaintiff

In any action for libel or slander the defendant may give evidence in mitigation of damages that the plaintiff has recovered damages, or has brought actions for damages, for libel or slander in respect of the publication of words to the same effect as the words on which the action is founded, or has received or agreed to receive compensation in respect of any such publication.

13 Consolidation of actions for slander, etc

Section five of the Law of Libel Amendment Act 1888 (which provides for the consolidation, on the application of the defendants, of two or more actions for libel by the same plaintiff) shall apply to actions for slander and to actions for slander of title, slander of goods or other malicious falsehood as it applies to actions for libel; and references in that section to the same, or substantially the same, libel shall be construed accordingly.

16 Interpretation

(1) Any reference in this Act to words shall be construed as including a reference to pictures, visual images, gestures and other methods of signifying meaning.

17 Proceedings affected and saving

(1) This Act applies for the purposes of any proceedings begun after the commencement of this Act, whenever the cause of action arose, but does not affect any proceedings begun before the commencement of this Act.

(2) Nothing in this Act affects the law relating to criminal libel.

As amended by the Revision of the Army and Air Force Acts (Transitional Provisions) Act 1955, s3, Schedule 2, para 16; British Nationality Act 1981, s52(6), Schedule 7; Local Government (Access to Information) Act 1985, s3(1), Schedule 2, para 2; Defamation Act 1996, s16, Schedule 2; Scotland Act 1998, s125(1), Schedule 8, para 10.

OCCUPIERS' LIABILITY ACT 1957
(5 & 6 Eliz 2 c 31)1

1   Preliminary

(1) The rules enacted by the two next following sections shall have effect, in place of the rules of the common law, to regulate the duty which an occupier of premises owes to his visitors in respect of dangers due to the state of the premises or to things done or omitted to be done on them.

(2) The rules so enacted shall regulate the nature of the duty imposed by law in consequence of a person's occupation or control of premises and of any invitation or permission he gives (or is to be treated as giving) to another to enter or use the premises, but they shall not alter the rules of the common law as to the persons on whom a duty is so imposed or to whom it is owed; and accordingly for the purpose of the rules so enacted the persons who are to be treated as an occupier and as his visitors are the same (subject to subsection (4) of this section) as the persons who would at common law be treated as an occupier and as his invitees or licensees.

(3) The rules so enacted in relation to an occupier of premises and his visitors shall also apply, in like manner and to the like extent as the principles applicable at common law to an occupier of premises and his invitees or licensees would apply, to regulate –

   (a) the obligations of a person occupying or having control over any fixed or movable structure, including any vessel, vehicle or aircraft; and

   (b) the obligations of a person occupying or having control over any premises or structure in respect of damage to property, including the property of persons who are not themselves his visitors.

(4) A person entering any premises in exercise of rights conferred by virtue of –

   (a) section 2(1) of the Countryside and Rights of Way Act 2000, or

   (b) an access agreement or order under the National Parks and Access to the Countryside Act 1949,

is not, for the purposes of this Act, a visitor of the occupier of the premises.

2   Extent of occupier's ordinary duty

(1) An occupier of premises owes the same duty, the 'common duty of care', to all his visitors, except in so far as he is free and does extend, restrict, modify or exclude his duty to any visitor or visitors by agreement or otherwise.

(2) The common duty of care is a duty to take such care as in all the circumstances of the case is reasonable to see that the visitor will be reasonably safe in using the premises for the purposes for which he is invited or permitted by the occupier to be there.

(3) The circumstances relevant for the present purpose include the degree of care and want of care, which would ordinarily be looked for in such a visitor, so that (for example) in proper cases –

(a) an occupier must be prepared for children to be less careful than adults; and

(b) an occupier may expect that a person, in the exercise of his calling, will appreciate and guard against any special risks ordinarily incident to it, so far as the occupier leaves him free to do so.

(4) In determining whether the occupier of premises has discharged the common duty of care to a visitor, regard is to be had to all the circumstances so that (for example) –

(a) where damage is caused to a visitor by a danger of which he had been warned by the occupier, the warning is not to be treated without more as absolving the occupier from liability, unless in all the circumstances it was enough to enable the visitor to be reasonably safe; and

(b) where damage is caused to a visitor by a danger due to the faulty execution of any work of construction, maintenance or repair by an independent contractor employed by the occupier, the occupier is not to be treated without more as answerable for the danger if in all the circumstances he had acted reasonably in entrusting the work to an independent contractor and had taken such steps (if any) as he reasonably ought in order to satisfy himself that the contractor was competent and that the work had been properly done.

(5) The common duty of care does not impose on an occupier any obligation to a visitor in respect of risks willingly accepted as his by the visitor (the question whether a risk was so accepted to be decided on the same principles as in other cases in which one person owes a duty of care to another).

(6) For the purposes of this section, persons who enter premises for any purpose in the exercise of a right conferred by law are to be treated as permitted by the occupier to be there for that purpose, whether they in fact have his permission or not.

3 Effect of contract on occupier's liability to third party

(1) Where an occupier of premises is bound by contract to permit persons who are strangers to the contract to enter or use the premises, the duty of care which he owes to them as his visitors cannot be restricted or excluded by that contract, but (subject to any provision of the contract to the contrary) shall include the duty to perform his obligations under the contract, whether undertaken for their protection or not, in so far as those obligations go beyond the obligations otherwise involved in that duty.

(2) A contract shall not by virtue of this section have the effect, unless it expressly so provides, of making an occupier who has taken all reasonable care answerable to strangers to the contract for dangers due to the faulty execution of any work of construction, maintenance or repair or other like operation by persons other than himself, his servants and persons acting under his direction and control.

(3) In this section 'stranger to the contract' means a person not for the time being entitled to the benefit of the contract as a party to it or as the successor by assignment or otherwise of a party to it, and accordingly includes a party to the contract who has ceased to be so entitled.

(4) Where by the terms or conditions governing any tenancy (including a statutory tenancy which does not in law amount to a tenancy) either the landlord or the tenant is bound, though not by contract, to permit persons to enter or use premises of which he is the occupier, this section shall apply as if the tenancy were a contract between the landlord and the tenant.

(5) This section, in so far as it prevents the common duty of care from being restricted or excluded, applies to contracts entered into and tenancies created before the commencement of this Act, as well as to those entered into or created after its commencement; but, in so far as it enlarges the duty owed by an occupier beyond the common duty of care, it shall have effect only in relation to obligations which are undertaken after that commencement or which are renewed by agreement (whether express or implied) after that commencement.

5   Implied term in contracts

(1) Where persons enter or use, or bring or send goods to, any premises in exercise of a right conferred by contract with a person occupying or having control of the premises, the duty he owes them in respect of dangers due to the state of the premises or to things done or omitted to be done on them, in so far as the duty depends on a term to be implied in the contract by reason of its conferring that right, shall be the common duty of care.

(2) The foregoing subsection shall apply to fixed and movable structures as it applies to premises.

(3) This section does not affect the obligations imposed on a person by or by virtue of any contract for the hire of, or for the carriage for reward of persons or goods in, any vehicle, vessel, aircraft or other means of transport, or by or by virtue of any contract of bailment.

6   Application to Crown

This Act shall bind the Crown, but as regards the Crown's liability in tort shall not bind the Crown further than the Crown is made liable in tort by the Crown Proceedings Act 1947, and that Act and in particular section two of it shall apply in relation to duties under sections two to four of this Act as statutory duties.

As amended by the Countryside and Rights of Way Act 2000, s13(1).

CORPORATE BODIES' CONTRACTS ACT 1960
(8 & 9 Eliz 2 c 46)

1   Cases where contracts need not be under seal

(1) Contracts may be made on behalf of any body corporate, wherever incorporated, as follows: –

(a) a contract which if made between private persons would be by law required to be in writing, signed by the parties to be charged therewith, may be made on behalf of the body corporate in writing signed by any person acting under its authority, express or implied, and

(b) a contract which if made between private persons would by law be valid although made by parol only, and not reduced into writing, may be made by parol on behalf of the body corporate by any person acting under its authority, express or implied.

(2) A contract made according to this section shall be effectual in law, and shall bind the body corporate and its successors and all other parties thereto.

(3) A contract made according to this section may be varied or discharged in the same manner in which it is authorised by this section to be made.

(4) Nothing in this section shall be taken as preventing a contract under seal from being made by or on behalf of a body corporate.

(5) This section shall not apply to the making, variation or discharge of a contract before the commencement of this Act but shall apply whether the body corporate gave its authority before or after the commencement of this Act.

2   Exclusion of companies under Companies Acts

This Act shall not apply to any company formed and registered under the Companies Act 1985 or an existing company as defined in that Act or to a limited liability partnership.

As amended by the Companies Consolidation (Consequential Provisions) Act 1985, s30, Schedule 2; Limited Liability Partnerships Regulations 2001, reg 9, Schedule 5, para 3.

LAW REFORM (HUSBAND AND WIFE) ACT 1962
(10 & 11 Eliz 2 c 48)

1 Actions in tort between husband and wife

(1) Subject to the provisions of this section, each of the parties to a marriage shall have the like right of action in tort against the other as if they were not married.

(2) Where an action in tort is brought by one of the parties to a marriage against the other during the subsistence of the marriage, the court may stay the action if it appears – (a) that no substantial benefit would accrue to either party from the continuation of the proceedings; or (b) that the question or questions in issue could more conveniently be disposed of on an application made under section seventeen of the Married Women's Property Act 1882 (determination of questions between husband and wife as to the title to or possession of property); and without prejudice to paragraph (b) of this subsection the court may, in such an action, either exercise any power which could be exercised on an application under the said section seventeen, or give such directions as it thinks fit for the disposal under that section of any question arising in the proceedings. ...

3 Short title, repeal, interpretation, saving and extent ...

(3) The references in subsection (1) of section one of this Act to the parties to a marriage include references to the persons who were parties to a marriage which has been dissolved. ...

As amended by the Civil Procedure (Modification of Enactments) Order 1998, art 4.

HIRE-PURCHASE ACT 1964
(1964 c 53)

27 Protection of purchasers of motor vehicles

(1) This section applies where a motor vehicle has been bailed or (in Scotland) hired under a hire-purchase agreement, or has been agreed to be sold under a conditional sale agreement, and, before the property in the vehicle has become vested in the debtor, he disposes of the vehicle to another person.

(2) Where the disposition referred to in subsection (1) above is to a private purchaser, and he is a purchaser of the motor vehicle in good faith, without notice of the hire-purchaser or conditional sale agreement (the 'relevant agreement') that disposition shall have effect as if the creditor's title to the vehicle has been vested in the debtor immediately before that disposition.

(3) Where the person to whom the disposition referred to in subsection (1) above is made (the 'original purchaser') is a trade or finance purchaser, then if the person who is the first private purchaser of the motor vehicle after that disposition (the 'first private purchaser') is a purchaser of the vehicle in good faith without notice of the relevant agreement, the disposition of the vehicle to the first private purchaser shall have effect as if the title of the creditor to the vehicle had been vested in the debtor immediately before he disposed of it to the original purchaser.

(4) Where, in a case within subsection (3) above –

(a) the disposition by which the first private purchaser becomes a purchaser of the motor vehicle in good faith without notice of the relevant agreement is itself a bailment or hiring under a hire-purchase agreement, and

(b) the person who is the creditor in relation to that agreement disposes of the vehicle to the first private purchaser, or a person claiming under him, by transferring to him the property in the vehicle in pursuance of a provision in the agreement in that behalf.

the disposition referred to in paragraph (b) above (whether or not the person to whom it is made is a purchaser in good faith without notice of the relevant agreement) shall as well as the disposition referred to in paragraph (a) above, have effect as mentioned in subsection (3) above.

(5) The preceding provisions of this section apply –

(a) notwithstanding anything in section 21 of the Sale of Goods Act 1979 (sale of goods by a person not the owner), but

(b) without prejudice to the provisions of the Factors Act (as defined by section 61(1) of the said Act of 1979) or of any other enactment enabling the apparent owner of goods to dispose of them as if he were the true owner.

(6) Nothing in this section shall exonerate the debtor from any liability (whether criminal or civil) to which he would be subject apart from this section; and, in a case where the debtor disposes of the motor vehicle to a trade or finance purchaser, nothing in this section shall exonerate –

(a) that trade or finance purchaser; or

(b) any other trade or finance purchaser who becomes a purchaser of the vehicle and is not a person claiming under the first private purchaser,

from any liability (whether criminal or civil) to which he would be subject apart from this section.

28 Presumptions relating to dealings with motor vehicles

(1) Where in any proceedings (whether criminal or civil) relating to a motor vehicle it is proved –

(a) that the vehicle was bailed or (in Scotland) hired under a hire-purchase agreement, or was agreed to be sold under a conditional sale agreement and

(b) that a person (whether a party to the proceedings or not) became a private purchaser of the vehicle in good faith without notice of the hire-purchase or conditional sale agreement (the 'relevant agreement'),

this section shall have effect for the purposes of the operation of section 27 of this Act in relation to those proceedings.

(2) It shall be presumed for those purposes, unless the contrary is proved, that the disposition of the vehicle to the person referred to in subsection (1)(b) above (the 'relevant purchaser') was made by the debtor.

(3) If it is proved that that disposition was not made by the debtor, then it shall be presumed for those purposes, unless the contrary is proved –

(a) that the debtor disposed of the vehicle to a private purchaser purchasing in good faith without notice of the relevant agreement, and

(b) that the relevant purchaser is or was a person claiming under the person to whom the debtor so disposed of the vehicle.

(4) If it is proved that the disposition of the vehicle to the relevant purchaser was not made by the debtor, and that the person to whom the debtor disposed of the vehicle (the 'original purchaser') was a trade or finance purchaser, then it shall be presumed for those purposes, unless the contrary is proved, –

(a) that the person who, after the disposition of the vehicle to the original purchaser, first became a private purchaser of the vehicle was a purchaser in good faith without notice of the relevant agreement, and

(b) that the relevant purchaser is or was a person claiming under the original purchaser.

(5) Without prejudice to any other method of proof, where in any proceedings a party thereto admits a fact, that fact shall, for the purposes of this section, be taken as against him to be proved in relation to those proceedings.

29   Interpretation of Part III

(1) In this Part of this Act –

'conditional sale agreement' means an agreement for the sale of goods under which the purchase price or part of it is payable by instalments, and the property in the goods is to remain in the seller (notwithstanding that the buyer is to be in possession of the goods) until such conditions as to the payment of instalments or otherwise as may be specified in the agreement are fulfilled;

'creditor' means the person by whom goods are bailed or (in Scotland) hired under a hire-purchase agreement or as the case may be, the seller under a conditional sale agreement, or the person to whom his rights and duties have passed by assignment or operation of law;

'disposition' means any sale or contract of sale (including a conditional sale agreement), any bailment or (in Scotland) hiring under a hire-purchase agreement and any transfer of the property in goods in pursuance of a provision in that behalf contained in a hire-purchase agreement, and includes any transaction purporting to be a disposition (as so defined), and 'dispose of' shall be construed accordingly.

'hire-purchase agreement' means an agreement, other than a conditional sale agreement, under which –

(a) goods are bailed or (in Scotland) hired in return for periodical payments by the person to whom they are bailed or hired, and

(b) the property in the goods will pass to that person if the terms of the agreement are complied with and one or more of the following occurs –

(i) the exercise of an option to purchase by that person,

(ii) the doing of any other specified act by any party to the agreement,

(iii) the happening of any other specified events; and

'motor vehicle' means a mechanically propelled vehicle intended or adapted for use on roads to which the public has access.

(2) In this Part of this Act, 'trade or finance purchaser' means a purchaser who, at the time of the disposition made to him, carries on a business which consists, wholly or partly, –

(a) of purchasing motor vehicles for the purpose of offering or exposing them for sale, or

(b) of providing finance by purchasing motor vehicles for the purpose of bailing or (in Scotland) hiring them under hire-purchase agreements or agreeing to sell them under conditional sale agreements,

and 'private purchaser' means a purchaser who, at the time of the disposition made to him, does not carry on any such business.

(3) For the purposes of this Part of this Act a person becomes a purchaser of a motor vehicle if, and at the time when, a disposition of the vehicle is made to him; and a person shall be taken to be a purchaser of a motor vehicle without notice of a hire-purchase agreement or conditional sale agreement if, at the time of the disposition made to him, he has no actual notice that the vehicle is or was the subject of any such agreement.

(4) In this Part of this Act the 'debtor' in relation to a motor vehicle which has been bailed or hired under a hire-purchase agreement, or, as the case may be, agreed to be sold under a conditional sale agreement, means the person who at the material time (whether the agreement has before that time been terminated or not) is either –

(a) the person to whom the vehicle is bailed or hired under that agreement, or

(b) is, in relation to the agreement, the buyer,

including a person who at the time is, by virtue of section 130(4) of the Consumer Credit Act 1974 treated as a bailee or (in Scotland) a custodier of the vehicle.

(5) In this Part of this Act any reference to the title of the creditor to a motor vehicle which has been bailed or (in Scotland) hired under a hire-purchase agreement, or agreed to be sold under a conditional sale agreement, and is disposed of by the debtor, is a reference to such title (if any) to the vehicle as, immediately before that disposition, was vested in the person who then was the creditor in relation to the agreement.

As substituted by the Consumer Credit Act 1974, s192(3)(a), Schedule 4, para 22 and amended by the Sale of Goods Act 1979, s63, Schedule 2, para 4.

MISREPRESENTATION ACT 1967
(1967 c 7)

1   Removal of certain bars to rescission for innocent misrepresentation

Where a person has entered into a contract after a misrepresentation has been made to him, and –

(a) the misrepresentation has become a term of the contract; or

(b) the contract has been performed;

or both, then, if otherwise he would be entitled to rescind the contract without alleging fraud, he shall be so entitled, subject to the provisions of this Act, notwithstanding the matters mentioned in paragraphs (a) and (b) of this section.

2   Damages for misrepresentation

(1) Where a person has entered into a contract after a misrepresentation has been made to him by another party thereto and as a result thereof he has suffered loss, then, if the person making the misrepresentation would be liable to damages in respect thereof had the misrepresentation been made fraudulently, that person shall be so liable notwithstanding that the misrepresentation was not made fraudulently, unless he proves that he had reasonable ground to believe and did believe up to the time the contract was made that the facts represented were true.

(2) Where a person has entered into a contract after a misrepresentation has been made to him otherwise than fraudulently, and he would be entitled, by reason of the misrepresentation, to rescind the contract, then, if it is claimed, in any proceedings arising out of the contract, that the contract ought to be or has been rescinded the court or arbitrator may declare the contract subsisting and award damages in lieu of rescission, if of opinion that it would be equitable to do so, having regard to the nature of the misrepresentation and the loss that would be caused by it if the contract were upheld, as well as to the loss that rescission would cause to the other party.

(3) Damages may be awarded against a person under subsection (2) of this section whether or not he is liable to damages under subsection (1) thereof, but where he is so liable any award under the said subsection (2) shall be taken into account in assessing his liability under the said subsection (1).

3   Avoidance of provision excluding liability for misrepresentation

If a contract contains a term which would exclude or restrict –

(a) any liability to which a party to a contract may be subject by reason of any misrepresentation made by him before the contract was made; or

(b) any remedy available to another party to the contract by reason of such misrepresentation,

that term shall be of no effect except in so far as it satisfies the requirement of reasonableness stated in section 11(1) of the Unfair Contract Terms Act 1977; and it is for those claiming that the term satisfies that requirement to show that it does.

As amended by the Unfair Contract Terms Act 1977, s8(1).

CRIMINAL LAW ACT 1967
(1967 c 58)

3   Use of force in making arrest, etc

(1) A person may use such force as is reasonable in the circumstances in the prevention of crime, or in effecting or assisting in the lawful arrest of offenders or suspected offenders or of persons unlawfully at large.

(2) Subsection (1) above shall replace the rules of the common law on the question when force used for a purpose mentioned in the subsection is justified by that purpose.

THEATRES ACT 1968
(1968 c 54)

4   Amendment of the law of defamation

(1) For the purposes of the law of libel and slander (including the law of criminal libel so far as it relates to the publication of defamatory matter) the publication of words in the course of a performance of a play shall, subject to section 7 of this Act, be treated as publication in permanent form.

(2) The foregoing subsection shall apply for the purposes of section 3 (slander of title, etc) of the Defamation Act 1952, as it applies for the purposes of the law of libel and slander.

(3) In this section 'words' includes pictures, visual images, gestures and other methods of signifying meaning. ...

7   Exceptions for performances given in certain circumstances

(1) Nothing in sections 2 to 4 of this Act shall apply in relation to a performance of a play given on a domestic occasion in a private dwelling.

(2) Nothing in sections 2 to 6 of this Act shall apply in relation to a performance of a play given solely or primarily for one or more of the following purposes, that is to say –

    (a) rehearsal; or

    (b) to enable –

        (i) a record or cinematograph film to be made from or by means of the performance; or

        (ii) the performance to be broadcast; or

        (iii) the performance to be included in a programme service (within the meaning of the Broadcasting Act 1990) other than a sound or television broadcasting service;

but in any proceedings for an offence under section 2 or 6 of this Act alleged to have been committed in respect of a performance of a play or an offence at common law alleged to have been committed in England and Wales by the publication of defamatory matter in the course of a performance of a play, if it is proved that the performance was attended by persons other than persons directly connected with the giving of the performance or the doing in relation thereto of any of the things mentioned in paragraph (b) above, the performance shall be taken to not have been given solely or primarily for one or more of the said purposes unless the contrary is shown.

(3) In this section –

'broadcast' means broadcast by wireless telegraphy (within the meaning of the Wireless Telegraphy Act 1949), whether by way of sound broadcasting or television;

'cinematograph film' means any print, negative, tape or other article on which a performance of a play or any part of such a performance is recorded for the purposes of visual reproduction;

'record' means any record or similar contrivance for reproducing sound, including the sound-track of a cinematograph film.

As amended by the Cable and Broadcasting Act 1984, s57, Schedule 5, para 21, Schedule 6; Public Order Act 1986, s40(3), Schedule 3; Broadcasting Act 1990, s203(1), Schedule 20, para 13.

CIVIL EVIDENCE ACT 1968
(1968 c 64)

13 Conclusiveness of convictions for purposes of defamation actions

(1) In an action for libel or slander in which the question whether the plaintiff did or did not commit a criminal offence is relevant to an issue arising in the action, proof that, at the date when that issue falls to be determined, he stands convicted of that offence shall be conclusive evidence that he committed that offence; and his conviction thereof shall be admissible in evidence accordingly.

(2) In any such action as aforesaid in which by virtue of this section the plaintiff is proved to have been convicted of an offence, the contents of any document which is admissible as evidence of the conviction, and the contents of the information, complaint, indictment or charge-sheet on which he was convicted, shall, without prejudice to the reception of any other admissible evidence for the purpose of identifying the facts on which the conviction was based, be admissible in evidence for the purpose of identifying those facts.

(2A) In the case of an action for libel or slander in which there is more than one plaintiff –

(a) the references in subsections (1) and (2) above to the plaintiff shall be construed as references to any of the plaintiffs, and

(b) proof that any of the plaintiffs stands convicted of an offence shall be conclusive evidence that he committed that offence so far as that fact is relevant to any issue arising in relation to his cause of action or that of any other plaintiff.

(3) For the purposes of this section a person shall be taken to stand convicted of an offence if but only if there subsists against him a conviction of that offence by or before a court in the United Kingdom or by a court-martial there or elsewhere ...

As amended by the Defamation Act 1996, s12(1).

GAMING ACT 1968
(1968 c 65)

1   Gaming to which Part I applies

(1) Except as provided by the next following subsection, this part of this Act applies to all gaming which takes place elsewhere than on premises in respect of which either –

    (a) a licence under this Act is for the time being in force, or

    (b) a club or miners' welfare institute is for the time being registered under Part II of this Act.

(2) This Part of this Act does not apply to –

    (a) gaming by means of any machine to which Part III of this Act applies, or

    (b) gaming to which section 41 of this Act applies [gaming at entertainments not held for private gain], or

    (c) gaming which constitutes the provision of amusements with prizes as mentioned in sectiion 15(1) or 16(1) of the Lotteries and Amusements Act 1976.

2   Nature of game

(1) Subject to the following provisions of this section, no gaming to which this Part of this Act applies shall take place where any one or more of the following conditions are fulfilled, that is to say –

    (a) the game involves playing or staking against a bank, whether the bank is held by one of the players or not;

    (b) the nature of the game is such that the chances in the game are not equally favourable to all the players;

    (c) the nature of the game is such that the chances in it lie between the player and some other person, or (if there are two or more players) lie wholly or partly between the players and some other person, and those chances are not as favourable to the player or players as they are to that other person.

(2) The preceding subsection shall not have effect in relation to gaming which takes place on a domestic occasion in a private dwelling, and shall not have effect in relation to any gaming where the gaming takes place in a hostel, hall of residence or similar establishment which is not carried on by way of a trade or business and the players consist exclusively or mainly of persons who are residents or inmates in that establishment.

16   Provision of credit for gaming

(1) Subject to subsections (2) to (2A) of this section, where gaming to which this Part of this Act applies takes place on premises in respect of which a licence under this Act is for the time being in force, neither the holder of the licence nor any person acting on his behalf or under any arrangement with him shall make any loan or otherwise provide or allow to any person any credit, or release, or discharge on another person's behalf, the whole or part of any debt, –

(a) for enabling any person to take part in the gaming, or

(b) in respect of any losses incurred by any person in the gaming.

(2) Neither the holder of the licence nor any person acting on his behalf or under any arrangement with him shall accept a cheque and give in exchange for it cash or tokens for enabling any person to take part in the gaming unless the following conditions are fulfilled, that is to say –

(a) the cheque is not a post-dated cheque, and

(b) it is exchanged for cash to an amount equal to the amount for which it is drawn, or is exchanged for tokens at the same rate as would apply if cash, to the amount for which the cheque is drawn, were given in exchange for them;

but, where those conditions are fulfilled, the giving of cash or tokens in exchange for a cheque shall not be taken to contravene subsection (1) of this section.

(2ZA) Neither the holder of the licence nor any person acting on his behalf or under any arrangement with him shall accept a debit card payment and give in exchange for it cash or tokens for enabling any person to take part in the gaming unless the following conditions are fulfilled, that is to say –

(a) the payment is exchanged for cash to an amount equal to the amount of the payment, or is exchanged for tokens at the same rate as would apply if cash, to the amount of the payment, were given in exchange for them, and

(b) the payment has been authorised by the holder of the card and by or on behalf of the issuer of the card;

but where those conditions are fulfilled, the giving of cash or tokens in exchange for a debit card payment shall not be taken to contravene subsection (1) above.

(2A) Neither the holder of a licence under this Act nor any person acting on his behalf or under any arrangement with him shall permit to be redeemed any cheque (not being a cheque which has been dishonoured) accepted in exchange for cash or tokens for enabling any person to take part in gaming to which this Part of this Act applies unless the following conditions are fulfilled, that is to say –

(a) the cheque is redeemed by the person from whom it was accepted giving in exchange for it cash, or tokens, or a substitute cheque or a debit card payment, or any combination of these, to an amount equal to the amount of the redeemed cheque or (where two or more cheques are redeemed) the aggregate amount of the redeemed cheques;

(b) it is redeemed during the playing session in which it was accepted, or within 30 minutes after the end of the session;

(c) where a substitute cheque is given in whole or in part exchange for the redeemed cheque the substitute cheque is not a post-dated cheque;

(d) where tokens are given in whole or in part exchange for the redeemed cheque, the value of each token is equal to the amount originally given in exchange for it or, if the token was won in the gaming, the value it represented when won;

but, where those conditions are fulfilled, the return of a redeemed cheque in exchange for cash, or tokens, or a substitute cheque, or any combination of these, shall not be taken to contravene subsection (1) of this section.

(3) Where the holder of a licence under this Act, or a person acting on behalf of or under any arrangement with the holder of such a licence, accepts a cheque in exchange for cash or tokens to be used by a player in gaming to which this Part of this Act applies or a substitute cheque, he shall not more than two banking days later cause the cheque to be delivered to a bank for payment or collection.

(3A) Subsection (3) of this section shall not apply to a redeemed cheque.

(3B) Where the holder of a licence under this Act, or a person acting on behalf of or under any arrangement with the holder of such a licence, accepts a debit card payment in exchange for cash or tokens to be used by a player in gaming to which this Part of this Act applies, or a substitute debit card payment, he shall not more than two banking days later do whatever is required under his arrangements with the issuer of the card to secure that he is credited with the amount of the payment.

(4) Nothing in the Gaming Act 1710, the Gaming Act 1835, the Gaming Act 1845, or the Gaming Act 1892, shall affect the validity of, or any remedy in respect of, any cheque or debit card payment which is accepted in exchange for cash or tokens to be used by a player in gaming to which this Part of this Act applies or any substitute cheque or substitute debit card payment.

(5) In this section 'banking day' means a day which is a business day in accordance with section 92 of the Bills of Exchange Act 1882.

'debit card' means a card which may be used as a means of payment under arrangements which do not provide for the extension of credit to the cardholder, but provide for amounts paid by means of the card to be debited to a specified account in his name (or in his name jointly with one or more others);

'debit card payment' means a payment by means of a debit card;

'playing session' means a continuous period during one day, or two consecutive days, throughout which gaming is permitted by or under this Act to take place on premises in respect of which a licence under this Act is for the time being in force;

'redeemed cheque' means a cheque accepted in fulfilment of the conditions specified in subsection (2) of this section and returned to the person from whom it was accepted in fulfilment of the conditions specified in subsection (2A) of this section;

'substitute cheque' means a cheque accepted in accordance with subsection (2A) of this section by either the holder of a licence under this Act or a person acting on behalf of or under any arrangement with the holder of such a licence;

'substitute debit card payment' means a debit card payment accepted in accordance with subsection (2A) of this section by either the holder of a licence under this Act or a person acting on behalf of or under any arrangement with the holder of such a licence.

52   Interpretation

(1) In this Act, except in so far as the context otherwise requires, the following expressions have the meanings hereby assigned to them respectively, that is to say:
...

'gaming' (subject to subsections (3) to (5) of this section) [which exclude certain lotteries (including the National Lottery), pool betting and certain games played by machines] means the playing of a game of chance for winnings in money or money's worth, whether any person playing the game is at risk of losing any money or money's worth or not; ...

As amended by the Lotteries and Amusements Act 1976, s25(2), Schedule 4, para 1; Gaming (Amendment) Act 1986, s1; Deregulation (Casinos and Bingo Clubs: Debit Cards) Order 1997, art 3.

EMPLOYERS' LIABILITY (DEFECTIVE EQUIPMENT) ACT 1969

(1969 c 37)

1   Extension of employer's liability for defective equipment

(1) Where after the commencement of this Act –

(a) an employee suffers personal injury in the course of his employment in consequence of a defect in equipment provided by his employer for the purposes of the employer's business; and

(b) the defect is attributable wholly or partly to the fault of a third party (whether identified or not),

the injury shall be deemed to be also attributable to negligence on the part of the employer (whether or not he is liable in respect of the injury apart from this subsection), but without prejudice to the law relating to contributory negligence and to any remedy by way of contribution or in contract or otherwise which is available to the employer in respect of the injury.

(2) In so far as any agreement purports to exclude or limit any liability of an employer arising under subsection (1) of this section, the agreement shall be void.

(3) In this section –

'business' includes the activities carried on by any public body;

'employee' means a person who is employed by another person under a contract of service or apprenticeship and is so employed for the purposes of a business carried on by that other person, and 'employer' shall be construed accordingly; 'equipment' includes any plant and machinery, vehicle, aircraft and clothing;

'fault' means negligence, breach of statutory duty or other act or omission which gives rise to liability in tort in England and Wales or which is wrongful and gives rise to liability in damages in Scotland; and

'personal injury' includes loss of life, any impairment of a person's physical or mental condition and any disease.

(4) This section binds the Crown, and persons in the service of the Crown shall accordingly be treated for the purposes of this section as employees of the Crown if they would not be so treated apart from this subsection.

FAMILY LAW REFORM ACT 1969
(1969 c 46)

1 Reduction of age of majority from 21 to 18

(1) As from the date on which this section comes into force a person shall attain full age on attaining the age of eighteen instead of on attaining the age of twenty-one; and a person shall attain full age on that date if he has then already attained the age of eighteen but not the age of twenty-one.

(2) The foregoing subsection applies for the purposes of any rule of law, and, in the absence of a definition or of any indication of a contrary intention, for the construction of 'full age', 'infant', 'infancy', 'minor', 'minority' and similar expressions in –

(a) any statutory provision, whether passed or made before, on or after the date on which this section comes into force; and

(b) any deed, will or other instrument of whatever nature (not being a statutory provision) made on or after that date. ...

(6) In this section 'statutory provision' means any enactment (including, except where the context otherwise requires, this Act) and any order, rule, regulation, byelaw or other instrument made in the exercise of a power conferred by any enactment. ...

9 Time at which a person attains a particular age

(1) The time at which a person attains a particular age expressed in years shall be the commencement of the relevant anniversary of the date of his birth.

(2) This section applies only where the relevant anniversary falls on a date after that on which this section comes into force, and, in relation to any enactment, deed, will or other instrument, has effect subject to any provision therein.

ADMINISTRATION OF JUSTICE ACT 1970
(1970 c 31)

44   Interest on judgment debts

(1) The Lord Chancellor may by order made with the concurrence of the Treasury direct that section 17 of the Judgments Act 1838 (as that enactment has effect for the time being whether by virtue of this subsection or otherwise) shall be amended so as to substitute for the rate specified in that section as the rate at which judgment debts shall carry interest such rate as may be specified in the order.

(2) An order under this section shall be made by statutory instrument which shall be laid before Parliament after being made.

44A   Interest on judgment debts expressed in currencies other than sterling

(1) Where a judgment is given for a sum expressed in a currency other than sterling and the judgment debt is one to which section 17 of the Judgments Act 1838 applies, the court may order that the interest rate applicable to the debt shall be such rate as the court thinks fit.

(2) Where the court makes such an order, section 17 of the Judgments Act 1838 shall have effect in relation to the judgment debt as if the rate specified in the order were substituted for the rate specified in that section.

Section 44A was inserted by the Private International Law (Miscellaneous Provisions) Act 1995, s1.

ANIMALS ACT 1971
(1971 c 22)

1 New provisions as to strict liability for damage done by animals

(1) The provisions of sections 2 to 5 of this Act replace –

(a) the rules of the common law imposing a strict liability in tort for damage done by an animal on the ground that the animal is regarded as ferae naturae or that its vicious or mischievous propensities are known or presumed to be known;

(b) subsections (1) and (2) of section I of the Dogs Act 1906 as amended by the Dogs (Amendment) Act 1928 (injury to cattle or poultry); and

(c) the rules of the common law imposing a liability for cattle trespass.

(2) Expressions used in those sections shall be interpreted in accordance with the provisions of section 6 (as well as those of section 11) of this Act.

2 Liability for damage done by dangerous animals

(1) Where any damage is caused by an animal which belongs to a dangerous species, any person who is a keeper of the animal is liable for the damage, except as otherwise provided by this Act.

(2) Where damage is caused by an animal which does not belong to a dangerous species, a keeper of the animal is liable for the damage, except as otherwise provided by this Act, if –

(a) the damage is of a kind which the animal, unless restrained, was likely to cause or which, if caused by the animal, was likely to be severe; and

(b) the likelihood of the damage or of its being severe was due to characteristics of the animal which are not normally found in animals of the same species or are not normally so found except at particular times or in particular circumstances; and

(c) those characteristics were known to that keeper or were at any time known to a person who at that time had charge of the animal as that keeper's servant or, where that keeper is the head of a household, were known to another keeper of the animal who is a member of that household and under the age of sixteen.

3 Liability for injury done by dogs to livestock

Where a dog causes damage by killing or injuring livestock, any person who is a keeper of the dog is liable for the damage, except as otherwise provided by this Act.

4 Liability for damage and expenses due to trespassing livestock

(1) Where livestock belonging to any person strays on to land in the ownership or occupation of another and –

(a) damage is done by the livestock to the land or to any property on it which is in the ownership or possession of the other person; or

(b) any expenses are reasonably incurred by that other person in keeping the livestock while it cannot be restored to the person to whom it belongs or while it is detained in pursuance of section 7 of this Act, or in ascertaining to whom it belongs;

the person to whom the livestock belongs is liable for the damage or expenses, except as otherwise provided by this Act.

(2) For the purposes of this section any livestock belongs to the person in whose possession it is.

5 Exceptions from liability under sections 2 to 4

(1) A person is not liable under sections 2 to 4 of this Act for any damage which is due wholly to the fault of the person suffering it.

(2) A person is not liable under section 2 of this Act for any damage suffered by a person who has voluntarily accepted the risk thereof.

(3) A person is not liable under section 2 of this Act for any damage caused by an animal kept on any premises or structure to a person trespassing there, if it is proved either –

(a) that the animal was not kept there for the protection of persons or property; or

(b) (if the animal was kept there for the protection of persons or property) that keeping it there for that purpose was not unreasonable.

(4) A person is not liable under section 3 of this Act if the livestock was killed or injured on land on to which it had strayed and either the dog belonged to the occupier or its presence on the land was authorised by the occupier.

(5) A person is not liable under section 4 of this Act where the livestock strayed from a highway and its presence there was a lawful use of the highway.

(6) In determining whether any liability for damage under section 4 of this Act is excluded by subsection (1) of this section the damage shall not be treated as due to the fault of the person suffering it by reason only that he could have prevented it by fencing; but a person is not liable under that section where it is proved that the straying of the livestock on to the land would not have occurred but for a breach by any other person, being a person having an interest in the land, of a duty to fence.

6 Interpretation of certain expressions used in sections 2 to 5

(1) The following provisions apply to the interpretation of sections 2 to 5 of this Act.

(2) A dangerous species is a species –

(a) which is not commonly domesticated in the British Islands; and

(b) whose fully grown animals normally have such characteristics that they are likely, unless restrained, to cause severe damage or that any damage they may cause is likely to be severe.

(3) Subject to subsection (4) of this section, a person is a keeper of an animal if –

(a) he owns the animal or has it in his possession; or

(b) he is the head of a household of which a member under the age of sixteen owns the animal or has it in his possession;

and if at any time an animal ceased to be owned by or to be in the possession of a person, any person who immediately before that time was a keeper thereof by virtue of the preceding provisions of this subsection continues to be a keeper of the animal until another person becomes a keeper thereof by virtue of those provisions.

(4) Where an animal is taken into and kept in possession for the purpose of preventing it from causing damage or of restoring it to its owner, a person is not a keeper of it by virtue only of that possession.

(5) Where a person employed as a servant by a keeper of an animal incurs a risk incidental to his employment he shall not be treated as accepting it voluntarily.

7 Detention and sale of trespassing livestock

(1) The right to seize and detain any animal by way of distress damage feasant is hereby abolished.

(2) Where any livestock strays on to any land and is not then under the control of any person the occupier of the land may detain it, subject to subsection (3) of this section, unless ordered to return it by a court.

(3) Where any livestock is detained in pursuance of this section the right to detain it ceases –

(a) at the end of a period of forty-eight hours, unless within that period notice of the detention has been given to the officer in charge of a police station and also, if the person detaining the livestock knows to whom it belongs, to that person; or

(b) when such amount is tendered to the person detaining the livestock as is sufficient to satisfy any claim he may have under section 4 of this Act in respect of the livestock; or

(c) if he has no such claim, when the livestock is claimed by a person entitled to its possession.

(4) Where livestock has been detained in pursuance of this section for a period of not

less than fourteen days the person detaining it may sell it at a market or by public auction, unless proceedings are then pending for the return of the livestock or for any claim under section 4 of this Act in respect of it.

(5) Where any livestock is sold in the exercise of the right conferred by this section and the proceeds of the sale, less the costs thereof and any costs incurred in connection with it, exceed the amount of any claim under section 4 of this Act which the vendor had in respect of the livestock, the excess shall be recoverable from him by the person who would be entitled to the possession of the livestock but for the sale.

(6) A person detaining any livestock in pursuance of this section is liable for any damage caused to it by a failure to treat it with reasonable care and supply it with adequate food and water while it is so detained.

(7) References in this section to a claim under section 4 of this Act in respect of any livestock do not include any claim under that section for damage done by or expenses incurred in respect of the livestock before the straying in connection with which it is detained under this section.

8   Duty to take care to prevent damage from animals straying on to the highway

(1) So much of the rules of the common law relating to liability for negligence as excludes or restricts the duty which a person might owe to others to take such care as is reasonable to see that damage is not caused by animals straying on to a highway is hereby abolished.

(2) Where damage is caused by animals straying from unfenced land to a highway a person who placed them on the land shall not be regarded as having committed a breach of the duty to take care by reason only of placing them there if –

(a) the land is common land, or is land situated in an area where fencing is not customary, or is a town or village green; and

(b) he had a right to place the animals on that land.

9   Killing of or injury to dogs worrying livestock

(1) In any civil proceedings against a person (in this section referred to as the defendant) for killing or causing injury to a dog it shall be a defence to prove –

(a) that the defendant acted for the protection of any livestock and was a person entitled to act for the protection of that livestock; and

(b) that within forty-eight hours of the killing or injury notice thereof was given by the defendant to the officer in charge of a police station.

(2) For the purposes of this section a person is entitled to act for the protection of any livestock if, and only if –

(a) the livestock or the land on which it is belongs to him or to any person under whose express or implied authority he is acting; and

(b) the circumstances are not such that liability for killing or causing injury to the livestock would be excluded by section 5(4) of this Act.

(3) Subject to subsection (4) of this section, a person killing or causing injury to a dog shall be deemed for the purposes of this section to act for the protection of any livestock if, and only if; either –

(a) the dog is worrying or is about to worry the livestock and there are no other reasonable means of ending or preventing the worrying; or

(b) the dog has been worrying livestock, has not left the vicinity and is not under the control of any person and there are no practicable means of ascertaining to whom it belongs.

(4) For the purposes of this section the condition stated in either of the paragraphs of the preceding subsection shall be deemed to have been satisfied if the defendant believed that it was satisfied and had reasonable ground for that belief.

(5) For the purposes of this section –

(a) an animal belongs to any person if he owns it or has it in his possession; and

(b) land belongs to any person if he is the occupier thereof.

10   Application of certain enactments to liability under sections 2 to 4

For the purposes of the Fatal Accidents Act 1976, the Law Reform (Contributory Negligence) Act 1945 and the Limitation Act 1980 any damage for which a person is liable under sections 2 to 4 of this Act shall be treated as due to his fault.

11   General interpretation

In this Act –

'common land', and 'town or village green' have the same meanings as in the Commons Registration Act 1965;

'damage' includes the death of, or injury to, any person (including any disease and any impairment of physical or mental condition);

'fault' has the same meaning as in the Law Reform (Contributory Negligence) Act 1945;

'fencing' includes the construction of any obstacle designed to prevent animals from straying;

'livestock' means cattle, horses, asses, mules, hinnies, sheep, pigs, goats and poultry, and also deer not in the wild state and, in sections 3 and 9, also, while in captivity, pheasants, partridges and grouse; 'poultry' means the domestic varieties of the following, that is to say, fowls, turkeys, geese, ducks, guineafowls, pigeons, peacocks and quails; and

'species' includes sub-species and variety.

12 Application to Crown

(1) This Act binds the Crown, but nothing in this section shall authorise proceedings to be brought against Her Majesty in her private capacity.

(2) Section 38 (3) of the Crown Proceedings Act 1947 (interpretation of references to Her Majesty in her private capacity) shall apply as if this section were contained in that Act.

As amended by the Limitation Act 1980, s40(2), Schedule 3, para 10.

POWERS OF ATTORNEY ACT 1971
(1971 c 27)

4 Powers of attorney given as security

(1) Where a power of attorney is expressed to be irrevocable and is given to secure –

(a) a proprietary interest of the donee of the power; or

(b) the performance of an obligation owed to the donee,

then, so long as the donee has that interest or the obligation remains undischarged, the power shall not be revoked –

(a) by the donor without the consent of the donee; or

(b) by the death, incapacity or bankruptcy of the donor or, if the donor is a body corporate, by its winding up or dissolution.

(2) A power of attorney given to secure a proprietary interest may be given to the person entitled to the interest and persons deriving title under him to that interest, and those persons shall be duly constituted donees of the power for all purposes of the power but without prejudice to any right to appoint substitutes given by the power.

(3) This section applies to powers of attorney whenever created.

DEFECTIVE PREMISES ACT 1972
(1972 c 35)

1 Duty to build dwellings properly

(1) A person taking on work for or in connection with the provision of a dwelling (whether the dwelling is provided by the erection or by the conversion or enlargement of a building) owes a duty –

(a) if the dwelling is provided to the order of any person, to that person; and

(b) without prejudice to paragraph (a) above, to every person who acquires an interest (whether legal or equitable) in the dwelling;

to see that the work which he takes on is done in a workmanlike or, as the case may be, professional manner, with proper materials and so that as regards that work the dwelling will be fit for habitation when completed.

(2) A person who takes on any such work for another on terms that he is to do it in accordance with instructions given by or on behalf of that other shall, to the extent to which he does it properly in accordance with those instructions, be treated for the purposes of this section as discharging the duty imposed on him by subsection (1) above except where he owes a duty to that other to warn him of any defects in the instructions and fails to discharge that duty.

(3) A person shall not be treated for the purposes of subsection (2) above as having given instructions for the doing of work merely because he has agreed to the work being done in a specified manner, with specified materials or to a specified design.

(4) A person who –

(a) in the course of a business which consists of or includes providing or arranging for the provision of dwellings or installations in dwellings; or

(b) in the exercise of a power of making such provision or arrangements conferred by or by virtue of any enactment;

arranges for another to take on work for or in connection with the provision of a dwelling shall be treated for the purposes of this section as included among the persons who have taken on the work.

(5) Any cause of action in respect of a breach of the duty imposed by this section shall be deemed, for the purposes of the Limitation Act 1980, to have accrued at the time when the dwelling was completed, but if after that time a person who has done work for or in connection with the provision of the dwelling does further work to rectify the work he has already done, any such cause of action in respect of that

further work shall be deemed for those purposes to have accrued at the time when the further work was finished.

2   Cases excluded from the remedy under section 1

(1) Where –

(a) in connection with the provision of a dwelling or its first sale or letting for habitation any rights in respect of defects in the state of the dwelling are conferred by an approved scheme to which this section applies on a person having or acquiring an interest in the dwelling; and

(b) it is stated in a document of a type approved for the purposes of this section that the requirements as to design or construction imposed by or under the scheme have, or appear to have, been substantially complied with in relation to the dwelling;

no action shall be brought by any person having or acquiring an interest in the dwelling for breach of the duty imposed by section 1 above in relation to the dwelling.

(2) A scheme to which this section applies –

(a) may consist of any number of documents and any number of agreements or other transactions between any number of persons; but

(b) must confer, by virtue of agreements entered into with persons having or acquiring an interest in the dwellings to which the scheme applies, rights on such persons in respect of defects in the state of the dwellings.

(3) In this section 'approved' means approved by the Secretary of State, and the power of the Secretary of State to approve a scheme or document for the purposes of this section shall be exercisable by order, except that any requirements as to construction or design imposed under a scheme to which this section applies may be approved by him without making any order or, if he thinks fit, by order.

(4) The Secretary of State –

(a) may approve a scheme or document for the purposes of this section with or without limiting the duration of his approval; and

(b) may by order revoke or vary a previous order under this section or, without such an order, revoke or vary a previous approval under this section given otherwise than by order.

(5) The production of a document purporting to be a copy of an approval given by the Secretary of State otherwise than by order and certified by an officer of the Secretary of State to be a true copy of the approval shall be conclusive evidence of the approval, and without proof of the handwriting or official position of the person purporting to sign the certificate.

(6) The power to make an order under this section shall be exercisable by statutory instrument which shall be subject to annulment in pursuance of a resolution by either House of Parliament.

(7) Where an interest in a dwelling is compulsorily acquired –

(a) no action shall be brought by the acquiring authority for breach of the duty imposed by section 1 above in respect of the dwelling; and

(b) if any work for or in connection with the provision of the dwelling was done otherwise than in the course of a business by the person in occupation of the dwelling at the time of the compulsory acquisition, the acquiring authority and not that person shall be treated as the person who took on the work and accordingly as owing that duty.

3   Duty of care with respect to work done on premises not abated by disposal of premises

(1) Where work of construction, repair, maintenance or demolition or any other work is done on or in relation to premises, any duty of care owed, because of the doing of the work, to persons who might reasonably be expected to be affected by defects in the state of the premises created by the doing of the work shall not be abated by the subsequent disposal of the premises by the person who owed the duty.

(2) This section does not apply –

(a) in the case of premises which are let, where the relevant tenancy of the premises commenced, or the relevant tenancy agreement of the premises was entered into, before the commencement of this Act;

(b) in the case of premises disposed of in any other way, when the disposal of the premises was completed, or a contract for their disposal was entered into, before the commencement of this Act; or

(c) in either case, where the relevant transaction disposing of the premises is entered into in pursuance of an enforceable option by which the consideration for the disposal was fixed before the commencement of this Act.

4   Landlord's duty of care in virtue of obligation or right to repair premises demised

(1) Where premises are let under a tenancy which puts on the landlord an obligation to the tenant for the maintenance or repair of the premises, the landlord owes to all persons who might reasonably be expected to be affected by defects in the state of the premises a duty to take such care as is reasonable in all the circumstances to see that they are reasonably safe from personal injury or from damage to their property caused by a relevant defect.

(2) The said duty is owed if the landlord knows (whether as the result of being notified by the tenant or otherwise) or if he ought in all the circumstances to have known of the relevant defect.

(3) In this section 'relevant defect' means a defect in the state of the premises existing at or after the material time and arising from, or continuing because of, an act or omission by the landlord which constitutes or would if he had had notice of the defect have constituted a failure by him to carry out his obligation to the

tenant for the maintenance or repair of the premises; and for the purposes of the foregoing provision 'the material time' means –

(a) where the tenancy commenced before this Act, the commencement of this Act; and

(b) in all other cases, the earliest of the following times, that is to say –

(i) the time when the tenancy commences;

(ii) the time when the tenancy agreement is entered into;

(iii) the time when possession is taken of the premises in contemplation of the letting.

(4) Where premises are let under a tenancy which expressly or impliedly gives the landlord the right to enter the premises to carry out any description of maintenance or repair of the premises, then, as from the time when he first is, or by notice or otherwise can put himself, in a position to exercise the right and so long as he is or can put himself in that position, he shall be treated for the purposes of subsections (1) to (3) above (but for no other purpose) as if he were under an obligation to the tenant for that description of maintenance or repair of the premises; but the landlord shall not owe the tenant any duty by virtue of this subsection in respect of any defect in the state of the premises arising from, or continuing because of, a failure to carry out an obligation expressly imposed on the tenant by the tenancy.

(5) For the purposes of this section obligations imposed or rights given by any enactment in virtue of a tenancy shall be treated as imposed or given by the tenancy.

(6) This section applies to a right of occupation given by contract or any enactment and not amounting to a tenancy as if the right were a tenancy, and 'tenancy' and cognate expressions shall be construed accordingly.

5 Application to Crown

This Act shall bind the Crown, but as regards the Crown's liability in tort shall not bind the Crown further than the Crown is made liable in tort by the Crown Proceedings Act 1947.

6 Supplemental

(1) In this Act –

'disposal', in relation to premises, includes a letting, and an assignment or surrender of a tenancy, of the premises and the creation by contract of any other right to occupy the premises and 'dispose' shall be construed accordingly;

'personal injury' includes any disease and any impairment of a person's physical or mental condition; 'tenancy' means –

(a) a tenancy created either immediately or derivatively out of the freehold, whether by a lease or underlease, by an agreement for a lease or underlease or by a tenancy agreement, but not including a mortgage term or any interest arising in favour of a mortgagor by his attorning tenant to his mortgagee; or

(b) a tenancy at will or a tenancy on sufferance; or

(c) a tenancy, whether or not constituting a tenancy at common law, created by or in pursuance of any enactment; and cognate expressions shall be construed accordingly.

(2) Any duty imposed by or enforceable by virtue of any provision of this Act is in addition to any duty a person may owe apart from that provision.

(3) Any term of an agreement which purports to exclude or restrict, or has the effect of excluding or restricting, the operation of any of the provisions of this Act, or any liability arising by virtue of any such provision, shall be void. ...

SUPPLY OF GOODS (IMPLIED TERMS) ACT 1973

(1973 c 13)

8   Implied terms as to title

(1) In every hire-purchase agreement, other than one to which subsection (2) below applies, there is –

    (a) an implied term on the part of the creditor that he will have a right to sell the goods at the time when the property is to pass; and

    (b) an implied term that –

        (i) the goods are free, and will remain free until the time when the property is to pass, from any charge or encumbrance not disclosed or known to the person to whom the goods are bailed or (in Scotland) hired before the agreement is made, and

        (ii) that person will enjoy quiet possession of the goods except so far as it may be disturbed by any person entitled to the benefit of any charge or encumbrance so disclosed or known.

(2) In a hire-purchase agreement, in the case of which there appears from the agreement or is to be inferred from the circumstances of the agreement an intention that the creditor should transfer only such title as he or a third person may have, there is –

    (a) an implied term that all charges or encumbrances known to the creditor and not known to the person to whom the goods are bailed or hired have been disclosed to that person before the agreement is made, and

    (b) an implied term that neither –

        (i) the creditor; nor

        (ii) in a case where the parties to the agreement intend that any title which may be transferred shall be only such title as a third person may have, that person; nor

        (iii) anyone claiming through or under the creditor or that third person otherwise than under a charge or encumbrance disclosed or known to the person to whom the goods are bailed or hired, before the agreement is made;

will disturb the quiet possession of the person to whom the goods are bailed or hired.

(3) As regards England and Wales and Northern Ireland, the term implied by subsection (1)(a) above is a condition and the terms implied by subsections (1)(b), (2)(a) and (2)(b) above are warranties.

9 Bailing or hiring by description

(1) Where under a hire-purchase agreement goods are bailed or (in Scotland) hired by description, there is an implied term that the goods will correspond with the description, and if under the agreement the goods are bailed or hired by reference to a sample as well as a description, it is not sufficient that the bulk of the goods corresponds with the sample if the goods do not also correspond with the description.

(1A) As regards England and Wales and Northern Ireland, the term implied by subsection (1) above is a condition.

(2) Goods shall not be prevented from being bailed or hired by description by reason only that, being exposed for sale, bailment or hire, they are selected by the person to whom they are bailed or hired.

10 Implied undertakings as to quality or fitness

(1) Except as provided by this section and section 11 below and subject to the provisions of any other enactment, including any enactment of the Parliament of Northern Ireland or the Northern Ireland Assembly, there is no implied term as to the quality or fitness for any particular purpose of goods bailed or (in Scotland) hired under a hire-purchase agreement.

(2) Where the creditor bails or hires goods under a hire-purchase agreement in the course of a business, there is an implied term that the goods supplied under the agreement are of satisfactory quality.

(2A) For the purposes of this Act, goods are of satisfactory quality if they meet the standard that a reasonable person would regard as satisfactory, taking account of any description of the goods, the price (if relevant) and all the other relevant circumstances.

(2B) For the purposes of this Act, the quality of goods includes their state and condition and the following (among others) are in appropriate cases aspects of the quality of goods –

    (a) fitness for all the purposes for which goods of the kind in question are commonly supplied,

    (b) appearance and finish,

    (c) freedom from minor defects,

    (d) safety, and

    (e) durability.

(2C) The term implied by subsection (2) above does not extend to any matter making the quality of goods unsatisfactory –

(a) which is specifically drawn to the attention of the person to whom the goods are bailed or hired before the agreement is made,

(b) where that person examines the goods before the agreement is made, which that examination ought to reveal, or

(c) where the goods are bailed or hired by reference to a sample, which would have been apparent on a reasonable examination of the sample.

(2D) If the person to whom the goods are bailed or hired deals as consumer or, in Scotland, if the goods are hired to a person under a consumer contract, the relevant circumstances mentioned in subsection (2A) above include any public statements on the specific characteristics of the goods made about them by the creditor, the producer or his representative, particularly in advertising or on labelling.

(2E) A public statement is not by virtue of subsection (2D) above a relevant circumstance for the purposes of subsection (2A) above in the case of a contract of hire-purchase, if the creditor shows that –

(a) at the time the contract was made, he was not, and could not reasonably have been, aware of the statement,

(b) before the contract was made, the statement had been withdrawn in public or, to the extent that it contained anything which was incorrect or misleading, it had been corrected in public, or

(c) the decision to acquire the goods could not have been influenced by the statement.

(2F) Subsections (2D) and (2E) above do not prevent any public statement from being a relevant circumstance for the purposes of subsection (2A) above (whether or not the person to whom the goods are bailed or hired deals as consumer or, in Scotland, whether or not the goods are hired to a person under a consumer contract) if the statement would have been such a circumstance apart from those subsections.

(3) Where the creditor bails or hires goods under a hire-purchase agreement in the course of a business and the person to whom the goods are bailed or hired, expressly or by implication, makes known –

(a) to the creditor in the course of negotiations conducted by the creditor in relation to the making of the hire-purchase agreement, or

(b) to a credit-broker in the course of negotiations conducted by that broker in relation to goods sold by him to the creditor before forming the subject matter of the hire-purchase agreement,

any particular purpose for which the goods are being bailed or hired, there is an implied term that the goods supplied under the agreement are reasonably fit for that purpose, whether or not that is a purpose for which such goods are commonly supplied, except where the circumstances show that the person to whom the goods are bailed or hired does not rely, or that it is unreasonable for him to rely, on the skill or judgment of the creditor or credit-broker.

(4) An implied term as to quality or fitness for a particular purpose may be annexed to a hire-purchase agreement by usage.

(5) The preceding provisions of this section apply to a hire-purchase agreement made by a person who in the course of a business is acting as agent for the creditor as they apply to an agreement made by the creditor in the course of a business, except where the creditor is not bailing or hiring in the course of a business and either the person to whom the goods are bailed or hired knows that fact or reasonable steps are taken to bring it to the notice of that person before the agreement is made.

(6) In subsection (3) above and this subsection –

(a) 'credit-broker' means a person acting in the course of a business of credit brokerage.

(b) 'credit brokerage' means the effecting of introductions of individuals desiring to obtain credit –

(i) to persons carrying on any business so far as it relates to the provision of credit, or

(ii) to other persons engaged in credit brokerage.

(7) As regards England and Wales and Northern Ireland, the terms implied by subsections (2) and (3) above are conditions. ...

11   Samples

(1) Where under a hire-purchase agreement goods are bailed or (in Scotland) hired by reference to a sample, there is an implied term –

(a) that the bulk will correspond with the sample in quality; and

(b) that the person to whom the goods are bailed or hired will have a reasonable opportunity of comparing the bulk with the sample; and

(c) that the goods will be free from any defect, making their quality unsatisfactory, which would not be apparent on reasonable examination of the sample.

(2) As regards England and Wales and Northern Ireland, the term implied by subsection (1) above is a condition.

11A   Modification of remedies for breach of statutory condition in non-consumer cases

(1) Where in the case of a hire-purchase agreement –

(a) the person to whom goods are bailed would, apart from this subsection, have the right to reject them by reason of a breach on the part of the creditor of a term implied by sections 9, 10, or 11(1)(a) or (c) above, but

(b) the breach is so slight that it would be unreasonable for him to reject them,

then, if the person to whom the goods are bailed does not deal as a consumer, the breach is not to be treated as a breach of condition but may be treated as a breach of warranty.

(2) This section applies unless a contrary intention appears in, or is to be implied from, the agreement.

(3) It is for the creditor to show –

    (a) that a breach fell within subsection (1)(b) above, and

    (b) that the person to whom the goods were bailed did not deal as consumer.

(4) The references in this section to dealing as consumer are to be construed in accordance with Part I of the Unfair Contract Terms Act 1977. ...

12   Exclusion of implied terms

An express term does not negative a term implied by this Act unless inconsistent with it.

14   Special provisions as to conditional sale agreements

(1) Section 11(4) of the Sale of Goods Act 1979 (whereby in certain circumstances a breach of a condition in a contract of sale is treated only as a breach of warranty) shall not apply to a conditional sale agreement where the buyer deals as consumer within Part I of the Unfair Contract Terms Act 1977.

(2) In England and Wales and Northern Ireland a breach of a condition (whether express or implied) to be fulfilled by the seller under any such agreement shall be treated as a breach of warranty, and not as grounds for rejecting the goods and treating the agreement as repudiated, if (but only if) it would have fallen to be so treated had the condition been contained or implied in a corresponding hire-purchase agreement as a condition to be fulfilled by the creditor.

15   Supplementary

(1) In sections 8 to 14 above and this section –

'business' includes a profession and the activities of any government department (including a Northern Ireland department), or local or public authority;

'buyer' and 'seller' includes a person to whom rights and duties under a conditional sale agreement have passed by assignment or operation of law;

'conditional sale agreement' means an agreement for the sale of goods under which the purchase price or part of it is payable by instalments, and the property in the goods is to remain in the seller (notwithstanding that the buyer is to be in possession of the goods) until such conditions as to the payment of instalments or otherwise as may be specified in the agreement are fulfilled;

'creditor' means the person by whom the goods are bailed or (in Scotland) hired under a hire-purchase agreement or the person to whom his rights and duties under the agreement have passed by assignment or operation of law; and

'hire-purchase agreement' means an agreement, other than a conditional sale agreement, under which –

(a) goods are bailed or (in Scotland) hired in return for periodical payments by the person to whom they are bailed or hired, and

(b) the property in the goods will pass to that person if the terms of the agreement are complied with and one or more of the following occurs –

(i) the exercise of an option to purchase by that person,

(ii) the doing of any other specified act by any party to the agreement,

(iii) the happening of any other specified event;

'producer' means the manufacturer of goods, the importer of goods into the European Economic Area or any person purporting to be a producer by placing his name, trade mark or other distinctive sign on the goods.

(3) In section 14(2) above 'corresponding hire-purchase agreement' means, in relation to a conditional sale agreement, a hire-purchase agreement relating to the same goods as the conditional sale agreement and made between the same parties and at the same time and in the same circumstances and, as nearly as may be, in the same terms as the conditional sale agreement.

(4) Nothing in sections 8 to 13 above shall prejudice the operation of any other enactment including any enactment of the Parliament of Northern Ireland or the Northern Ireland Assembly or any rule of law whereby any term, other than one relating to quality or fitness, is to be implied in any hire-purchase agreement.

As amended by the Consumer Credit Act 1974, s192(3)(a), Schedule 4, paras 35 and 36; Unfair Contract Terms Act 1977, s31(3), Schedule 3; Sale of Goods Act 1979, s63, Schedule 2, para 16; Statute Law (Repeals) Act 1981, Schedule 1, Part XII; Sale and Supply of Goods Act 1994, s7(1), Schedule 2, para 4, Schedule 3 (with effect from 3 January 1995); Sale and Supply of Goods to Consumers Regulations 2002, reg 13(1), (2), (4).

MATRIMONIAL CAUSES ACT 1973
(1973 c 18)

34 Validity of maintenance agreements

(1) If a maintenance agreement includes a provision purporting to restrict any right to apply to a court for an order containing financial arrangements, then –

(a) that provision shall be void; but

(b) any other financial arrangements contained in the agreement shall not thereby be rendered void or unenforceable and shall, unless they are void or unenforceable for any other reason (and subject to sections 35 and 36 below [which apply to the alteration of agreements by the court during the lives of parties and after the death of one party]), be binding on the parties to the agreement.

(2) In this section and in section 35 below –

'maintenance agreement' means any agreement in writing made, whether before or after the commencement of this Act, between the parties to a marriage, being –

(a) an agreement containing financial arrangements, whether made during the continuance or after the dissolution or annulment of the marriage; or

(b) a separation agreement which contains no financial arrangements in a case where no other agreement in writing between the same parties contains such arrangements

'financial arrangements' means provisions governing the rights and liabilities towards one another when living separately of the parties to a marriage (including a marriage which has been dissolved or annulled) in respect of the making or securing of payments or the disposition or use of any property, including such rights and liabilities with respect to the maintenance or education of any child, whether or not a child of the family.

CONSUMER CREDIT ACT 1974
(1974 c 39)

56   Antecedent negotiations

(1) In this Act 'antecedent negotiations' means any negotiations with the debtor or hirer –

　　(a) conducted by the creditor or owner in relation to the making of any regulated agreement, or

　　(b) conducted by a credit-broker in relation to goods sold or proposed to be sold by the credit-broker to the creditor before forming the subject-matter of a debtor-creditor-supplier agreement within section 12(a), or

　　(c) conducted by the supplier in relation to a transaction financed or proposed to be financed by a debtor-creditor-supplier agreement within section 12(b) or (c).

and 'negotiator' means the person by whom negotiations are so conducted with the debtor or hirer.

(2) Negotiations with the debtor in a case falling within subsection (1)(b) or (c) shall be deemed to be conducted by the negotiator in the capacity of agent of the creditor as well as in his actual capacity.

(3) An agreement is void if, and to the extent that, it purports in relation to an actual or prospective regulated agreement –

　　(a) to provide that a person acting as, or on behalf of, a negotiator is to be treated as the agent of the debtor or hirer, or

　　(b) to relieve a person from liability for acts or omissions of any person acting as, or on behalf of, a negotiator.

(4) For the purposes of this Act, antecedent negotiations shall be taken to begin when the negotiator and the debtor or hirer first enter into communication (including communication by advertisement), and to include any representations made by the negotiator to the debtor or hirer and any other dealings between them.

137   Extortionate credit bargains

(1) If the court finds a credit bargain extortionate it may reopen the credit agreement so as to do justice between the parties.

(2) In this section and sections 138 to 140 –

　　(a) 'credit agreement' means any agreement (other than an agreement which is an exempt agreement as a result of section 16(6C)) between an individual (the 'debtor') and any other person (the 'creditor') by which the creditor provides the debtor with credit of any amount, and

(b) 'credit bargain' –

(i) where no transaction other than the credit agreement is to be taken into account in computing the total charge for credit, means the credit agreement, or

(ii) where one or more other transactions are to be so taken into account, means the credit agreement and those other transactions, taken together.

138 When bargains are extortionate

(1) A credit bargain is extortionate if it –

(a) requires the debtor or a relative of his to make payments (whether unconditionally, or on certain contingencies) which are grossly exorbitant, or

(b) otherwise grossly contravenes ordinary principles of fair dealing.

(2) In determining whether a credit bargain is extortionate, regard shall be had to such evidence as is adduced concerning –

(a) interest rates prevailing at the time it was made,

(b) the factors mentioned in subsections (3) to (5), and

(c) any other relevant considerations.

(3) Factors applicable under subsection (2) in relation to the debtor include –

(a) his age, experience, business capacity and state of health; and

(b) the degree to which, at the time of making the credit bargain, he was under financial pressure, and the nature of that pressure.

(4) Factors applicable under subsection (2) in relation to the creditor include –

(a) the degree of risk accepted by him, having regard to the value of any security provided;

(b) his relationship to the debtor; and

(c) whether or not a colourable cash price was quoted for any goods or services included in the credit bargain.

(5) Factors applicable under subsection (2) in relation to a linked transaction include the question how far the transaction was reasonably required for the protection of debtor or creditor, or was in the interest of the debtor.

139 Reopening of extortionate agreements

(1) A credit agreement may, if the court thinks just, be reopened on the ground that the credit bargain is extortionate –

(a) on an application for the purpose made by the debtor or any surety to the High Court, county court or sheriff court; or

(b) at the instance of the debtor or a surety in any proceedings to which the debtor and creditor are parties, being proceedings to enforce the agreement, any security relating to it, or any linked transaction; or

(c) at the instance of the debtor or a surety in other proceedings in any court where the amount paid or payable under the credit agreement is relevant.

(2) In reopening the agreement, the court may, for the purpose of relieving the debtor or a surety from payment of any sum in excess of that fairly due and reasonable, by order –

(a) direct accounts to be taken, or (in Scotland) an accounting to be made, between any persons,

(b) set aside the whole or part of any obligation imposed on the debtor or a surety by the credit bargain or any related agreement,

(c) require the creditor to repay the whole or part of any sum paid under the credit bargain or any related agreement by the debtor or a surety, whether paid to the creditor or any other person,

(d) direct the return to the surety of any property provided for the purposes of the security, or

(e) alter the terms of the credit agreement or any security instrument.

(3) An order may be made under subsection (2) notwithstanding that its effect is to place a burden on the creditor in respect of an advantage unfairly enjoyed by another person who is a party to a linked transaction.

(4) An order under subsection (2) shall not alter the effect of any judgment.

(5) In England and Wales an application under subsection (1)(a) shall be brought only in the county court in the case of –

(a) a regulated agreement, or

(b) an agreement (not being a regulated agreement) under which the creditor provides the debtor with a fixed-sum credit or running-account credit. ...

NB Section 16(6C) provides: 'This Act does not regulate a consumer credit agreement if –

(a) it is secured by a land mortgage; and

(b) entering into that agreement as lender is a regulated activity for the purposes of the Financial Services and Markets Act 2000.'

As amended by the High Court and County Courts Jurisdiction Order 1991; Financial Services and Markets Act 2000 (Regulated Activities) Order 2001, reg 90(1), (6).

GUARD DOGS ACT 1975
(1975 c 50)

1   Control of guard dogs

(1) A person shall not use or permit the use of a guard dog at any premises unless a person ('the handler') who is capable of controlling the dog is present on the premises and the dog is under the control of the handler at all times while it is being so used except while it is secured so that it is not at liberty to go freely about the premises.

(2) The handler of a guard dog shall keep the dog under his control at all times while it is being used as a guard dog at any premises except –

(a) while another handler has control over the dog; or

(b) while the dog is secured so that it is not at liberty to go freely about the premises.

(3) A person shall not use or permit the use of a guard dog at any premises unless a notice containing a warning that a guard dog is present is clearly exhibited at each entrance to the premises.

5   Offences, penalties and civil liability

(1) A person who contravenes section 1 or 2 of this Act shall be guilty of an offence and liable on summary conviction to a fine not exceeding level 5 on the standard scale.

(2) The provisions of this Act shall not be construed as –

(a) conferring a right of action in any civil proceedings (other than proceedings for the recovery of a fine or any prescribed fee) in respect of any contravention of this Act or of any regulations made under this Act or of any of the terms or conditions of a licence granted under section 3 of this Act; or

(b) derogating from any right of action or other remedy (whether civil or criminal) in proceedings instituted otherwise than by virtue of this Act.

7   Interpretation

In this Act unless the context otherwise requires – ...

'guard dog' means a dog which is being used to protect –

(a) premises; or

(b) property kept on the premises; or

(c) a person guarding the premises of such property; ...

'premises' means land other than agricultural land and land within the curtilage of a dwelling-house, and buildings, including parts of buildings, other than dwellinghouses. ...

CONGENITAL DISABILITIES (CIVIL LIABILITY) ACT 1976
(1976 c 28)

1   Civil liability to child born disabled

(1) If a child is born disabled as the result of such an occurrence before its birth as is mentioned in subsection (2) below, and a person (other than the child's own mother) is under this section answerable to the child in respect of the occurrence, the child's disabilities are to be regarded as damage resulting from the wrongful act of that person and actionable accordingly at the suit of the child.

(2) An occurrence to which this section applies is one which –

(a) affected either parent of the child in his or her ability to have a normal, healthy child; or

(b) affected the mother during her pregnancy, or affected her or the child in the course of its birth, so that the child is born with disabilities which would not otherwise have been present.

(3) Subject to the following subsections, a person (here referred to as 'the defendant') is answerable to the child if he was liable in tort to the parent or would, if sued in due time, have been so; and it is no answer that there could not have been such liability because the parent suffered no actionable injury, if there was a breach of legal duty which, accompanied by injury, would have given rise to the liability.

(4) In the case of an occurrence preceding the time of conception, the defendant is not answerable to the child if at that time either or both of the parents knew the risk of their child being born disabled (that is to say, the particular risk created by the occurrence); but should it be the child's father who is the defendant, this subsection does not apply if he knew of the risk and the mother did not.

(5) The defendant is not answerable to the child, for anything he did or omitted to do when responsible in a professional capacity for treating or advising the parent, if he took reasonable care having regard to then received professional opinion applicable to the particular class of case; but this does not mean that he is answerable only because he departed from received opinion.

(6) Liability to the child under this section may be treated as having been excluded or limited by contract made with the parent affected, to the same extent and subject to the same restrictions as liability in the parent's own case; and a contract term which could have been set up by the defendant in an action by the parent, so as to

exclude or limit his liability to him or her, operates in the defendant's favour to the same, but no greater, extent in an action under this section by the child.

(7) If in the child's action under this section it is shown that the parent affected shared the responsibility for the child being born disabled, the damages are to be reduced to such extent as the court thinks just and equitable having regard to the extent of the parent's responsibility.

1A   Extension of section 1 to cover infertility treatments

(1) In any case where –

(a) a child carried by a woman as the result of the placing in her of an embryo or of sperm and eggs or her artificial insemination is born disabled,

(b) the disability results from an act or omission in the course of the selection, or the keeping or use outside the body, of the embryo carried by her or of the gametes used to bring about the creation of the embryo, and

(c) a person is under this section answerable to the child in respect of the act or omission,

the child's disabilities are to be regarded as damage resulting from the wrongful act of that person and actionable accordingly at the suit of the child.

(2) Subject to subsection (3) below and the applied provisions of section 1 of this Act, a person (here referred to as 'the defendant') is answerable to the child if he was liable in tort to one or both of the parents (here referred to as 'the parent or parents concerned') or would, if sued in due time, have been so; and it is no answer that there could not have been such liability because the parent or parents concerned suffered no actionable injury, if there was a breach of legal duty which, accompanied by injury, would have given rise to the liability.

(3) The defendant is not under this section answerable to the child if at the time the embryo, or the sperm and eggs, are placed in the woman or the time of her insemination (as the case may be) either or both of the parents knew the risk of their child being born disabled (that is to say, the particular risk created by the act or omission).

(4) Subsections (5) to (7) of section 1 of this Act apply for the purposes of this section as they apply for the purposes of that but as if references to the parent or the parent affected were references to the parent or parents concerned.

2   Liability of women driving when pregnant

A woman driving a motor vehicle when she knows (or ought reasonably to know) herself to be pregnant is to be regarded as being under the same duty to take care for the safety of her unborn child as the law imposes on her with respect to the safety of other people; and if in consequence of her breach of that duty her child is born with disabilities which would not otherwise have been present, those disabilities are to be regarded as damage resulting from her wrongful act and actionable accordingly at the suit of the child.

3   Disabled birth due to radiation

(1) Section 1 of this Act does not affect the operation of the Nuclear Installations Act 1965 as to liability for, and compensation in respect of, injury or damage caused by occurrences involving nuclear matter or the emission of ionising radiations.

(2) For the avoidance of doubt anything which –

(a) affects a man in his ability to have a normal, healthy child; or

(b) affects a woman in that ability, or so affects her when she is pregnant that her child is born with disabilities which would not otherwise have been present, is an injury for the purposes of that Act.

(3) If a child is born disabled as the result of an injury to either of its parents caused in breach of a duty imposed by any of sections 7 to 11 of that Act (nuclear site licensees and others to secure that nuclear incidents do not cause injury to persons, etc), the child's disabilities are to be regarded under the subsequent provisions of that Act (compensation and other matters) as injuries caused on the same occasion, and by the same breach of duty, as was the injury to the parent.

(4) As respects compensation to the child, section 13(6) of that Act (contributory fault of person injured by radiation) is to be applied as if the reference there to fault were to the fault of the parent.

(5) Compensation is not payable in the child's case if the injury to the parent preceded the time of the child's conception and at that time either or both of the parents knew the risk of their child being born disabled (that is to say, the particular risk created by the injury).

4   Interpretation and other supplementary provisions

(1) References in this Act to a child being born disabled or with disabilities are to its being born with any deformity, disease or abnormality, including predisposition (whether or not susceptible of immediate prognosis) to physical or mental defect in the future.

(2) In this Act –

(a) 'born' means born alive (the moment of a child's birth being when it first has a life separate from its mother), and 'birth' has a corresponding meaning; and

(b) 'motor vehicle' means a mechanically propelled vehicle intended or adapted for use on roads

and references to embryos shall be construed in accordance with section 1 of the Human Fertilisation and Embryology Act 1990.

(3) Liability to a child under section 1, 1A or 2 of this Act is to be regarded –

(a) as respects all its incidents and any matters arising or to arise out of it; and

(b) subject to any contrary context or intention, for the purpose of construing references in enactments and documents to personal or bodily injuries and cognate matters,

as liability for personal injuries sustained by the child immediately after its birth.

(4) No damages shall be recoverable under any of those sections in respect of any loss of expectation of life, nor shall any such loss be taken into account in the compensation payable in respect of a child under the Nuclear Installations Act 1965 as extended by section 3, unless (in either case) the child lives for at least 48 hours.

(4A) In any case where a child carried by a woman as the result of the placing in her of an embryo or of sperm and eggs or her artificial insemination is born disabled, any reference in section 1 of this Act to a parent includes a reference to a person who would be a parent but for sections 27 to 29 of the Human Fertilisation and Embryology Act 1990.

(5) This Act applies in respect of births after (but not before) its passing, and in respect of any such birth it replaces any law in force before its passing, whereby a person could be liable to a child in respect of disabilities with which it might be born; but in section 1(3) of this Act the expression 'liable in tort' does not include any reference to liability by virtue of this Act, or to liability by virtue of any such law.

(6) References to the Nuclear Installations Act 1965 are to that Act as amended; and for the purposes of section 28 of that Act (power by Order in Council to extend the Act to territories outside the United Kingdom) section 3 of this Act is to be treated as if it were a provision of that Act.

5   Crown application

This Act binds the Crown.

As amended by the Human Fertilisation and Embryology Act 1990, ss35(4), 44(1), (2).

FATAL ACCIDENTS ACT 1976
(1976 c 30)

1   Right of action for wrongful act causing death

(1) If death is caused by any wrongful act, neglect or default which is such as would (if death had not ensued) have entitled the person injured to maintain an action and recover damages in respect thereof, the person who would have been liable if death had not ensued shall be liable to an action for damages, notwithstanding the death of the person injured.

(2) Subject to section 1A(2) below, every such action shall be for the benefit of the dependants of the person ('the deceased') whose death has been so caused.

(3) In this Act 'dependant' means –

(a) the wife or husband or former wife or husband of the deceased;

(b) any person who –

(i) was living with the deceased in the same household immediately before the date of the death; and

(ii) had been living with the deceased in the same household for at least two years before that date; and

(iii) was living during the whole of that period as the husband or wife of the deceased;

(c) any parent or other ascendant of the deceased;

(d) any person who was treated by the deceased as his parent;

(e) any child or other descendant of the deceased;

(f) any person (not being a child of the deceased) who, in the case of any marriage to which the deceased was at any time a party was treated by the deceased as a child of the family in relation to that marriage;

(g) any person who is, or is the issue of, a brother, sister, uncle or aunt of the deceased.

(4) The reference to the former wife or husband of the deceased in subsection (3) (a) above includes a reference to a person whose marriage to the deceased has been annulled or declared void as well as a person whose marriage to the deceased has been dissolved.

(5) In deducing any relationship for the purposes of subsection (3) above –

(a) any relationship by affinity shall be treated as a relationship by consanguinity, any relationship of the half blood as a relationship of the whole blood, and the stepchild of any person as his child, and

(b) an illegitimate person shall be treated as the legitimate child of his mother and reputed father.

(6) Any reference in this Act to injury includes any disease and any impairment of a person's physical or mental condition.

1A   Bereavement

(1) An action under this Act may consist of or include a claim for damages for bereavement.

(2) A claim for damages for bereavement shall only be for the benefit –

(a) of the wife or husband of the deceased; and

(b) where the deceased was a minor who was never married –

(i) of his parents, if he was legitimate; and

(ii) of his mother, if he was illegitimate.

(3) Subject to subsection (5) below, the sum to be awarded as damages under this section shall be £10,000.

(4) Where there is a claim for damages under this section for the benefit of both the parents of the deceased, the sum awarded shall be divided equally between them (subject to any deduction falling to be made in respect of costs not recovered from the defendant).

(5) The Lord Chancellor may by order made by statutory instrument, subject to annulment in pursuance of a resolution of either House of Parliament, amend this section by varying the sum for the time being specified in subsection (3) above.

2   Persons entitled to bring the action

(1) The action shall be brought by and in the name of the executor or administrator of the deceased.

(2) If –

(a) there is no executor or administrator of the deceased, or

(b) no action is brought within six months after the death by and in the name of an executor or administrator of the deceased,

the action may be brought by and in the name of all or any of the persons for whose benefit an executor or administator could have brought it.

(3) Not more than one action shall lie for and in respect of the same subject matter of complaint.

(4) The plaintiff in the action shall be required to deliver to the defendant or his solicitor full particulars of the persons for whom and on whose behalf the action is

brought and of the nature of the claim in respect of which damages are sought to be recovered.

3   Assessment of damages

(1) In the action such damages, other than damages for bereavement, may be awarded as are proportioned to the injury resulting from the death to the dependants respectively.

(2) After deducting the costs not recovered from the defendant any amount recovered otherwise than as damages for bereavement shall be divided among the dependants in such shares as may be directed.

(3) In an action under this Act where there fall to be assessed damages payable to a widow in respect of the death of her husband there shall not be taken into account the re-marriage of the widow or her prospects of re-marriage.

(4) In an action under this Act where there fall to be assessed damages payable to a person who is a dependant by virtue of section 1(3)(b) above in respect of the death of the person with whom the dependant was living as husband or wife there shall be taken into account (together with any other matter that appears to the court to be relevant to the action) the fact that the dependant had no enforceable right to financial support by the deceased as a result of their living together.

(5) If the dependants have incurred funeral expenses in respect of the deceased, damages may be awarded in respect of those expenses.

(6) Money paid into court in satisfaction of a cause of action under this Act may be in one sum without specifying any person's share.

4   Assessment of damages: disregard of benefits

In assessing damages in respect of a person's death in an action under this Act, benefits which have accrued or will or may accrue to any person from his estate or otherwise as a result of his death shall be disregarded.

5   Contributory negligence

Where any person dies as the result partly of his own fault and partly of the fault of any other person or persons, and accordingly if an action were brought for the benefit of the estate under the Law Reform (Miscellaneous Provisions) Act 1934 the damages recoverable would be reduced under section 1(1) of the Law Reform (Contributory Negligence) Act 1945, any damages recoverable in an action under this Act shall be reduced to a proportionate extent.

As amended by the Administration of Justice Act 1982, ss3(1), (2), 75, Schedule 9, Pt I; Damages for Bereavement (Variation of Sum) (England and Wales) Order 2002, art 2.

TORTS (INTERFERENCE WITH GOODS) ACT 1977
(1977 c 32)

1 Definition of 'wrongful interference with goods'

In this Act 'wrongful interference', or 'wrongful interference with goods', means –

(a) conversion of goods (also called trover),

(b) trespass to goods,

(c) negligence so far as it results in damage to goods or to an interest in goods,

(d) subject to section 2, any other tort so far as it results in damage to goods or to an interest in goods

and references in this Act (however worded) to proceedings for wrongful interference or to a claim or right to claim for wrongful interference shall include references to proceedings by virtue of Part I of the Consumer Protection Act 1987 ... (product liability) in respect of any damage to goods or to an interest in goods or, as the case may be, to a claim or right to claim by virtue of that Part in respect of any such damage.

2 Abolition of detinue

(1) Detinue is abolished.

(2) An action lies in conversion for loss or destruction of goods which a bailee has allowed to happen in breach of his duty to his bailor (that is to say it lies in a case which is not otherwise conversion, but would have been detinue before detinue was abolished).

3 Form of judgment where goods are detained

(1) In proceedings for wrongful interference against a person who is in possession or in control of the goods relief may be given in accordance with this section, so far as appropriate.

(2) The relief is –

(a) an order for delivery of the goods, and for payment of any consequential damages, or

(b) an order for delivery of the goods, but giving the defendant the alternative of paying damages by reference to the value of the goods, together in either alternative with payment of any consequential damages, or

(c) damages.

(3) Subject to rules of court –

(a) relief shall be given under only one of paragraphs (a), (b) and (c) of subsection (2),

(b) relief under paragraph (a) of subsection (2) is at the discretion of the court, and the claimant may choose between the others.

(4) If it is shown to the satisfaction of the court that an order under subsection (2)(a) has not been complied with, the court may –

(a) revoke the order, or the relevant part of it, and

(b) make an order for payment of damages by reference to the value of the goods.

(5) Where an order is made under subsection (2)(b) the defendant may satisfy the order by returning the goods at any time before execution of judgment, but without prejudice to liability to pay any consequential damages.

(6) An order for delivery of the goods under subsection (2)(a) or (b) may impose such conditions as may be determined by the court, or pursuant to rules of court, and in particular, where damages by reference to the value of the goods would not be the whole of the value of the goods, may require an allowance to be made by the claimant to reflect the difference.

For example, a bailor's action against the bailee may be one in which the measure of damages is not the full value of the goods, and then the court may order delivery of the goods, but require the bailor to pay the bailee a sum reflecting the difference.

(7) Where under subsection (1) or subsection (2) of section 6 an allowance is to be made in respect of an improvement of the goods, and an order is made under subsection (2)(a) or (b), the court may assess the allowance to be made in respect of the improvement, and by the order require, as a condition for delivery of the goods, that allowance to be made by the claimant.

(8) This section is without prejudice –

(a) to the remedies afforded by section 133 of the Consumer Credit Act 1974, or

(b) to the remedies afforded by section 35, 42 and 44 of the Hire-Purchase Act 1965, ... (so long as those sections respectively remain in force), or

(c) to any jurisdiction to afford ancillary or incidental relief.

4   Interlocutory relief where goods are detained

(1) In this section 'proceedings' means proceedings for wrong interference.

(2) On the application of any person in accordance with rules of court, the High Court shall, in such circumstances as may be specified in the rules, have power to

make an order providing for the delivery up of any goods which are or may become the subject matter of subsequent proceedings in the court, or as to which any question may arise in proceedings.

(3) Delivery shall be, as the order may provide, to the claimant or to a person appointed by the court for the purpose, and shall be on such terms and conditions as may be specified in the order. ...

5 Extinction of title on satisfaction of claim for damages

(1) Where damages for wrongful interference are, or would fall to be, assessed on the footing that the claimant is being compensated –

(a) for the whole of his interest in the goods, or

(b) for the whole of his interest in the goods subject to a reduction for contributory negligence,

payment of the assessed damages (under all heads), or as the case may be settlement of a claim for damages for the wrong (under all heads), extinguishes the claimant's title to that interest.

(2) In subsection (1) the reference to the settlement of the claim includes –

(a) where the claim is made in court proceedings, and the defendant has paid a sum into court to meet the whole claim, the taking of that sum by the claimant, and

(b) where the claim is made in court proceedings, and the proceedings are settled or compromised, the payment of what is due in accordance with the settlement or compromlse, and

(c) where the claim is made out of court and is settled or compromised, the payment of what is due in accordance with the settlement or compromise.

(3) It is hereby declared that subsection (1) does not apply where damages are assessed on the footing that the claimant is being compensated for the whole of his interest in the goods, but the damages paid are limited to some lesser amount by virtue of any enactment or rule of law.

(4) Where under section 7(3) the claimant accounts over to another person (the 'third party') so as to compensate (under all heads) the third party for the whole of his interest in the goods, the third party's title to that interest is extinguished.

(5) This section has effect subject to any agreement varying the respective rights of the parties to the agreement, and where the claim is made in court proceedings has effect subject to any order of the court.

6 Allowances for improvement of the goods

(1) If in proceedings for wrongful interference against a person (the 'improver') who has improved the goods, it is shown that the improver acted in the mistaken but honest belief that he had a good title to them, an allowance shall be made for the

extent to which, at the time as at which the goods fall to be valued in assessing damages, the value of the goods is attributable to the improvement.

(2) If, in proceedings for wrongful interference against a person ('the purchaser') who has purported to purchase the goods –

(a) from the improver, or

(b) where after such a purported sale the goods passed by a further purported sale on one or more occasions, on any such occasion,

it is shown that the purchaser acted in good faith, an allowance shall be made on the principle set out in subsection (1).

For example, where a person in good faith buys a stolen car from the improver and is sued in conversion by the true owner the damages may be reduced to reflect the improvement, but if the person who bought the stolen car from the improver sues the improver for failure of consideration, and the improver acted in good faith, subsection (3) below will ordinarily make a comparable reduction in the damages he recovers from the improver.

(3) If in a case within subsection (2) the person purporting to sell the goods acted in good faith, then in proceedings by the purchaser for recovery of the purchase price because of failure of consideration, or in any other proceedings founded on that failure of consideration, an allowance shall, where appropriate, be made on the principle set out in subsection (1).

(4) This section applies, with the necessary modifications, to a purported bailment or other disposition of goods as it applies to a purported sale of goods.

7   Double liability

(1) In this section 'double liability' means the double liability of the wrongdoer which can arise–

(a) where one of two or more rights of action for wrongful interference is founded on a possessory title, or

(b) where the measure of damages in an action for wrongful interference founded on a proprietary title is or includes the entire value of the goods, although the interest is one of two or more interests in the goods.

(2) In proceedings to which any two or more claimants are parties, the relief shall be such as to avoid double liability of the wrongdoer as between those claimants.

(3) On satisfaction, in whole or in part, of any claim for an amount exceeding that recoverable if subsection (2) applied, the claimant is liable to account over to the other person having a right to claim to such extent as will avoid double liability.

(4) Where, as the result of enforcement of a double liability, any claimant is unjustly enriched to any extent, he shall be liable to reimburse the wrongdoer to that extent.

For example, if a converter of goods pays damages first to a finder of the goods, and then to the true owner, the finder is unjustly enriched unless he accounts over to the true owner under subsection (3); and then the true owner is unjustly enriched and becomes liable to reimburse the converter of the goods.

8   Competing rights to the goods

(1) The defendant in an action for wrongful interference shall be entitled to show, in accordance with rules of court, that a third party has a better right than the plaintiff as respects all or any part of the interest claimed by the plaintiff, or in right of which he sues, and any rule of law (sometimes called jus tertii) to the contrary is abolished.

(2) Rules of court relating to proceedings for wrongful interference may –

(a) require the plaintiff to give particulars of his title,

(b) require the plaintiff to identify any person who, to his knowledge, has or claims any interest in the goods,

(c) authorise the defendant to apply for directions as to whether any person should be joined with a view to establishing whether he has a better right than the plaintiff, or has a claim as a result of which the defendant might be doubly liable,

(d) where a party fails to appear on an application within paragraph (c), or to comply with any direction given by the court on such an application, authorise the court to deprive him of any right of action against the defendant for the wrong either unconditionally, or subject to such terms or conditions as may be specified.

(3) Subsection (2) is without prejudice to any other power of making rules of court.

9   Concurrent actions

(1) This section applies where goods are the subject of two or more claims for wrongful interference (whether or not the claims are founded on the same wrongful act, and whether or not any of the claims relates also to other goods).

(2) Where goods are the subject of two or more claims under section 6 this section shall apply as if any claim under section 6(3) were a claim for wrongful interference.

(3) If proceedings have been brought in a county court on one of those claims, county court rules may waive, or allow a court to waive, any limit (financial or territorial) on the jurisdiction of county courts in the County Courts Act 1984 ... so as to allow another of those claims to be brought in the same county court.

(4) If proceedings are brought on one of the claims in the High Court and proceedings on any other are brought in a county court, whether prior to the High Court proceedings or not, the High Court may, on the application of the defendant, after notice has been given to the claimant in the county court proceedings –

(a) order that the county court proceedings be transferred to the High Court, and

(b) order security for costs or impose such other terms as the court thinks fit.

10   Co-owners

(1) Co-ownership is no defence to an action founded on conversion or trespass to goods where the defendant without the authority of the other co-owner –

(a) destroys the goods, or disposes of the goods in a way giving a good title to the entire property in the goods, or otherwise does anything equivalent to the destruction of the other's interest in the goods, or

(b) purports to dispose of the goods in a way which would give a good title to the entire property in the goods if he was acting with the authority of all co-owners of the goods.

(2) Subsection (1) shall not effect the law concerning execution or enforcement of judgments, or concerning any form of distress.

(3) Subsection (1)(a) is by way of restatement of existing law so far as it relates to conversion.

11   Minor amendments

(1) Contributory negligence is no good defence in proceedings founded on conversion, or on intentional trespass to goods.

(2) Receipt of goods by way of pledge is conversion if the delivery of the goods is conversion.

(3) Denial of title is not of itself conversion.

12   Bailee's power of sale

(1) This section applies to goods in the possession or under the control of a bailee where –

(a) the bailor is in breach of an obligation to take delivery of the goods or, if the terms of the bailment so provide, to give directions as to their delivery, or

(b) the bailee could impose such an obligation by giving notice to the bailor, but is unable to trace or communicate with the bailor, or

(c) the bailee can reasonably expect to be relieved of any duty to safeguard the goods on giving notice to the bailor, but is unable to trace or communicate with the bailor.

(2) In the cases in Part I of Schedule 1 to this Act a bailee may, for the purposes of subsection (1), impose an obligation on the bailor to take delivery of the goods, or as the case may be to give directions as to their delivery, and in those cases the said Part I sets out the methods of notification.

(3) If the bailee –

(a) has in accordance with Part II of Schedule 1 to this Act given notice to the bailor of his intention to sell the goods under this subsection, or

(b) has failed to trace or communicate with the bailor with a view to giving him such a notice, after having taken reasonable steps for the purpose, and is reasonably satisfied that the bailor owns the goods, he shall be entitled, as against the bailor, to sell the goods.

(4) Where subsection (3) applies but the bailor did not in fact own the goods, a sale under this section, or under section 13, shall not give a good title as against the owner, or as against a person claiming under the owner.

(5) A bailee exercising his powers under subsection (3) shall be liable to account to the bailor for the proceeds of sale, less any costs of sale, and –

(a) the account shall be taken on the footing that the bailee should have adopted the best method of sale reasonably available in the circumstances, and

(b) where subsection (3)(a) applies, any sum payable in respect of the goods by the bailor to the bailee which accrued due before the bailee gave notice of intention to sell the goods shall be deductible from the proceeds of sale.

(6) A sale duly made under this section gives a good title to the purchaser as against the bailor.

(7) In this section, section 13, and Schedule 1 to this Act,

(a) 'bailor' and 'bailee' include their respective successors in title, and

(b) references to what is payable, paid or due to the bailee in respect of the goods include references to what would be payable by the bailor to the bailee as a condition of delivery of the goods at the relevant time.

(8) This section, and Schedule 1 to this Act, have effect subject to the terms of the bailment.

(9) This section shall not apply where the goods were bailed before the commencement of this Act.

13 Sale authorised by the court

(1) If a bailee of the goods to which section 12 applies satisfies the court that he is entitled to sell the goods under section 12, or that he would be so entitled if he had given any notice required in accordance with Schedule 1 to this Act, the court –

(a) may authorise the sale of the goods subject to such terms and conditions, if any, as may be specified in the order, and

(b) may authorise the bailee to deduct from the proceeds of sale any costs of sale and any amount due from the bailor to the bailee in respect of the goods, and

(c) may direct the payment into court of the net proceeds of sale, less any amount deducted under paragraph (b), to be held to the credit of the bailor.

(2) A decision of the court authorising a sale under this section shall, subject to any right of appeal, be conclusive, as against the bailor, of the bailee's entitlement to sell the goods, and gives a good title to the purchaser as against the bailor.

(3) In this section 'the court' means the High Court or a county court and a county court shall have jurisdiction in the proceedings ...

14 Interpretation

(1) In this Act, unless the context otherwise requires – ...

'goods' includes all chattels personal other than things in action and money, ...

16 Extent and application to the Crown

(3) This Act shall bind the Crown, but as regards the Crown's liability in tort shall not bind the Crown further than the Crown is made liable in tort by the Crown Proceedings Act 1947.

SCHEDULE 1

UNCOLLECTED GOODS

PART I

POWER TO IMPOSE OBLIGATIONS TO COLLECT GOODS

1. – (1) For the purposes of section 12(1) a bailee may, in the circumstances specified in this Part of this Schedule, by notice given to the bailor impose on him an obligation to take delivery of the goods.

(2) The notice shall be in writing, and may be given either –

   (a) by delivering it to the bailor, or

   (b) by leaving it at his proper address, or

   (c) by post.

(3) The notice shall –

   (a) specify the name and address of the bailee, and give suffficient particulars of the goods and the address or place where they are held, and

   (b) state that the goods are ready for delivery to the bailor, or where combined with a notice terminating the contract of bailment, will be ready for delivery when the contract is terminated, and

   (c) specify the amount, if any, which is payable by the bailor to the bailee in respect of the goods and which became due before the giving of the notice.

(4) Where the notice is sent by post it may be combined with a notice under Part II of this Schedule if the notice is sent by post in a way complying with paragraph 6(4).

(5) References in this Part of this Schedule to taking delivery of the goods include, where the terms of the bailment admit, references to giving directions as to their delivery.

(6) This Part of this Schedule is without prejudice to the provisions of any contract requiring the bailor to take delivery of the goods.

2. If a bailee has accepted goods for repair or other treatment on the terms (expressed or implied) that they will be re-delivered to the bailor when the repair or

other treatment has been carried out, the notice may be given at any time after the repair or other treatment has been carried out.

3. If a bailee has accepted goods in order to value or appraise them, the notice may be given at any time after the bailee has carried out the valuation or appraisal.

4. – (1) If a bailee is in possession of goods which he has held as custodian, and his obligation as custodian has come to an end, the notice may be given at any time after the ending of the obligation, or may be combined with any notice terminating his obligation as custodian.

(2) This paragraph shall not apply to goods held by a person as mercantile agent, that is to say by a person having in the customary course of his business as a mercantile agent authority either to sell goods or to consign goods for the purpose of sale, or to buy goods, or to raise money on the security of goods.

5. Paragraphs 2, 3 and 4 apply whether or not the bailor has paid any amount due to the bailee in respect of the goods, and whether or not the bailment is for reward, or in the course of business, or gratuitous.

PART II

NOTICE OF INTENTION TO SELL GOODS

6. – (1) A notice under section 12(3) shall –

    (a) specify the name and address of the bailee, and give sufficient particulars of the goods and the address or place where they are held, and

    (b) specify the date on or after which the bailee proposes to sell the goods, and

    (c) specify the amount, if any, which is payable by the bailor to the bailee in respect of the goods, and which became due before the giving of the notice.

(2) The period between giving of the notice and the date specified in the notice as that on or after which the bailee proposes to exercise the power of sale shall be such as will afford the bailor a reasonable opportunity of taking delivery of the goods.

(3) If any amount is payable in respect of the goods by the bailor to the bailee, and became due before giving of the notice, the said period shall be not less than three months.

(4) This notice shall be in writing and shall be sent by post in a registered letter, or by the recorded delivery service.

7. – (1) The bailee shall not give a notice under section 12(3), or exercise his right to sell the goods pursuant to such a notice, at a time when he has notice that, because of a dispute concerning the goods, the bailor is questioning or refusing to pay all or any part of what the bailee claims to be due to him in respect of the goods.

(2) This paragraph shall be left out of account in determining under section 13(1)

whether a bailee of goods is entitled to sell the goods under section 12, or would be so entitled if he had given any notice required in accordance with this Schedule.

8. For the purposes of this Schedule, and of section 26 of the Interpretation Act 1889 in its application to this Schedule, the proper address of the person to whom a notice is to be given shall be –

(a) in the case of a body corporate, a registered or principal office of the body corporate, and

(b) in any other case, the last known address of the person.

As amended by the Consumer Protection Act 1987, s48(1), Schedule 4, para 5; High Court and County Courts Jurisdiction Order 1991, art 2(8), Schedule.

RENT ACT 1977
(1977 c 42)

125 Recovery of premiums and loans unlawfully required or received

(1) Where under any agreement (whether made before or after the commencement of this Act) any premium is paid after the commencement of this Act and the whole or any part of the premium could not lawfully be required or received under the preceding provisions of this Part of this Act, the amount of the premium, or, as the case may be, so much of it as could not lawfully be required or received, shall be recoverable by the person by whom it was paid.

(2) Nothing in section 119 [prohibition of premiums and loans on grant of protected tenancies] or 120 [prohibition of premiums and loans on assignment of protected tenancies] of this Act shall invalidate any agreement for the making of a loan or any security issued in pursuance of such an agreement but, notwithstanding anything in the agreement for the loan, any sum lent in circumstances involving a contravention of either of those sections shall be repayable to the lender on demand.

UNFAIR CONTRACT TERMS ACT 1977
(1977 c 50)

PART I

AMENDMENT OF LAW FOR ENGLAND AND WALES AND NORTHERN IRELAND

1   Scope of Part I

(1) For the purposes of this Part of this Act, 'negligence' means the breach –

(a) of any obligation, arising from the express or implied terms of a contract, to take reasonable care or exercise reasonable skill in the performance of the contract;

(b) of any common law duty to take reasonable care or exercise reasonable skill (but not any stricter duty);

(c) of the common duty of care imposed by the Occupiers' Liability Act 1957 or the Occupiers' Liability Act (Northern Ireland) 1957.

(2) This Part of this Act is subject to Part III; and in relation to contracts, the operation of sections 2 to 4 and 7 is subject to the exceptions made by Schedule 1.

(3) In the case of both contract and tort, sections 2 to 7 apply except where the contrary is stated in section 6 (4) only to business liability, that is liability for breach of obligations or duties arising –

(a) from things done or to be done by a person in the course of a business (whether his own business or another's);

(b) from the occupation of premises used for business purposes of the occupier;

and references to liability are to be read accordingly but liability of an occupier of premises for breach of an obligation or duty towards a person obtaining access to the premises for recreational or educational purposes, being liability for loss or damage suffered by reason of the dangerous state of the premises, is not a business liability of the occupier unless granting that person such access for the purposes concerned falls within the business purposes of the occupier.

(4) In relation to any breach of duty or obligation, it is immaterial for any purpose of this part of this Act whether the breach was inadvertent or intentional, or whether liability for it arises directly or vicariously.

2   Negligence liability

(1) A person cannot by reference to any contract term or to a notice given to persons generally or to particular persons exclude or restrict his liability for death or personal injury resulting from negligence.

(2) In the case of other loss or damage, a person cannot so exclude or restrict his liability for negligence except in so far as the term or notice satisfies the requirement of reasonableness.

(3) Where a contract term or notice purports to exclude or restrict liability for negligence a person's agreement to or awareness of it is not of itself to be taken as indicating his voluntary acceptance of any risk.

3   Liability arising in contract

(1) This section applies as between contracting parties where one of them deals as consumer or on the other's written standard terms of business.

(2) As against that party, the other cannot by reference to any contract term –

(a) when himself in breach of contract, exclude or restrict any liability of his in respect of the breach; or

(b) claim to be entitled –

(i) to render a contractual performance substantially different from that which was reasonably expected of him, or

(ii) in respect of the whole or any part of his contractual obligation, to render no performance at all,

except in so far as (in any of the cases mentioned above in this subsection) the contract term satisfies the requirement of reasonableness.

4   Unreasonable indemnity clauses

(1) A person dealing as consumer cannot by reference to any contract term be made to indemnify another person (whether a party to the contract or not) in respect of liability that may be incurred by the other for negligence or breach of contract, except in so far as the contract term satisfies the requirement of reasonableness.

(2) This section applies whether the liability in question –

(a) is directly that of the person to be indemnified or is incurred by him vicariously;

(b) is to the person dealing as consumer or to someone else.

5   'Guarantee' of consumer goods

(1) In the case of goods of a type ordinarily supplied for private use or consumption, where loss or damage

(a) arises from the goods proving defective while in consumer use; and

(b) results from the negligence of a person concerned in the manufacture or distribution of the goods,

liability for the loss or damage cannot be excluded or restricted by reference to any contract term or notice contained in or operating by reference to a guarantee of the goods.

(2) For these purposes –

(a) goods are to be regarded as 'in consumer use' when a person is using them, or has them in his possession for use, otherwise than exclusively for the purposes of a business; and

(b) anything in writing is a guarantee if it contains or purports to contain some promise or assurance (however worded or presented) that defects will be made good by complete or partial replacement, or by repair, monetary compensation or otherwise.

(3) This section does not apply as between the parties to a contract under or in pursuance of which possession or ownership of the goods passed.

6   Sale and hire-purchase

(1) Liability for breach of the obligations arising from –

(a) section 12 of the Sale of Goods Act 1979 (seller's implied undertakings as to title, etc);

(b) section 8 of the Supply of Goods (Implied Terms) Act 1973 (the corresponding thing in relation to hire-purchase);

cannot be excluded or restricted by reference to any contract term.

(2) As against a person dealing as consumer, liability for breach of the obligations arising from –

(a) section 13, 14 and 15 of the 1979 Act (seller's implied undertakings as to conformity of goods with description or sample, or as to their quality or fitness for a particular purpose);

(b) section 9, 10 or 11 of the 1973 Act (the corresponding things in relation to hire-purchase),

cannot be excluded or restricted by reference to any contract term.

(3) As against a person dealing otherwise than as consumer, the liability specified in subsection (2) above can be excluded or restricted by reference to a contract term, but only in so far as the term satisfies the requirement of reasonableness.

(4) The liabilities referred to in this section are not only the business liabilities defined by section 1(3), but include those arising under any contract of sale of goods or hire-purchase agreement.

7   Miscellaneous contracts under which goods pass

(1) Where the possession or ownership of goods passes under or in pursuance of a contract not governed by the law of sale of goods or hire-purchase, subsections (2) to (4) below apply as regards the effect (if any) to be given to contract terms excluding or restricting liability for breach of obligation arising by implication of law from the nature of the contract.

(2) As against a person dealing as consumer, liability in respect of the goods' correspondence with description or sample, or their quality or fitness for any particular purpose, cannot be excluded or restricted by reference to any such term.

(3) As against a person dealing otherwise than as consumer, that liability can be excluded or restricted by reference to such a term, but only in so far as the term satisfies the requirement of reasonableness.

(3A) Liability for breach of the obligations arising under section 2 of the Supply of Goods and Services Act 1982 (implied terms about title etc in certain contracts for the transfer of the property in goods) cannot be excluded or restricted by references to any such term.

(4) Liability in respect of –

    (a) the right to transfer ownership of the goods, or give possession; or

    (b) the assurance of quiet possession to a person taking goods in pursuance of the contract,

cannot (in a case to which subsection (3A) above does not apply) be excluded or restricted by reference to any such term except in so far as the term satisfies the requirement of reasonableness.

(5) This section does not apply in the case of goods passing on a redemption of trading stamps within the Trading Stamps Act 1964 or the Trading Stamps Act (Northern Ireland) 1965.

9   Effect of breach

(1) Where for reliance upon it a contract term has to satisfy the requirement of reasonableness, it may be found to do so and be given effect accordingly notwithstanding that the contract has been terminated either by breach or by a party electing to treat it as repudiated .

(2) Where on a breach the contract is nevertheless affirmed by a party entitled to treat it as repudiated, this does not of itself exclude the requirement of reasonableness in relation to any contract term.

10   Evasion by means of secondary contract

A person is not bound by any contract term prejudicing or taking away rights of his which arise under, or in connection with the performance of, another contract, so far as those rights extend to the enforcement of another's liability which this Part of this Act prevents that other from excluding or restricting.

11   The 'reasonableness' test

(1) In relation to a contract term, the requirement of reasonableness for the purposes of this Part of this Act, section 3 of the Misrepresentation Act 1967 and section 3 of the Misrepresentation Act (Northern Ireland) 1967 is that the term shall have been a fair and reasonable one to be included having regard to the circumstances which were, or ought reasonably to have been, known to or in the contemplation of the parties when the contract was made.

(2) In determining for the purposes of section 6 or 7 above whether a contract term satisfies the requirement of reasonableness, regard shall be had in particular to the matters specified in Schedule 2 to this Act; but this subsection does not prevent the court or arbitrator from holding, in accordance with any rule of law, that a term which purports to exclude or restrict any relevant liability is not a term of the contract.

(3) In relation to a notice (not being a notice having contractual effect), the requirement of reasonableness under this Act is that it should be fair and reasonable to allow reliance on it, having regard to all the circumstances obtaining when the liability arose or (but for the notice) would have arisen.

(4) Where by reference to a contract term or notice a person seeks to restrict liability to a specified sum of money, and the question arises (under this or any other Act) whether the term or notice satisfies the requirement of reasonableness, regard shall be had in particular (but without prejudice to subsection (2) above in the case of contract terms) to –

  (a) the resources which he could expect to be available to him for the purpose of meeting the liability should it arise; and

  (b) how far it was open to him to cover himself by insurance.

(5) It is for those claiming that a contract term or notice satisfies the requirement of reasonableness to show that it does.

12   'Dealing as consumer'

(1) A party to a contract 'deals as consumer' in relation to another party if –

  (a) he neither makes the contract in the course of a business nor holds himself out as doing so; and

  (b) the other party does make the contract in the course of a business; and

  (c) in the case of a contract governed by the law of sale of goods or hire-purchase, or by section 7 of this Act, the goods passing under or in pursuance of the contract are of a type ordinarily supplied for private use or consumption.

(1A) But if the first party mentioned in subsection (1) is an individual paragraph (c) of that subsection must be ignored.

(2) But the buyer is not in any circumstances to be regarded as dealing as consumer –

  (a) if he is an individual and the goods are second hand goods sold at public auction at which individuals have the opportunity of attending the sale in person;

(b) if he is not an individual and the goods are sold by auction or by competitive tender.

(3) Subject to this, it is for those claiming that a party does not deal as consumer to show that he does not.

13 Varieties of exemption clause

(1) To the extent that this Part of this Act prevents the exclusion or restriction of any liability it also prevents –

(a) making the liability or its enforcement subject to restrictive or onerous conditions;

(b) excluding or restricting any right or remedy in respect of the liability, or subjecting a person to any prejudice in consequence of his pursuing any such right or remedy;

(c) excluding or restricting rules of evidence or procedure; and (to that extent) sections 2 and 7 also prevent excluding or restricting liability by reference to terms and notices which exclude or restrict the relevant obligation or duty.

(2) But an agreement in writing to submit present or future differences to arbitration is not to be treated under this Part of this Act as excluding or restricting any liability.

14 Interpretation of Part I

In this Part of this Act –

'business' includes a profession and the activities of any government department or local or public authority;

'goods' has the same meaning as in the Sale of Goods Act 1979;

'hire-purchase agreement' has the same meaning as in the Consumer Credit Act 1974; 'negligence' has the meaning given by section 1(1);

'notice' includes an announcement, whether or not in writing, and any other communication or pretended communication; and

'personal injury' includes any disease and any impairment of physical or mental condition.

PART III

PROVISIONS APPLYING TO WHOLE OF UNITED KINGDOM

26 International supply contracts

(1) The limits imposed by this Act on the extent to which a person may exclude or

restrict liability by reference to a contract term do not apply to liability arising under such a contract as is described in subsection (3) below.

(2) The terms of such a contract are not subject to any requirement of reasonableness under section 3 or 4 ...

(3) Subject to subsection (4), that description of contract is one whose characteristics are the following –

(a) either it is a contract of sale of goods or it is one under or in pursuance of which the possession or ownership of goods passes; and

(b) it is made by parties whose places of business (or, if they have none, habitual residences) are in the territories of different States (the Channel Islands and the Isle of Man being treated for this purpose as different States from the United Kingdom).

(4) A contract falls within subsection (3) above only if either:

(a) the goods in question are, at the time of the conclusion of the contract, in the course of carriage, or will be carried, from the territory of one State to the territory of another; or

(b) the acts constituting the offer and acceptance have been done in the territories of different States; or

(c) the contract provides for the goods to be delivered to the territory of a State other than that within whose territory those acts were to be done.

27 Choice of law clauses

(1) Where the law applicable to a contract is the law of any part of the United Kingdom only by choice of the parties (and apart from that choice would be the law of some country outside the United Kingdom) sections 2 to 7 and 16 to 21 of this Act do not operate as part of the law applicable to the contract.

(2) This Act has effect notwithstanding any contract term which applies or purports to apply the law of some country outside the United Kingdom, where (either or both) –

(a) the term appears to the court, or arbitrator or arbiter to have been imposed wholly or mainly for the purpose of enabling the party imposing it to evade the operation of this Act; or

(b) in the making of the contract one of the parties dealt as consumer, and he was then habitually resident in the United Kingdom, and the essential steps necessary for the making of the contract were taken there, whether by him or by others on his behalf.

29 Saving for other relevant legislation

(1) Nothing in this Act removes or restricts the effect of, or prevents reliance upon, any contractual provision which –

(a) is authorised or required by the express terms or necessary implication of an enactment; or

(b) being made with a view to compliance with an international agreement to which the United Kingdom is a party, does not operate more restrictively than is contemplated by the agreement.

(2) A contract term is to be taken –

(a) for the purposes of Part I of this Act, as satisfying the requirement of reasonableness …

if it is incorporated or approved by, or incorporated pursuant to a decision or ruling of, a competent authority acting in the exercise of any statutory jurisdiction or function and is not a term in a contract to which the competent authority is itself a party.

(3) In this section:

'competent authority' means any court, arbitrator or arbiter, government department or public authority;

'enactment' means any legislation (including subordinate legislation) of the United Kingdom or Northern Ireland and any instrument having effect by virtue of such legislation; and

'statutory' means conferred by an enactment.

SCHEDULE 1

SCOPE OF SECTIONS 2 TO 4 AND 7

1. Sections 2 to 4 of this Act do not extend to

(a) any contract of insurance (including a contract to pay an annuity on human life);

(b) any contract so far as it relates to the creation or transfer of an interest in land, or to the termination of such an interest, whether by extinction, merger, surrender, forfeiture or otherwise;

(c) any contract so far as it relates to the creation or transfer of a right or interest in any patent, trade mark, copyright or design right, registered design, technical or commercial information or other intellectual property, or relates to the termination of any such right or interest;

(d) any contract so far as it relates –

(i) to the formation or dissolution of a company (which means any body corporate or unincorporated association and includes a partnership), or

(ii) to its constitution or the rights or obligations of its corporators or members;

(e) any contract so far as it relates to the creation or transfer of securities or of any right or interest in securities.

2. Section 2(1) extends to

(a) any contract of marine salvage or towage;

(b) any charterparty of a ship or hovercraft; and

(c) any contract for the carriage of goods by ship or hovercraft;

but subject to this sections 2 to 4 and 7 do not extend to any such contract except in favour of a person dealing as consumer.

3. Where goods are carried by ship or hovercraft in pursuance of a contract which either –

(a) specifies that as the means of carriage over part of the journey to be covered, or

(b) makes no provision as to the means of carriage and does not exclude that means,

then sections 2(2), 3 and 4 do not, except in favour of a person dealing as consumer, extend to the contract as it operates for and in relation to the carriage of the goods by that means.

4. Section 2(1) and (2) do not extend to a contract of employment, except in favour of the employee.

5. Section 2(1) does not affect the validity of any discharge and indemnity given by a person, on or in connection with an award to him of compensation for pneumoconiosis attributable to employment in the coal industry, in respect of any further claim arising from his contracting that disease.

SCHEDULE 2

'GUIDELINES' FOR APPLICATION OF REASONABLENESS TEST

The matters to which regard is to be had in particular for the purposes of sections 6(3), 7(3) and (4), 20 and 21 are any of the following which appear to be relevant –

(a) the strength of the bargaining positions of the parties relative to each other, taking into account (among other things) alternative means by which the customer's requirements could have been met;

(b) whether the customer received an inducement to agree to the term, or in accepting it had an opportunity of entering into a similar contract with other persons, but without having to accept a similar term;

(c) whether the customer knew or ought reasonably to have known of the existence and extent of the term (having regard, among other things, to any custom of the trade and any previous course of dealing between the parties);

(d) where the term excludes or restricts any relevant liability if some condition is not complied with, whether it was reasonable at the time of the contract to expect that compliance with that condition would be practicable;

(e) whether the goods were manufactured, processed or adapted to the special order of the customer.

As amended by the Sale of Goods Act 1979, s63, Schedule 2, paras 19, 20; Supply of Goods and Services Act 1982, s17(2), (3); Occupiers' Liability Act 1984, s2; Copyright, Designs and Patents Act 1988, s303(1), Schedule 7, para 24; Contracts (Applicable Law) Act 1990, Schedule 4, para 4; Sale and Supply of Goods to Consumers Regulations 2002, reg 14(1)–(3).

CIVIL LIABILITY (CONTRIBUTION) ACT 1978

(1978 c 47)

1   Entitlement to contribution

(1) Subject to the following provisions of this section, any person liable in respect of any damage suffered by another person may recover contribution from any other person liable in respect of the same damage (whether jointly with him or otherwise).

(2) A person shall be entitled to recover contribution by virtue of subsection (1) above notwithstanding that he has ceased to be liable in respect of the damage in question since the time when the damage occurred, provided that he was so liable immediately before he made or was ordered or agreed to make the payment in respect of which the contribution is sought.

(3) A person shall be liable to make contribution by virtue of subsection (1) above notwithstanding that he has ceased to be liable in respect of the damage in question since the time when the damage occurred, unless he ceased to be liable by virtue of the expiry of a period of limitation or prescription which extinguished the right on which the claim against him in respect of the damage was based.

(4) A person who has made or agreed to make any payment in bona fide settlement or compromise of any claim made against him in respect of any damage (including a payment into court which has been accepted) shall be entitled to recover contribution in accordance with this section without regard to whether or not he himself is or ever was liable in respect of the damage provided, however, that he would have been liable assuming that the factual basis of the claim against him could be established.

(5) A judgment given in any action brought in any part of the United Kingdom by or on behalf of the person who suffered the damage in question against any person from whom contribution is sought under this section shall be conclusive in the proceedings for contribution as to any issue determined by that judgment in favour of the person from whom the contribution is sought.

(6) References in this section to a person's liability in respect of any damage are references to any such liability which has been or could be established in an action brought against him in England and Wales by or on behalf of the person who suffered the damage; but it is immaterial whether any issue arising in any such action was or would be determined (in accordance with the rules of private international law) by reference to the law of a country outside England and Wales.

2   Assessment of contribution

(1) Subject to subsection (3) below, in any proceedings for contribution under section 1 above the amount of the contribution recoverable from any person shall be such as may be found by the court to be just and equitable having regard to the extent of that person's responsibility for the damage in question.

(2) Subject to subsection (3) below, the court shall have power in any such proceedings to exempt any person from liability to make contribution, or to direct that the contribution to be recovered from any person shall amount to a complete indemnity.

(3) Where the amount of the damages which have or might have been awarded in respect of the damage in question in any action brought in England and Wales by or on behalf of the person who suffered it against the person from whom the contribution is sought was or would have been subject to –

(a) any limit imposed by or under any enactment or by any agreement made before the damage occurred;

(b) any reduction by virtue of section 1 of the Law Reform (Contributory Negligence) Act 1945 or section 5 of the Fatal Accidents Act 1976; or

(c) any corresponding limit or reduction under the law of a country outside England and Wales; the person from whom the contribution is sought shall not by virtue of any contribution awarded under section 1 above be required to pay in respect of the damage a greater amount than the amount to those damages as so limited or reduced.

3   Proceedings against persons jointly liable for the same debt or damage

Judgment recovered against any person liable in respect of any debt or damage shall not be a bar to an action, or to the continuance of an action, against any other person who is (apart from any such bar) jointly liable with him in respect of the same debt or damage.

4   Successive actions against persons liable (jointly or otherwise) for the same damage

If more than one action is brought in respect of any damage by or on behalf of the person by whom it was suffered against persons liable in respect of the damage (whether jointly or otherwise) the plaintiff shall not be entitled to costs in any of those actions, other than that in which judgment is first given, unless the court is of the opinion that there was reasonable ground for bringing the action.

5   Application to Crown

Without prejudice to section 4(1) of the Crown Proceedings Act 1947 (indemnity and contribution), this Act shall bind the Crown, but nothing in this Act shall be construed as in any way affecting Her Majesty in Her private capacity (including in right of Her Duchy of Lancaster) or the Duchy of Cornwall.

6 Interpretation

(1) A person is liable in respect of any damage for the purposes of this Act if the person who suffered it (or anyone representing his estate or dependants) is entitled to recover compensation from him in respect of that damage (whatever the legal basis of his liability, whether tort, breach of contract, breach of trust or otherwise).

(2) References in this Act to an action brought by or on behalf of the person who suffered any damage include references to an action brought for the benefit of his estate or dependants.

(3) In this Act 'dependants' has the same meaning as in the Fatal Accidents Act 1976.

(4) In this Act, except in section 1(5) above, 'action' means an action brought in England and Wales.

7 Savings

(1) Nothing in this Act shall affect any case where the debt in question became due or (as the case may be) the damage in question occurred before the date on which it comes into force.

(2) A person shall not be entitled to recover contribution or liable to make contribution in accordance with section 1 above by reference to any liability based on breach of any obligation assumed by him before the date on which this Act comes into force.

(3) The right to recover contribution in accordance with section 1 above supersedes any right, other than an express contractual right, to recover contribution (as distinct from indemnity) otherwise than under this Act in corresponding circumstances; but nothing in this Act shall affect –

(a) any express or implied contractual or other right to indemnity; or

(b) any express contractual provision regulating or excluding contribution;

which would be enforceable apart from this Act (or render enforceable any agreement for indemnity or contribution which would not be enforceable apart from this Act).

SALE OF GOODS ACT 1979
(1979 c 54)

PART II

FORMATION OF THE CONTRACT

2 Contract of sale

(1) A contract of sale of goods is a contract by which the seller transfers or agrees to transfer the property in goods to the buyer for a money consideration, called the price.

(2) There may be a contract of sale between one part owner and another.

(3) A contract of sale may be absolute or conditional.

(4) Where under a contract of sale the property in the goods is transferred from the seller to the buyer the contract is called a sale.

(5) Where under a contract of sale the transfer of the property in the goods is to take place at a future time or subject to some condition later to be fulfilled the contract is called an agreement to sell.

(6) An agreement to sell becomes a sale when the time elapses or the conditions are fulfilled subject to which the property in the goods is to be transferred.

3 Capacity to buy and sell

(1) Capacity to buy and sell is regulated by the general law concerning capacity to contract and to transfer and acquire property.

(2) Where necessaries are sold and delivered to a minor or to a person who by reason of mental incapacity or drunkenness is incompetent to contract, he must pay a reasonable price for them.

(3) In subsection (2) above 'necessaries' means goods suitable to the condition in life of the minor or other person concerned and to his actual requirements at the time of the sale and delivery.

4 How contract of sale is made

(1) Subject to this and any other Act, a contract of sale may be made in writing (either with or without seal), or by word of mouth, or partly in writing and partly by word of mouth, or may be implied from the conduct of the parties.

(2) Nothing in this section affects the law relating to corporations.

5   Existing or future goods

(1) The goods which form the subject of a contract of sale may be either existing goods, owned or possessed by the seller, or goods to be manufactured or acquired by him after the making of the contract of sale, in this Act called future goods.

(2) There may be a contract for the sale of goods the acquisition of which by the seller depends on a contingency which may or may not happen.

(3) Where by a contract of sale the seller purports to effect a present sale of future goods, the contract operates as an agreement to sell the goods.

6   Goods which have perished

Where there is a contract for the sale of specific goods, and the goods without the knowledge of the seller have perished at the time when the contract is made, the contract is void.

7   Goods perishing before sale but after agreement to sell

Where there is an agreement to sell specific goods and subsequently the goods, without any fault on the part of the seller or buyer, perish before the risk passes to the buyer, the agreement is avoided.

8   Ascertainment of price

(1) The price in a contract of sale may be fixed by the contract, or may be left to be fixed in a manner agreed by the contract, or may be determined by the course of dealing between the parties.

(2) Where the price is not determined as mentioned in subsection (1) above the buyer must pay a reasonable price.

(3) What is a reasonable price is a question of fact dependent on the circumstances of each particular case.

9   Agreement to sell at valuation

(1) Where there is an agreement to sell goods on the terms that the price is to be fixed by the valuation of a third party, and he cannot or does not make the valuation, the agreement is avoided; but if the goods or any part of them have been delivered to and appropriated by the buyer he must pay a reasonable price for them.

(2) Where the third party is prevented from making the valuation by the fault of the seller or buyer, the party not at fault may maintain an action for damages against the party at fault.

10   Stipulations about time

(1) Unless a different intention appears from the terms of the contract, stipulations as to time of payment are not of the essence of a contract of sale.

(2) Whether any other stipulation as to time is or is not of the essence of the contract depends on the terms of the contract.

(3) In a contract of sale 'month' prima facie means calendar month.

11   When condition to be treated as warranty ...

(2) Where a contract of sale is subject to a condition to be fulfilled by the seller, the buyer may waive the condition, or may elect to treat the breach of the condition as a breach of warranty and not as a ground for treating the contract as repudiated.

(3) Whether a stipulation in a contract of sale is a condition, the breach of which may give rise to a right to treat the contract as repudiated, or a warranty, the breach of which may give rise to a claim for damages but not to a right to reject the goods and treat the contract as repudiated, depends in each case on the construction of the contract; and a stipulation may be a condition, though called a warranty in the contract.

(4) Subject to section 35A below where a contract of sale is not severable and the buyer has accepted the goods or part of them, the breach of a condition to be fulfilled by the seller can only be treated as a breach of warranty, and not as a ground for rejecting the goods and treating the contract as repudiated, unless there is an express or implied term of the contract to that effect.

(6) Nothing in this section affects a condition or warranty whose fulfilment is excused by law by reason of impossibility or otherwise.

12   Implied terms about title, etc

(1) In a contract of sale, other than one to which subsection (3) below applies, there is an implied term on the part of the seller that in the case of a sale he has a right to sell the goods, and in the case of an agreement to sell he will have such a right at the time when the property is to pass.

(2) In a contract of sale, other than one to which subsection (3) below applies, there is also an implied term that –

(a) the goods are free, and will remain free until the time when the property is to pass, from any charge or encumbrance not disclosed or known to the buyer before the contract is made, and

(b) the buyer will enjoy quiet possession of the goods except so far as it may be disturbed by the owner or other person entitled to the benefit of any charge or encumbrance so disclosed or known.

(3) This subsection applies to a contract of sale in the case of which there appears from the contract or is to be inferred from its circumstances an intention that the seller should transfer only such title as he or a third person may have.

(4) In a contract to which subsection (3) above applies there is an implied term that all charges or encumbrances known to the seller and not known to the buyer have been disclosed to the buyer before the contract is made.

(5) In a contract to which subsection (3) above applies there is also an implied term that none of the following will disturb the buyer's quiet possession of the goods, namely –

(a) the seller;

(b) in a case where the parties to the contract intend that the seller should transfer only such title as a third person may have, that person;

(c) anyone claiming through or under the seller or that third person otherwise than under a charge or encumbrance disclosed or known to the buyer before the contract is made.

(5A) As regards England and Wales and Northern Ireland, the term implied by subsection (1) above is a condition and the terms implied by subsections (2), (4) and (5) above are warranties.

13   Sale by description

(1) Where there is a contract for the sale of goods by description, there is an implied term that the goods will correspond with the description.

(1A) As regards England and Wales and Northern Ireland, the term implied by subsection (1) above is a condition.

(2) If the sale is by sample as well as by description it is not sufficient that the bulk of the goods corresponds with the sample if the goods do not also correspond with the description.

(3) A sale of goods is not prevented from being a sale by description by reason only that, being exposed for sale or hire, they are selected by the buyer.

14   Implied terms about quality or fitness

(1) Except as provided by this section and section 15 below and subject to any other enactment, there is no implied term about the quality or fitness for any particular purpose of goods supplied under a contract of sale.

(2) Where the seller sells goods in the course of a business, there is an implied term that the goods supplied under the contract are of satisfactory quality.

(2A) For the purposes of this Act, goods are of satisfactory quality if they meet the standard that a reasonable person would regard as satisfactory, taking account of any description of the goods, the price (if relevant) and all the other relevant circumstances.

(2B) For the purposes of this Act, the quality of goods includes their state and condition and the following (among others) are in appropriate cases aspects of the quality of goods –

(a) fitness for all the purposes for which goods of the kind in question are commonly supplied,

(b) appearance and finish,

(c) freedom from minor defects,

(d) safety, and

(e) durability.

(2C) The term implied by subsection (2) above does not extend to any matter making the quality of goods unsatisfactory –

(a) which is specifically drawn to the buyer's attention before the contract is made,

(b) where the buyer examines the goods before the contract is made, which that examination ought to reveal, or

(c) in the case of a contract for sale by sample, which would have been apparent on a reasonable examination of the sample.

(2D) If the buyer deals as consumer … the relevant circumstances mentioned in subsection (2A) above include any public statements on the specific characteristics of the goods made about them by the seller, the producer or his representative, particularly in advertising or on labelling.

(2E) A public statement is not by virtue of subsection (2D) above a relevant circumstance for the purposes of subsection (2A) above in the case of a contract of sale, if the seller shows that –

(a) at the time the contract was made, he was not, and could not reasonably have been, aware of the statement,

(b) before the contract was made, the statement had been withdrawn in public or, to the extent that it contained anything which was incorrect or misleading, it had been corrected in public, or

(c) the decision to buy the goods could not have been influenced by the statement.

(2F) Subsections (2D) and (2E) above do not prevent any public statement from being a relevant circumstance for the purposes of subsection (2A) above (whether or not the buyer deals as consumer …) if the statement would have been such a circumstance apart from those subsections.

(3) Where the seller sells goods in the course of a business and the buyer, expressly or by implication, makes known –

(a) to the seller, or

(b) where the purchase price or part of it is payable by instalments and the goods were previously sold by a credit-broker to the seller, to that credit-broker,

any particular purpose for which the goods are being bought, there is an implied term that the goods supplied under the contract are reasonably fit for that purpose, whether or not that is a purpose for which such goods are commonly supplied, except where the circumstances show that the buyer does not rely, or that it is unreasonable for him to rely, on the skill or judgment of the seller or credit-broker.

(4) An implied term about quality or fitness for a particular purpose may be annexed to a contract of sale by usage.

(5) The preceding provisions of this section apply to a sale by a person who in the course of a business is acting as agent for another as they apply to a sale by a principal in the course of a business, except where that other is not selling in the course of a business and either the buyer knows that fact or reasonable steps are taken to bring it to the notice of the buyer before the contract is made.

(6) As regards England and Wales and Northern Ireland, the terms implied by subsections (2) and (3) above are conditions. ...

15   Sale by sample

(1) A contract of sale is a contract for sale by sample where there is an express or implied term to that effect in the contract.

(2) In the case of a contract for sale by sample there is an implied term –

(a) that the bulk will correspond with the sample in quality;

(c) that the goods will be free from any defect, making their quality unsatisfactory, which would not be apparent on reasonable examination of the sample.

(3) As regards England and Wales and Northern Ireland, the term implied by subsection (2) above is a condition. ...

15A Modification of remedies for breach of condition in non-consumer cases

(1) Where in the case of a contract of sale –

(a) the buyer would, apart from this subsection, have the right to reject goods by reason of a breach on the part of the seller of a term implied by sections 13, 14 or 15 above, but

(b) the breach is so slight that it would be unreasonable for him to reject them,

then, if the buyer does not deal as consumer, the breach is not to be treated as a breach of condition but may be treated as a breach of warranty.

(2) This section applies unless a contrary intention appears in, or is to be implied from, the contract.

(3) It is for the seller to show that a breach fell within subsection (1)(b) above. ...

PART III

EFFECTS OF THE CONTRACT

16   Goods must be ascertained

Subject to section 20A below where there is a contract for the sale of unascertained goods no property in the goods is transferred to the buyer unless and until the goods are ascertained.

17   Property passes when intended to pass

(1) Where there is a contract for the sale of specific or ascertained goods the property in them is transferred to the buyer at such time as the parties to the contract intend it to be transferred.

(2) For the purpose of ascertaining the intention of the parties regard shall be had to the terms of the contract, the conduct of the parties and the circumstances of the case.

18   Rules for ascertaining intention

Unless a different intention appears, the following are rules for ascertaining the intention of the parties as to the time at which the property in the goods is to pass to the buyer.

Rule 1. – Where there is an unconditional contract for the sale of specific goods in a deliverable state the property in the goods passes to the buyer when the contract is made, and it is immaterial whether the time of payment or the time of delivery, or both, be postponed.

Rule 2. – Where there is a contract for the sale of specific goods and the seller is bound to do something to the goods for the purpose of putting them into a deliverable state, the property does not pass until the thing is done and the buyer has notice that it has been done.

Rule 3. – Where there is a contract for the sale of specific goods in a deliverable state but the seller is bound to weigh, measure, test, or do some other act or thing with reference to the goods for the purpose of ascertaining the price, the property does not pass until the act or thing is done and the buyer has notice that it has been done.

Rule 4. – When goods are delivered to the buyer on approval or on sale or return or other similar terms the property in the goods passes to the buyer: –

(a) when he signifies his approval or acceptance to the seller or does any other act adopting the transaction;

(b) if he does not signify his approval or acceptance to the seller but retains the goods without giving notice of rejection, then, if a time has been fixed for the return of the goods, on the expiration of that time, and, if no time has been fixed, on the expiration of a reasonable time.

Rule 5. – (1) Where there is a contract for the sale of unascertained or future goods by description, and goods of that description and in a deliverable state are unconditionally appropriated to the contract, either by the seller with the assent of the buyer or by the buyer with the assent of the seller, the property in the goods then passes to the buyer; and the assent may be express or implied, and may be given either before or after the appropriation is made.

(2) Where, in pursuance of the contract, the seller delivers the goods to the buyer or to a carrier or other bailee or custodier (whether named by the buyer or not) for the purpose of transmission to the buyer, and does not reserve the right of disposal, he is to be taken to have unconditionally appropriated the goods to the contract.

(3) Where there is a contract for the sale of a specified quantity of unascertained goods in a deliverable state forming part of a bulk which is identified either in the contract or by subsequent agreement between the parties and the bulk is reduced to (or to less than) that quantity, then, if the buyer under that contract is the only buyer to whom goods are then due out of the bulk –

(a) the remaining goods are to be taken as appropriated to that contract at the time when the bulk is so reduced; and

(b) the property in those goods then passes to that buyer.

(4) Paragraph (3) above applies also (with the necessary modifications) where a bulk is reduced to (or to less than) the aggregate of the quantities due to a single buyer under separate contracts relating to that bulk and he is the only buyer to whom goods are then due out of that bulk.

19 Reservation of right of disposal

(1) Where there is a contract for the sale of specific goods or where goods are subsequently appropriated to the contract, the seller may, by the terms of the contract or appropriation, reserve the right of disposal of the goods until certain conditions are fulfilled; and in such a case, notwithstanding the delivery of the goods to the buyer, or to a carrier or other bailee or custodier for the purpose of transmission to the buyer, the property in the goods does not pass to the buyer until the conditions imposed by the seller are fulfilled.

(2) Where goods are shipped, and by the bill of lading the goods are deliverable to the order of the seller or his agent, the seller is prima facie to be taken to reserve the right of disposal.

(3) Where the seller of goods draws on the buyer for the price, and transmits the bill of exchange and bill of lading to the buyer together to secure acceptance or payment of the bill of exchange, the buyer is bound to return the bill of lading if he does not honour the bill of exchange, and if he wrongfully retains the bill of lading the property in the goods does not pass to him.

20   Passing of risk

(1) Unless otherwise agreed, the goods remain at the seller's risk until the property in them is transferred to the buyer, but when the property in them is transferred to the buyer the goods are at the buyer's risk whether delivery has been made or not.

(2) But where delivery has been delayed through the fault of either buyer or seller the goods are at the risk of the party at fault as regards any loss which might not have occurred but for such fault.

(3) Nothing in this section affects the duties or liabilities of either seller or buyer as a bailee or custodier of the goods of the other party.

(4) In a case where the buyer deals a consumer ... subsections (1) to (3) above must be ignored and the goods remain at the seller's risk until they are delivered to the consumer.

20A Undivided shares in goods forming part of a bulk

(1) This section applies to a contract for the sale of a specified quantity of unascertained goods if the following conditions are met –

  (a) the goods or some of them form part of a bulk which is identified either in the contract or by subsequent agreement between the parties; and

  (b) the buyer has paid the price for some or all of the goods which are the subject of the contract and which form part of the bulk.

(2) Where this section applies, then (unless the parties agree otherwise), as soon as the conditions specified in paragraphs (a) and (b) of subsection (1) above are met or at such later time as the parties may agree –

  (a) property in an undivided share in the bulk is transferred to the buyer, and

  (b) the buyer becomes an owner in common of the bulk.

(3) Subject to subsection (4) below, for the purposes of this section, the undivided share of a buyer in a bulk at any time shall be such share as the quantity of goods paid for and due to the buyer out of the bulk bears to the quantity of goods in the bulk at that time.

(4) Where the aggregate of the undivided shares of buyers in a bulk determined under subsection (3) above would at any time exceed the whole of the bulk at that time, the undivided share in the bulk of each buyer shall be reduced proportionately so that the aggregate of the undivided shares is equal to the whole bulk.

(5) Where a buyer has paid the price for only some of the goods due to him out of a bulk, any delivery to the buyer out of the bulk shall, for the purposes of this section, be ascribed in the first place to the goods in respect of which payment has been made.

(6) For the purposes of this section payment of part of the price for any goods shall be treated as payment for a corresponding part of the goods.

20B Deemed consent by co-owner to dealings in bulk goods

(1) A person who has become an owner in common of a bulk by virtue of section 20A above shall be deemed to have consented to –

(a) any delivery of goods out of the bulk to any other owner in common of the bulk, being goods which are due to him under his contract;

(b) any dealing with or removal, delivery or disposal of goods in the bulk by any other person who is an owner in common of the bulk in so far as the goods fall within that co-owner's undivided share in the bulk at the time of the dealing, removal, delivery or disposal.

(2) No cause of action shall accrue to anyone against a person by reason of that person having acted in accordance with paragraph (a) or (b) of subsection (1) above in reliance on any consent deemed to have been given under that subsection.

(3) Nothing in this section or section 20A above shall –

(a) impose an obligation on a buyer of goods out of a bulk to compensate any other buyer of goods out of that bulk for any shortfall in the goods received by that other buyer;

(b) affect any contractual arrangement between buyers of goods out of a bulk for adjustments between themselves; or

(c) affect the rights of any buyer under his contract.

21 Sale by person not the owner

(1) Subject to this Act, where goods are sold by a person who is not their owner, and who does not sell them under the authority or with the consent of the owner, the buyer acquires no better title to the goods than the seller had, unless the owner of the goods is by his conduct precluded from denying the seller's authority to sell.

(2) Nothing in this Act affects –

(a) the provisions of the Factors Acts or any enactment enabling the apparent owner of goods to dispose of them as if he were their true owner;

(b) the validity of any contract of sale under any special common law or statutory power of sale or under the order of a court of competent jurisdiction.

23 Sale under voidable title

When the seller of goods has a voidable title to them, but his title has not been avoided at the time of the sale, the buyer acquires a good title to the goods, provided he buys them in good faith and without notice of the seller's defect of title.

24 Seller in possession after sale

Where a person having sold goods continues or is in possession of the goods, or of the documents of title to the goods, the delivery or transfer by that person, or by a mercantile agent acting for him, of the goods or documents of title under any sale, pledge, or other disposition thereof, to any person receiving the same in good faith and without notice of the previous sale, has the same effect as if the person making the delivery or transfer were expressly authorised by the owner of the goods to make the same.

25   Buyer in possession after sale

(1) Where a person having bought or agreed to buy goods obtains, with the consent of the seller, possession of the goods or the documents of title to the goods, the delivery or transfer by that person, or by a mercantile agent acting for him, of the goods or documents of title, under any sale, pledge, or other disposition thereof, to any person receiving the same in good faith and without notice of any lien or other right of the original seller in respect of the goods, has the same effect as if the person making the delivery or transfer were a mercantile agent in possession of the goods or documents of title with the consent of the owner.

(2) For the purposes of subsection (1) above –

(a) the buyer under a conditional sale agreement is to be taken not to be a person who has bought or agreed to buy goods, and

(b) 'conditional sale agreement' means an agreement for the sale of goods which is a consumer credit agreement within the meaning of the Consumer Credit Act 1974 under which the purchase price or part of it is payable by instalments, and the property in the goods is to remain in the seller (notwithstanding that the buyer is to be in possession of the goods) until such conditions as to the payment of instalments or otherwise as may be specified in the agreement are fulfilled.

(3) Paragraph 9 of Schedule 1 below applies in relation to a contract under which a person buys or agrees to buy goods and which is made before the appointed day.

(4) In subsection (3) above and paragraph 9 of Schedule 1 below references to the appointed day are to the day appointed for the purposes of those provisions by an order of the Secretary of State made by statutory instrument.

26   Supplementary to sections 24 and 25

In sections 24 and 25 above 'mercantile agent' means a mercantile agent having in the customary course of his business as such agent authority either –

(a) to sell goods, or

(b) to consign goods for the purpose of sale, or

(c) to buy goods, or

(d) to raise money on the security of goods.

PART IV

PERFORMANCE OF THE CONTRACT

27   Duties of seller and buyer

It is the duty of the seller to deliver the goods, and of the buyer to accept and pay for them, in accordance with the terms of the contract of sale.

28   Payment and delivery are concurrent conditions

Unless otherwise agreed, delivery of the goods and payment of the price are concurrent conditions, that is to say, the seller must be ready and willing to give possession of the goods to the buyer in exchange for the price and the buyer must be ready and willing to pay the price in exchange for possession of the goods.

29   Rules about delivery

(1) Whether it is for the buyer to take possession of the goods or for the seller to send them to the buyer is a question depending in each case on the contract, express or implied, between the parties.

(2) Apart from any such contract, express or implied, the place of delivery is the seller's place of business if he has one, and if not, his residence; except that, if the contract is for the sale of specific goods, which to the knowledge of the parties when the contract is made are in some other place, then that place is the place of delivery.

(3) Where under the contract of sale the seller is bound to send the goods to the buyer, but no time for sending them is fixed, the seller is bound to send them within a reasonable time.

(4) Where the goods at the time of sale are in the possession of a third person, there is no delivery by seller to buyer unless and until the third person acknowledges to the buyer that he holds the goods on his behalf; and nothing in this section affects the operation of the issue or transfer of any document of title to goods.

(5) Demand or tender of delivery may be treated as ineffectual unless made at a reasonable hour; and what is a reasonable hour is a question of fact.

(6) Unless otherwise agreed, the expenses of and incidental to putting the goods into a deliverable state must be borne by the seller.

30   Delivery of shortfall or excess

(1) Where the seller delivers to the buyer a quantity of goods less than he contracted to sell, the buyer may reject them, but if the buyer accepts the goods so delivered he must pay for them at the contract rate.

(2) Where the seller delivers to the buyer a quantity of goods larger than he contracted to sell, the buyer may accept the goods included in the contract and reject the rest, or he may reject the whole.

(2A) A buyer who does not deal as consumer may not –

(a) where the seller delivers a quantity of goods less than he contracted to sell, reject the goods under subsection (1) above, or

(b) where the seller delivers a quantity of goods larger than he contracted to sell, reject the whole under subsection (2) above,

if the shortfall or, as the case may be, excess is so slight that it would be unreasonable for him to do so.

(2B) It is for the seller to show that a shortfall or excess fell within subsection (2A) above. ...

(3) Where the seller delivers to the buyer a quantity of goods larger than he contracted to sell and the buyer accepts the whole of the goods so delivered he must pay for them at the contract rate.

(5) This section is subject to any usage of trade, special agreement, or course of dealing between the parties.

31   Instalment deliveries

(1) Unless otherwise agreed, the buyer of goods is not bound to accept delivery of them by instalments.

(2) Where there is a contract for the sale of goods to be delivered by stated instalments, which are to be separately paid for, and the seller makes defective deliveries in respect of one or more instalments, or the buyer neglects or refuses to take delivery of or pay for one or more instalments, it is a question in each case depending on the terms of the contract and the circumstances of the case whether the breach of contract is a repudiation of the whole contract or whether it is a severable breach giving rise to a claim for compensation but not to a right to treat the whole contract as repudiated.

32   Delivery to carrier

(1) Where, in pursuance of a contract of sale, the seller is authorised or required to send the goods to the buyer, delivery of the goods to a carrier (whether named by the buyer or not) for the purpose of transmission to the buyer is prima facie deemed to be a delivery of the goods to the buyer.

(2) Unless otherwise authorised by the buyer, the seller must make such contract with the carrier on behalf of the buyer as may be reasonable having regard to the nature of the goods and the other circumstances of the case; and if the seller omits to do so, and the goods are lost or damaged in course of transit; the buyer may decline to treat the delivery to the carrier as a delivery to himself or may hold the seller responsible in damages.

(3) Unless otherwise agreed, where goods are sent by the seller to the buyer by a route involving sea transit, under circumstances in which it is usual to insure, the seller must give such notice to the buyer as may enable him to insure them during

their sea transit; and if the seller fails to do so, the goods are at his risk during such sea transit.

(4) In a case where the buyer deals as consumer ... subsections (1) to (3) above must be ignored, but if in pursuance of a contract of sale the seller is authorised or required to send the goods to the buyer, delivery of the goods to the carrier is not delivery of the goods to the buyer.

33   Risk where goods are delivered at distant place

Where the seller of goods agrees to deliver them at his own risk at a place other than that where they are when sold, the buyer must nevertheless (unless otherwise agreed) take any risk of deterioration in the goods necessarily incident to the course of transit.

34   Buyer to have opportunity to examine goods

Unless otherwise agreed, when the seller tenders delivery of goods to the buyer, he is bound on request to afford the buyer a reasonable opportunity of examining the goods for the purpose of ascertaining whether they are in conformity with the contract and, in the case of a contract for sale by sample, of comparing the bulk with the sample.

35   Acceptance

(1) The buyer is deemed to have accepted the goods subject to subsection (2) below –

   (a) when he intimates to the seller that he has accepted them, or
   (b) when the goods have been delivered to him and he does any act in relation to them which is inconsistent with the ownership of the seller.

(2) Where goods are delivered to the buyer, and he has not previously examined them, he is not deemed to have accepted them under subsection (1) above until he has had a reasonable opportunity of examining them for the purpose –

   (a) of ascertaining whether they are in conformity with the contract, and
   (b) in the case of a contract for sale by sample, of comparing the bulk with the sample.

(3) Where the buyer deals as a consumer or (in Scotland) the contract of sale is a consumer contract, the buyer cannot lose his right to rely on subsection (2) above by agreement, waiver or otherwise.

(4) The buyer is also deemed to have accepted the goods when after the lapse of a reasonable time he retains the goods without intimating to the seller that he has rejected them.

(5) The questions that are material in determining for the purposes of subsection (4) above whether a reasonable time has elapsed include whether the buyer has had a reasonable opportunity of examining the goods for the purpose mentioned in subsection (2) above.

(6) The buyer is not by virtue of this section deemed to have accepted the goods merely because –

(a) he asks for, or agrees to, their repair by or under an arrangement with the seller, or

(b) the goods are delivered to another under a sub-sale or other disposition.

(7) Where the contract is for the sale of goods making one or more commercial units, a buyer accepting any goods included in a unit is deemed to have accepted all the goods making the unit; and in this subsection 'commercial unit' means a unit division of which would materially impair the value of the goods or the character of the unit ...

35A Right of partial rejection

(1) If the buyer –

(a) has the right to reject the goods by reason of a breach on the part of the seller that affects some or all of them, but

(b) accepts some of the goods, including, where there are any goods unaffected by the breach, all such goods,

he does not by accepting them lose his right to reject the rest.

(2) In the case of a buyer having the right to reject an instalment of goods, subsection (1) above applies as if references to the goods were references to the goods comprised in the instalment.

(3) For the purposes of subsection (1) above, goods are affected by breach if by reason of the breach they are not in conformity with the contract.

(4) This section applies unless a contrary intention appears in, or is to be implied from, the contract.

36 Buyer not bound to return rejected goods

Unless otherwise agreed, where goods are delivered to the buyer, and he refuses to accept them, having the right to do so, he is not bound to return them to the seller, but it is sufficient if he intimates to the seller that he refuses to accept them.

37 Buyer's liability for not taking delivery of goods

(1) When the seller is ready and willing to deliver the goods, and requests the buyer to take delivery, and the buyer does not within a reasonable time after such request take delivery of the goods, he is liable to the seller for any loss occasioned by his neglect or refusal to take delivery, and also for a reasonable charge for the care and custody of the goods.

(2) Nothing in this section affects the rights of the seller where the neglect or refusal of the buyer to take delivery amounts to a repudiation of the contract.

PART V

RIGHTS OF UNPAID SELLER AGAINST THE GOODS

38 Unpaid seller defined

(1) The seller of goods is an unpaid seller within the meaning of this Act –

(a) when the whole of the price has not been paid or tendered;

(b) when a bill of exchange or other negotiable instrument has been received as conditional payment, and the condition on which it was received has not been fulfilled by reason of the dishonour of the instrument or otherwise.

(2) In this Part of this Act 'seller' includes any person who is in the position of a seller, as, for instance, an agent of the seller to whom the bill of lading has been indorsed, or a consignor or agent who has himself paid (or is directly responsible for) the price.

39 Unpaid seller's rights

(1) Subject to this and any other Act, notwithstanding that the property in the goods may have passed to the buyer, the unpaid seller of goods, as such, has by implication of law –

(a) a lien on the goods or right to retain them for the price while he is in possession of them;

(b) in case of the insolvency of the buyer, a right of stopping the goods in transit after he has parted with the possession of them;

(c) a right of re-sale as limited by this Act.

(2) Where the property in goods has not passed to the buyer, the unpaid seller has (in addition to his other remedies) a right of withholding delivery similar to and co-extensive with his rights of lien or retention and stoppage in transit where the property has passed to the buyer.

41 Seller's lien

(1) Subject to this Act, the unpaid seller of goods who is in possession of them is entitled to retain possession of them until payment or tender of the price in the following cases –

(a) where the goods have been sold without any stipulation as to credit;

(b) where the goods have been sold on credit but the term of credit has expired;

(c) where the buyer becomes insolvent.

(2) The seller may exercise his lien or right of retention notwithstanding that he is in possession of the goods as agent or bailee or custodier for the buyer.

42   Part delivery

Where an unpaid seller has made part delivery of the goods, he may exercise his lien or right of retention on the remainder, unless such part delivery has been made under such circumstances as to show an agreement to waive the lien or right of retention.

43   Termination of lien

(1) The unpaid seller of goods loses his lien or right of retention in respect of them –

(a) when he delivers the goods to a carrier or other bailee or custodier for the purpose of transmission to the buyer without reserving the right of disposal of the goods;

(b) when the buyer or his agent lawfully obtains possession of the goods;

(c) by waiver of the lien or right of retention.

(2) An unpaid seller of goods who has a lien or right of retention in respect of them does not lose his lien or right of retention by reason only that he has obtained judgment or decree for the price of the goods.

44   Right of stoppage in transit

Subject to this Act, when the buyer of goods becomes insolvent the unpaid seller who has parted with the possession of the goods has the right of stopping them in transit, that is to say, he may resume possession of the goods as long as they are in course of transit, and may retain them until payment or tender of the price.

45   Duration of transit

(1) Goods are deemed to be in course of transit from the time when they are delivered to a carrier or other bailee or custodier for the purpose of transmission to the buyer, until the buyer or his agent in that behalf takes deliver of them from the carrier or other bailee or custodier.

(2) If the buyer or his agent in that behalf obtains delivery of the goods before their arrival at the appointed destination, the transit is at an end.

(3) If, after the arrival of the goods at the appointed destination, the carrier or other bailee or custodier acknowledges to the buyer or his agent that he holds the goods on his behalf and continues in possession of them as bailee or custodier for the buyer or his agent, the transit is at an end, and it is immaterial that a further destination for the goods may have been indicated by the buyer.

(4) If the goods are rejected by the buyer, and the carrier or other bailee or custodier continues in possession of them, the transit is not deemed to be at an end, even if the seller has refused to receive them back.

(5) When goods are delivered to a ship chartered by the buyer it is a question depending on the circumstances of the particular case whether they are in the possession of the master as a carrier or as agent to the buyer.

(6) Where the carrier or other bailee or custodier wrongfully refuses to deliver the gods to the buyer or his agent in that behalf, the transit is deemed to be at an end.

(7) Where part delivery of the goods has been made to the buyer or his agent in that behalf, the remainder of the goods may be stopped in transit, unless such part delivery has been made under such circumstances as to show an agreement to give up possession of the whole of the goods.

46   How stoppage in transit is effected

(1) The unpaid seller may exercise his right of stoppage in transit either by taking actual possession of the goods or by giving notice of his claim to the carrier or other bailee or custodier in whose possession the goods are.

(2) The notice may be given either to the person in actual possession of the goods or to his principal.

(3) If given to the principal, the notice is ineffective unless given at such time and under such circumstances that the principal, by the exercise of reasonable diligence, may communicate it to his servant or agent in time to prevent a delivery to the buyer.

(4) When notice of stoppage in transit is given by the seller to the carrier or other bailee or custodier in possession of the goods, he must re-deliver the goods to, or according to the directions of, the seller; and the expenses of the re-delivery must be borne by the seller.

47   Effect of sub-sale, etc by buyer

(1) Subject to this Act, the unpaid seller's right of lien or retention or stoppage in transit is not affected by any sale or other disposition of the goods which the buyer may have made, unless the seller has assented to it.

(2) Where a document of title to goods has been lawfully transferred to any person as buyer or owner of the goods, and that person transfers the document to a person who takes it in good faith and for valuable consideration, then –

   (a) if the last-mentioned transfer was by way of sale the unpaid seller's right of lien or retention or stoppage in transit is defeated; and

   (b) if the last-mentioned transfer was made by way of pledge or other disposition for value, the unpaid seller's right of lien or retention or stoppage in transit can only be exercised subject to the rights of the transferee.

48   Rescission: and re-sale by seller

(1) Subject to this section, a contract of sale is not rescinded by the mere exercise by an unpaid seller of his right of lien or retention or stoppage in transit.

(2) Where an unpaid seller who has exercised his right of lien or retention or stoppage in transit re-sells the goods, the buyer acquires a good title to them as against the original buyer.

(3) Where the goods are of a perishable nature, or where the unpaid seller gives notice to the buyer of his intention to re-sell, and the buyer does not within a reasonable time pay or tender the price, the unpaid seller may re-sell the goods and recover from the original buyer damages for any loss occasioned by his breach of contract.

(4) Where the seller expressly reserves the right of re-sale in case the buyer should make default, and on the buyer making default re-sells the goods, the original contract of sale is rescinded but without prejudice to any claim the seller may have for damages.

PART 5A

ADDITIONAL RIGHTS OF BUYER IN CONSUMER CASES

48A Introductory

(1) This section applies if –

    (a) the buyer deals as consumer ..., and

    (b) the goods do not conform to the contract of sale at the time of delivery.

(2) If this section applies, the buyer has the right –

    (a) under and in accordance with section 48B below, to require the seller to repair or replace the goods, or

    (b) under and in accordance with section 48C below –

        (i) to require the seller to reduce the purchase price of the goods to the buyer by an appropriate amount, or

        (ii) to rescind the contract with regard to the goods in question.

(3) For the purposes of subsection (1)(b) above goods which do not conform to the contract of sale at any time within the period of six months starting with the date on which the goods were delivered to the buyer must be taken not to have so conformed at that date.

(4) Subsection (3) above does not apply if –

    (a) it is established that the goods did so conform at that date;

    (b) its application is incompatible with the nature of the goods or the nature of the lack of conformity.

48B Repair or replacement of the goods

(1) If section 48A above applies, the buyer may require the seller –

    (a) to repair the goods, or

    (b) to replace the goods.

(2) If the buyer requires the seller to repair or replace the goods, the seller must –

(a) repair or, as the case may be, replace the goods within a reasonable time but without causing significant inconvenience to the buyer;

(b) bear any necessary costs incurred in doing so (including in particular the cost of any labour, materials or postage).

(3) The buyer must not require the seller to repair or, as the case may be, replace the goods if that remedy is –

(a) impossible, or

(b) disproportionate in comparison to the other of those remedies, or

(c) disproportionate in comparison to an appropriate reduction in the purchase price under paragraph (a), or rescission under paragraph (b), of section 48C(1) below.

(4) One remedy is disproportionate in comparison to the other if the one imposes costs on the seller which, in comparison to those imposed on him by the other, are unreasonable, taking into account –

(a) the value which the goods would have if they conformed to the contract of sale,

(b) the significance of the lack of conformity, and

(c) whether the other remedy could be effected without significant inconvenience to the buyer.

(5) Any question as to what is a reasonable time or significant inconvenience is to be determined by reference to –

(a) the nature of the goods, and

(b) the purpose for which the goods were acquired.

48C Reduction of purchase price or rescission of contract

(1) If section 48A above applies, the buyer may –

(a) require the seller to reduce the purchase price of the goods in question to the buyer by an appropriate amount, or

(b) rescind the contract with regard to those goods,

if the condition in subsection (2) below is satisfied.

(2) The condition is that –

(a) by virtue of section 48B(3) above the buyer may require neither repair nor replacement of the goods; or

(b) the buyer has required the seller to repair or replace the goods, but the seller is in breach of the requirement of section 48B(2)(a) above to do so within a reasonable time and without significant inconvenience to the buyer.

(3) For the purposes of this Part, if the buyer rescinds the contract, any reimbursement to the buyer may be reduced to take account of the use he has had of the goods since they were delivered to him.

48D Relation to other remedies, etc

(1) If the buyer requires the seller to repair or replace the goods the buyer must not act under subsection (2) until he has given the seller a reasonable time in which to repair or replace (as the case may be) the goods.

(2) The buyer acts under this subsection if –

(a) in England and Wales or Northern Ireland he rejects the goods and terminates the contract for breach of condition;

(c) he requires the goods to be replaced or repaired (as the case may be).

48E Powers of the court

(1) In any proceedings in which a remedy is sought by virtue of this Part the court, in addition to any other power it has, may act under this section.

(2) On the application of the buyer the court may make an order requiring specific performance ... by the seller of any obligation imposed on him by virtue of section 48B above.

(3) Subsection (4) applies if –

(a) the buyer requires the seller to give effect to a remedy under section 48B or 48C above or has claims to rescind under section 48C, but

(b) the court decides that another remedy under section 48B or 48C is appropriate.

(4) The court may proceed –

(a) as if the buyer had required the seller to give effect to the other remedy, or if the other remedy is rescission under section 48C

(b) as if the buyer had claimed to rescind the contract under that section.

(5) If the buyer has claimed to rescind the contract the court may order that any reimbursement to the buyer is reduced to take account of the use he has had of the goods since they were delivered to him.

(6) The court may make an order under this section unconditionally or on such terms and conditions as to damages, payment of the price and otherwise as it thinks just.

48F Conformity with the contract

For the purposes of this Part, goods do not conform to a contract of sale if there is, in relation to the goods, a breach of an express term of the contract or a term implied by section 13, 14 or 15 above.

PART VI

ACTIONS FOR BREACH OF THE CONTRACT

49 Action for price

(1) Where, under a contract of sale, the property in the goods has passed to the buyer and he wrongfully neglects or refuses to pay for the goods according to the terms of the contract, the seller may maintain an action against him for the price of the goods.

(2) Where, under a contract of sale, the price is payable on a day certain irrespective of delivery and the buyer wrongfully neglects or refuses to pay such price, the seller may maintain an action for the price, although the property in the goods has not passed and the goods have not been appropriated to the contract. ...

50 Damages for non-acceptance

(1) Where the buyer wrongfully neglects or refuses to accept and pay for the goods, the seller may maintain an action against him for damages for non-acceptance.

(2) The measure of damages is the estimated loss directly and naturally resulting, in the ordinary course of events, from the buyer's breach of contract.

(3) Where there is an available market for the goods in question the measure of damages is prima facie to be ascertained by the difference between the contract price and the market or current price at the time or times when the goods ought to have been accepted or (if no time was fixed for acceptance) at the time of the refusal to accept.

51 Damages for non-delivery

(1) Where the seller wrongfully neglects or refuses to deliver the goods to the buyer, the buyer may maintain an action against the seller for damages for non-delivery.

(2) The measure of damages is the estimated loss directly and naturally resulting, in the ordinary course of events, from the seller's breach of contract.

(3) Where there is an available market for the goods in question the measure of damages is prima facie to be ascertained by the difference between the contract price and the market or current price of the goods at the time or times when they ought to have been delivered or (if no time was fixed) at the time of the refusal to deliver.

52 Specific performance

(1) In any action for breach of contract to deliver specific or ascertained goods the court may, if it thinks fit, on the plaintiff's application, by its judgment or decree direct that the contract shall be performed specifically, without giving the defendant the option of retaining the goods on payment of damages.

(2) The plaintiff's application may be made at any time before judgment or decree.

(3) The judgment or decree may be unconditional, or on such terms and conditions as to damages, payment of the price and otherwise as seem just to the court. ...

53 Remedy for breach of warranty

(1) Where there is a breach of warranty by the seller, or where the buyer elects (or is compelled) to treat any breach of a condition on the part of the seller as a breach of warranty, the buyer is not by reason only of such breach of warranty entitled to reject the goods; but he may –

(a) set up against the seller the breach of warranty in diminution or extinction of the price, or

(b) maintain an action against the seller for damages for the breach of warranty.

(2) The measure of damages for breach of warranty is the estimated loss directly and naturally resulting, in the ordinary course of events, from the breach of warranty.

(3) In the case of breach of warranty of quality such loss is prima facie the difference between the value of the goods at the time of delivery to the buyer and the value they would have had if they had fulfilled the warranty.

(4) The fact that the buyer has set up the breach of warranty in diminution or extinction of the price does not prevent him from maintaining an action for the same breach of warranty if he has suffered further damage. ...

54 Interest

Nothing in this Act affects the right of the buyer or the seller to recover interest or special damages in any case where by law interest or special damages may be recoverable, or to recover money paid where the consideration for the payment of it has failed.

PART VII

SUPPLEMENTARY

55 Exclusion of implied terms

(I) Where a right, duty or liability would arise under a contract of sale of goods by implication of law, it may (subject to the Unfair Contract Terms Act 1977) be negatived or varied by express agreement, or by the course of dealing between the parties, or by such usage as binds both parties to the contract.

(2) An express term does not negative a term implied by this Act unless inconsistent with it. ...

57 Auction sales

(1) Where goods are put up for sale by auction in lots, each lot is prima facie deemed to be the subject of a separate contract of sale.

(2) A sale by auction is complete when the auctioneer announces its completion by the fall of the hammer, or in other customary manner; and until the announcement is made any bidder may retract his bid.

(3) A sale by auction may be notified to be subject to a reserve or upset price, and a right to bid may also be reserved expressly by or on behalf of the seller.

(4) Where a sale by auction is not notified to be subject to a right to bid by or on behalf of the seller, it is not lawful for the seller to bid himself or to employ any person to bid at the sale, or for the auctioneer knowingly to take any bid from the seller or any such person.

(5) A sale contravening subsection (4) above may be treated as fraudulent by the buyer.

(6) Where, in respect of a sale by auction, a right to bid is expressly reserved (but not otherwise) the seller or any one person on his behalf may bid at the auction.

59 Reasonable time a question of fact

Where a reference is made in this Act to a reasonable time the question what is a reasonable time is a question of fact.

60 Rights, etc enforceable by action

Where a right, duty or liability is declared by this Act, it may (unless otherwise provided by this Act) be enforced by action.

61 Interpretation

(1) In this Act, unless the context or subject matter otherwise requires –

'action' includes counterclaim and set-off, and in Scotland condescendence and claim and compensation;

'bulk' means a mass or collection of goods of the same kind which –

    (a) is contained in a defined space or area; and

    (b) is such that any goods in the bulk are interchangeable with any other goods therein of the same number or quantity;

'business' includes a profession and the activities of any government department (including a Northern Ireland department) or local or public authority;

'buyer' means a person who buys or agrees to buy goods;

'consumer contract' has the same meaning as in section 25(1) of the Unfair Contract Terms Act 1977; and for the purposes of this Act the onus of proving that a contract is not to be regarded as a consumer contract shall lie on the seller;

'contract of sale' includes an agreement to sell as well as a sale;

'credit-broker' means a person acting in the course of a business of credit brokerage carried on by him, that is a business of effecting introductions of individuals desiring to obtain credit –

(a) to persons carrying on any business so far as it relates to the provision of credit, or

(b) to other persons engaged in credit brokerage;

'delivery' means voluntary transfer of possession from one person to another except that in relation to sections 20A and 20B above it includes such appropriation of goods to the contract as results in property in the goods being transferred to the buyer;

'document of title to goods' has the same meaning as it has in the Factors Acts;

'Factors Acts' means the Factors Act 1889, the Factors (Scotland) Act 1890, and any enactment amending or substituted for the same;

'fault' means wrongful act or default;

'future goods' means goods to be manufactured or acquired by the seller after the making of the contract of sale;

'goods' includes all personal chattels other than things in action and money, and in Scotland all corporeal moveables except money; and in particular 'goods' includes emblements, industrial growing crops, and things attached to or forming part of the land which are agreed to be severed before sale or under the contract of sale and includes an undivided share in goods;

'plaintiff' includes pursuer, complainer, claimant in a multiplepoinding and defendant or defender counter-claiming;

'producer' means the manufacturer of goods, the importer of goods into the European Economic Area or any person purporting to be a producer by placing his name, trade mark or other distinctive sign on the goods;

'property' means the general property in goods, and not merely a special property;

'repair' means, in cases where there is a lack of conformity in goods for the purposes of section 48F of this Act, to bring the goods into conformity with the contract;

'sale' includes a person who sells or agrees to sell goods;

'specific goods' means goods identified and agreed on at the time a contract of sale is made and includes an undivided share, specified as a fraction or percentage, of goods identified and agreed on as aforesaid;

'warranty' (as regards England and Wales and Northern Ireland) means an agreement with reference to goods which are the subject of a contract of sale, but collateral to the main purpose of such contract, the breach of which gives rise to a claim for damages, but not to a right to reject the goods and treat the contract as repudiated.

(3) A thing is deemed to be done in good faith within the meaning of this Act when it is in fact done honestly, whether it is done negligently or not.

(4) A person is deemed to be insolvent within the meaning of this Act if he has either ceased to pay his debts in the ordinary course of business or he cannot pay his debts as they become due.

(5) Goods are in a deliverable state within the meaning of this Act when they are in such a state that the buyer would under the contract be bound to take delivery of them.

(5A) References in this Act to dealing as consumer are to be construed in accordance with Part I of the Unfair Contract Terms Act 1977; and, for the purposes of this Act, it is for a seller claiming that the buyer does not deal as consumer to show that he does not.

62   Savings: rules of law, etc

(1) The rules in bankruptcy relating to contracts of sale apply to those contracts, notwithstanding anything in this Act.

(2) The rules of the common law, including the law merchant, except in so far as they are inconsistent with the provisions of this Act,and in particular the rules relating to the law of principal and agent and the effect of fraud, misrepresentation, duress or coercion, mistake, or other invalidating cause, apply to contracts for the sale of goods.

(3) Nothing in this Act or the Sale of Goods Act 1893 affects the enactments relating to bills of sale, or any enactment relating to the sale of goods which is not expressly repealed or amended by this Act or that.

(4) The provisions of this Act about contracts of sale do not apply to a transaction in the form of a contract of sale which is intended to operate by way of mortgage, pledge, charge, or other security. ...

As amended by the Insolvency Act 1985, s235(3), Schedule 10, Part III; Sale and Supply of Goods Act 1994, ss1–4, 7(1), Schedule 2, para 5, Schedule 3 (with effect from 3 January 1995); Sale of Goods (Amendment) Act 1995, ss1(1), (2), (3), 2; Sale and Supply of Goods to Consumers Regulations 2002, regs 3–6.

LIMITATION ACT 1980
(1980 c 58)

PART I

ORDINARY TIME LIMITS FOR DIFFERENT CLASSES OF ACTION

1 Time limits under Part I subject to extension or exclusion under Part II

(1) This Part of this Act gives the ordinary time limits for bringing actions of the various classes mentioned in the following provisions of this Part.

(2) The ordinary time limits given in this Part of this Act are subject to extension or exclusion in accordance with the provisions of Part 11 of this Act.

2 Time limit for actions founded on tort

An action founded on tort shall not be brought after the expiration of six years from the date on which the cause of action accrued.

3 Time limit in case of successive conversions and extinction of title of owner of converted goods

(1) Where any cause of action in respect of the conversion of a chattel has accrued to any person and, before he recovers possession of the chattel, a further conversion takes place, no action shall be brought in respect of the further conversion after the expiration of six years from the accrual of the cause of action in respect of the original conversion.

(2) Where any such cause of action has accrued to any person and the period prescribed for bringing that action has expired and he has not during that period recovered possession of the chattel, the title of that person to the chattel shall be extinguished.

4 Special time limit in case of theft

(1) The right of any person from whom a chattel is stolen to bring an action in respect of the theft shall not be subject to the time limits under sections 2 and 3(1) of this Act, but if his title to the chattel is extinguished under section 3(2) of this Act he may not bring an action in respect of a theft preceding the loss of his title, unless

the theft in question preceded the conversion from which time began to run for the purposes of section 3(2).

(2) Subsection (1) above shall apply to any conversion related to the theft of a chattel as it applies to the theft of a chattel; and, except as provided below, every conversion following the theft of a chattel before the person from whom it is stolen recovers possession of it shall be regarded for the purposes of this section as related to the theft. If anyone purchases the stolen chattel in good faith neither the purchase nor any conversion following it shall be regarded as related to the theft.

(3) Any cause of action accruing in respect of the theft or any conversion related to the theft of a chattel to any person from whom the chattel is stolen shall be disregarded for the purpose of applying section 3(1) or (2) of this Act to his case.

(4) Where in any action brought in respect of the conversion of a chattel it is proved that the chattel was stolen from the plaintiff or anyone through whom he claims it shall be presumed that any conversion following the theft is related to the theft unless the contrary is shown.

(5) In this section 'theft' includes –

(a) any conduct outside England and Wales which would be theft if committed in England and Wales; and

(b) obtaining any chattel (in England and Wales or elsewhere) in the circumstances described in section 15(1) of the Theft Act 1968 (obtaining by deception) or by blackmail within the meaning of section 21 of that Act;

and references in this section to a chattel being 'stolen' shall be construed accordingly.

4A   Time limit for actions for defamation or malicious falsehood

The time limit under section 2 of this Act shall not apply to an action for –

(a) libel or slander, or

(b) slander of title, slander of goods or other malicious falsehood,

but no such action shall be brought after the expiration of one year from the date on which the cause of action accrued.

5   Time limit for actions founded on simple contract

An action founded on simple contract shall not be brought after the expiration of six years from the date on which the cause of action accrued.

6   Special time limit for actions in respect of certain loans

(1) Subject to subsection (3) below, section 5 of this Act shall not bar the right of action on a contract of loan to which this section applies.

(2) This section applies to any contract of loan which –

(a) does not provide for repayment of the debt on or before a fixed or determinable date; and

(b) does not effectively (whether or not it purports to do so) make the obligation to repay the debt conditional on a demand for repayment made by or on behalf of the creditor or on any other matter;

except where in connection with taking the loan the debtor enters into any collateral obligation to pay the amount of the debt or any part of it (as, for example, by delivering a promissory note as security for the debt) on terms which would exclude the application of this section to the contract of loan if they applied directly to repayment of the debt.

(3) Where a demand in writing for repayment of the debt under a contract of loan to which this section applies is made by or on behalf of the creditor (or, where there are joint creditors, by or on behalf of any one of them) section 5 of this Act shall thereupon apply as if the cause of action to recover the debt had accrued on the date on which the demand was made.

(4) In this section 'promissory note' has the same meaning as in the Bills of Exchange Act 1882.

7   Time limit for actions to enforce certain awards

An action to enforce an award, where the submission is not by an instrument under seal, shall not be brought after the expiration of six years from the date on which the cause of action accrued.

8   Time limit for actions on a specialty

(1) An action upon a specialty shall not be brought after the expiration of twelve years from the date on which the cause of action accrued.

(2) Subsection (1) above shall not affect any action for which a shorter period of limitation is prescribed by any other provision of this Act.

9   Time limit for actions for sums recoverable by statute

(1) An action to recover any sum recoverable by virtue of any enactment shall not be brought after the expiration of six years from the date on which the cause of action accrued.

(2) Subsection (1) above shall not affect any action to which section 10 of this Act applies.

10   Special time limit for claiming contribution

(1) Where under section 1 of the Civil Liability (Contribution) Act 1978 any person becomes entitled to a right to recover contribution in respect of any damage from any other person, no action to recover contribution by virtue of that right shall be brought after the expiration of two years from the date on which that right accrued.

(2) For the purposes of this section the date on which a right to recover contribution in respect of any damage accrues to any person (referred to below in this section as 'the relevant date') shall be ascertained as provided in subsections (3) and (4) below.

(3) If the person in question is held liable in respect of that damage –

    (a) by a judgment given in any civil proceedings; or

    (b) by an award made on any arbitration;

the relevant date shall be the date on which the judgment is given, or the date of the award (as the case may be).

For the purposes of this subsection no account shall be taken of any judgment or award given or made on appeal in so far as it varies the amount of damages awarded against the person in question.

(4) If, in any case not within subsection (3) above, the person in question makes or agrees to make any payment to one or more persons in compensation for that damage (whether he admits any liability in respect of the damage or not), the relevant date shall be the earliest date on which the amount to be paid by him is agreed between him (or his representative) and the person (or each of the persons, as the case may be) to whom the payment is to be made.

(5) An action to recover contribution shall be one to which sections 28, 32 and 35 of this Act apply, but otherwise Parts II and III of this Act (except sections 34, 37 and 38) shall not apply for the purposes of this section.

11   Special time limit for actions in respect of personal injuries

(1) This section applies to any action for damages for negligence, nuisance or breach of duty (whether the duty exists by virtue of a contract or of provision made by or under a statute or independently of any contract or any such provision) where the damages claimed by the plaintiff for the negligence, nuisance or breach of duty consist of or include damages in respect of personal injuries to the plaintiff or any other person.

(1A) This section does not apply to any action brought for damages under section 3 of the Protection from Harassment Act 1997.

(2) None of the time limits given in the preceding provisions of this Act shall apply to an action to which this section applies.

(3) An action to which this section applies shall not be brought after the expiration of the period applicable in accordance with subsection (4) or (5) below.

(4) Except where subsection (5) below applies, the period applicable is three years from –

    (a) the date on which the cause of action accrued; or

    (b) the date of knowledge (if later) of the person injured.

(5) If the person injured dies before the expiration of the period mentioned in subsection (4) above, the period applicable as respects the cause of action surviving

for the benefit of his estate by virtue of section 1 of the Law Reform (Miscellaneous Provisions) Act 1934 shall be three years from –

    (a) the date of death; or

    (b) the date of the personal representative's knowledge;

whichever is the later.

(6) For the purposes of this section 'personal representative' includes any person who is or has been a personal representative of the deceased, including an executor who has not proved the will (whether or not he has renounced probate) but not anyone appointed only as a special personal representative in relation to settled land; and regard shall be had to any knowledge acquired by any such person while a personal representative or previously.

(7) If there is more than one personal representative, and their dates of knowledge are different, subsection (5)(b) above shall be read as referring to the earliest of those dates.

11A Actions in respect of defective products

(1) This section shall apply to an action for damages by virtue of any provision of Part I of the Consumer Protection Act 1987.

(2) None of the time limits given in the preceding provisions of this Act shall apply to an action to which this section applies.

(3) An action to which this section applies shall not be brought after the expiration of the period of ten years from the relevant time, within the meaning of section 4 of the said Act of 1987; and this subsection shall operate to extinguish a right of action and shall do so whether or not that right of action had accrued, or time under the following provisions of this Act had begun to run, at the end of the said period of ten years.

(4) Subject to subsection (5) below, an action to which this section applies in which the damages claimed by the plaintiff consist of or include damages in respect of personal injuries to the plaintiff or any other person or loss of or damage to any property, shall not be brought after the expiration of the period of three years from whichever is the later of –

    (a) the date on which the cause of action accrued; and

    (b) the date of knowledge of the injured person or, in the case of loss of or damage to property, the date of knowledge of the plaintiff or (if earlier) of any person in whom his cause of action was previously vested.

(5) If in a case where the damages claimed by the plaintiff consist of or include damages in respect of personal injuries to the plaintiff or any other person the injured person died before the expiration of the period mentioned in subsection (4) above, that subsection shall have effect as respects the cause of action surviving for the benefit of his estate by virtue of section 1 of the Law Reform (Miscellaneous

Provisions) Act 1934 as if for the reference to that period there were substituted a reference to the period of three years from whichever is the later of –

(a) the date of death; and

(b) the date of the personal representative's knowledge.

(6) For the purposes of this section 'personal representative' includes any person who is or has been a personal representative of the deceased, including an executor who has not proved the will (whether or not he had renounced probate) but not anyone appointed only as a special personal representative in relation to settled land; and regard shall be had to any knowledge acquired by any such person while a personal representative or previously.

(7) If there is more than one personal representative and their dates of knowledge are different, subsection (5)(b) above shall be read as referring to the earliest of those dates.

(8) Expressions used in this section or section 14 of this Act and in Part I of the Consumer Protection Act 1987 have the same meanings in this section or that section as in that Part; and section 1(1) of that Act (Part I to be construed as enacted for the purpose of complying with the product liability Directive) shall apply for the purpose of construing this section and the following provisions of this Act so far as they relate to an action by virtue of any provision of that Part as it applies for the purpose of construing that Part.

12   Special time limit for actions under Fatal Accidents legislation

(1) An action under the Fatal Accidents Act 1976 shall not be brought if the death occurred when the person injured could no longer maintain an action and recover damages in respect of the injury (whether because of a time limit in this Act or in any other Act, or for any other reason).

Where any such action by the injured person would have been barred by the time limit in section 11 or 11A of this Act, no account shall be taken of the possibility of that time limit being overridden under section 33 of this Act.

(2) None of the time limits given in the preceding provisions of this Act shall apply to an action under the Fatal Accidents Act 1976, but no such action shall be brought after the expiration of three years from –

(a) the date of death; or

(b) the date of knowledge of the person for whose benefit the action is brought;

whichever is the later.

(3) An action under the Fatal Accidents Act 1976 shall be one to which sections 28, 33 and 35 of this Act apply, and the application to any such action of the time limit under subsection (2) above shall be subject to section 39; but otherwise Parts II and III of this Act shall not apply to any such action.

13 Operation of time limit under section 12 in relation to different dependants

(1) Where there is more than one person for whose benefit an action under the Fatal Accidents Act 1976 is brought, section 12(2)(b) of this Act shall be applied separately to each of them.

(2) Subject to subsection (3) below, if by virtue of subsection (1) above the action would be outside the time limit given by section 12(2) as regards one or more, but not all, of the persons for whose benefit it is brought, the court shall direct that any person as regards whom the action would be outside that limit shall be excluded from those for whom the action is brought.

(3) The court shall not give such a direction if it is shown that if the action were brought exclusively for the benefit of the person in question it would not be defeated by a defence of limitation (whether in consequence of section 28 of this Act or an agreement between the two parties not to raise the defence, or otherwise).

14 Definition of date of knowledge for purposes of sections 11 and 12

(1) Subject to subsection (1A) below, in sections 11 and 12 of this Act references to a person's date of knowledge are references to the date on which he first had knowledge of the following facts –

(a) that the injury in question was significant; and

(b) that the injury was attributable in whole or in part to the act or omission which is alleged to constitute negligence, nuisance or breach of duty; and

(c) the identity of the defendant; and

(d) if it is alleged that the act or omission was that of a person other than the defendant, the identity of that person and the additional facts supporting the bringing of an action against the defendant;

and knowledge that any acts or omissions did or did not, as a matter of law, involve negligence, nuisance or breach of duty is irrelevant.

(1A) In section 11A of this Act and in section 12 of this Act so far as that section applies to an action by virtue of section 6(1)(a) of the Consumer Protection Act 1987 (death caused by defective produce) references to a person's date of knowledge are references to the date on which he first had knowledge of the following facts –

(a) such facts about the damage caused by the defect as would lead a reasonable person who had suffered such damage to consider it sufficiently serious to justify his instituting proceedings for damages against a defendant who did not dispute liability and was able to satisfy a judgment; and

(b) that the damage was wholly or partly attributable to the facts and circumstances alleged to constitute the defect; and

(c) the identity of the defendant;

but, in determining the date on which a person first had such knowledge there shall be disregarded both the extent (if any) of that person's knowledge on any date of whether particular facts or circumstances would or would not, as a matter of law, constitute a defect and, in a case relating to loss of or damage to property, any knowledge which that person had on a date on which he had no right of action by virtue of Part I of that Act in respect of the loss or damage.

(2) For the purposes of this section an injury is significant if the person whose date of knowledge is in question would reasonably have considered it sufficiently serious to justify his instituting proceedings for damages against a defendant who did not dispute liability and was able to satisfy a judgment.

(3) For the purposes of this section a person's knowledge includes knowledge which he might reasonably have been expected to acquire –

(a) from facts observable or ascertainable by him; or

(b) from facts ascertainable by him with the help of medical or other appropriate expert advice which it is reasonable for him to seek;

but a person shall not be fixed under this subsection with knowledge of a fact ascertainable only with the help of expert advice so long as he has taken all reasonable steps to obtain (and, where appropriate, to act on) that advice.

14A Special time limit for negligence actions where facts relevant to cause of action are not known at date of accrual

(1) This section applies to any action for damages for negligence, other than one to which section 11 of this Act applies, where the starting date for reckoning the period of limitation under subsection (4)(b) below falls after the date on which the cause of action accrued.

(2) Section 2 of this Act shall not apply to an action to which this section applies.

(3) An action to which this section applies shall not be brought after the expiration of the period applicable in accordance with subsection (4) below.

(4) That period is either –

(a) six years from the date on which the cause of action accrued; or

(b) three years from the starting date as defined by subsection (5) below, if that period expires later than the period mentioned in paragraph (a) above.

(5) For the purposes of this section, the starting date for reckoning the period of limitation under subsection (4)(b) above is the earliest date on which the plaintiff or any person in whom the cause of action was vested before him first had both the knowledge required for bringing an action for damages in respect of the relevant damage and a right to bring such an action.

(6) In subsection (5) above 'the knowledge required for bringing an action for damages in respect of the relevant damage' means knowledge both –

(a) of the material facts about the damage in respect of which damages are claimed; and

(b) of the other facts relevant to the current action mentioned in subsection (8) below.

(7) For the purposes of subsection (6)(a) above, the material facts about the damage are such facts about the damage as would lead a reasonable person who had suffered such damage to consider it sufficiently serious to justify his instituting proceedings for damages against the defendant who did not dispute liability and was able to satisfy a judgment.

(8) The other facts referred to in subsection (6)(b) above are –

(a) that the damage was attributable in whole or in part to the act or omission which is alleged to constitute negligence; and

(b) the identity of the defendant; and

(c) if it is alleged that the act or omission was that of a person other than the defendant, the identity of that person and the additional facts supporting the bringing of an action against the defendant.

(9) Knowledge that any acts or omissions did or did not, as a matter of law, involve negligence is irrelevant for the purposes of subsection (5) above.

(10) For the purposes of this section a person's knowledge includes knowledge which he might reasonably have been expected to acquire –

(a) from facts observable or ascertainable by him; or

(b) from facts ascertainable by him with the help of appropriate expert advice which it is reasonable for him to seek;

but a person shall not be taken by virtue of this subsection to have knowledge of a fact ascertainable only with the help of expert advice so long as he has taken all reasonable steps to obtain (and, where appropriate, to act on) that advice.

14B Overriding time limit for negligence actions not involving personal injuries

(1) An action for damages for negligence, other than one to which section 11 of this Act applies, shall not be brought after the expiration of fifteen years from the date (or, if more than one, from the last of the dates) on which there occurred any act or omission –

(a) which is alleged to constitute negligence; and

(b) to which the damage in respect of which damages are claimed is alleged to be attributable (in whole or in part).

(2) This section bars the right of action in a case to which subsection (1) above applies notwithstanding that –

(a) the cause of action has not yet accrued; or

(b) where section 14A of this Act applies to the action, the date which is for the purposes of that section the starting date for reckoning the period mentioned in subsection (4)(b) of that section has not yet occurred;

before the end of the period of limitation prescribed by this section.

24 Time limit for actions to enforce judgments

(1) An action shall not be brought upon any judgment after the expiration of six years from the date on which the judgment became enforceable.

(2) No arrears of interest in respect of any judgment debt shall be recovered after the expiration of six years from the date on which the interest became due.

PART II

EXTENSION OR EXCLUSION OF ORDINARY TIME LIMITS

28 Extension of limitation period in case of disability

(1) Subject to the following provisions of this section, if on the date when any right of action accrued for which a period of limitation is prescribed by this Act, the person to whom it accrued was under a disability, the action may be brought at any time before the expiration of six years from the date when he ceased to be under a disability or died (whichever first occurred) notwithstanding that the period of limitation has expired.

(2) This section shall not affect any case where the right of action first accrued to some person (not under a disability) through whom the person under a disability claims.

(3) When a right of action which has accrued to a person under a disability accrues, on the death of that person while still under a disability, to another person under a disability, no further extension of time shall be allowed by reason of the disability of the second person.

(4) No action to recover land or money charged on land shall be brought by virtue of this section by any person after the expiration of thirty years from the date on which the right of action accrued to that person or some person through whom he claims.

(4A) If the action is one to which section 4A of this Act applies, subsection (1) above shall have effect –

(a) in the case of an action for libel or slander, as if for the words from 'at any time' to 'occurred)' there were substituted the words 'by him at any time before the expiration of one year from the date on which he ceased to be under a disability'; and

(b) in the case of an action for slander of title, slander of goods or other malicious falsehood, as if for the words 'six years' there were substituted the words 'one year'.

(5) If the action is one to which section 10 of this Act applies, subsection (1) above shall have effect as if for the words 'six years' there were substituted the words 'two years'.

(6) If the action is one to which section 11 or 12(2) of this Act applies, subsection

(1) above shall have effect as if for the words 'six years' there were substituted the words 'three years'.

(7) If the action is one to which section 11A of this Act applies or one by virtue of section 6(1)(a) of the Consumer Protection Act 1987 (death caused by defective product), subsection (1) above –

(a) shall not apply to the time limit prescribed by subsection (3) of the said section 11A or to that time limit as applied by virtue of section 12(1) of this Act; and

(b) in relation to any other time limit prescribed by this Act shall have effect as if for the words 'six years' there were substituted the words 'three years'.

28A Extension for cases where the limitation period is the period under section 14A(4)(b)

(1) Subject to subsection (2) below, if in the case of any action for which a period of limitation is prescribed by section 14A of this Act –

(a) the period applicable in accordance with subsection (4) of that section is the period mentioned in paragraph (b) of that subsection;

(b) on the date which is for the purposes of that section the starting date for reckoning that period the person by reference to whose knowledge that date fell to be determined under subsection (5) of that section was under a disability; and

(c) section 28 of this Act does not apply to the action;

the action may be brought at any time before the expiration of three years from the date when he ceased to be under a disability or died (whichever first occurred) notwithstanding that the period mentioned above has expired.

(2) An action may not be brought by virtue of subsection (1) above after the end of the period of limitation prescribed by section 14B of this Act.

29 Fresh accrual of action on acknowledgment or part payment ...

(5) Subject to subsection (6) below, where any right of action has accrued to recover –

(a) any debt or other liquidated pecuniary claim; or

(b) any claim to the personal estate of a deceased person or to any share or interest in any such estate;

and the person liable or accountable for the claim acknowledges the claim or makes any payment in respect of it the right shall be treated as having accrued on and not before the date of the acknowledgment or payment.

(6) A payment of a part of the rent or interest due at any time shall not extend the period for claiming the remainder then due, but any payment of interest shall be treated as a payment in respect of the principal debt.

(7) Subject to subsection (6) above, a current period of limitation may be repeatedly extended under this section by further acknowledgements or payments, but a right

of action, once barred by this Act, shall not be revived by any subsequent acknowledgment or payment.

30   Formal provisions as to acknowledgments and part payments

(1) To be effective for the purposes of section 29 of this Act, an acknowledgment must be in writing and signed by the person making it.

(2) For the purposes of section 29, any acknowledgment or payment –

(a) may be made by the agent of the person by whom it is required to be made under that section; and

(b) shall be made to the person, or to an agent of the person, whose title or claim is being acknowledged or, as the case may be, in respect of whose claim the payment is being made.

31   Effect of acknowledgement or part payment on persons other than the maker or recipient ...

(6) An acknowledgement of any debt or other liquidated pecuniary claim shall bind the acknowledgor and his successors but not any other person.

(7) A payment made in respect of any debt or other liquidated pecuniary claim shall bind all persons liable in respect of the debt or claim.

(8) An acknowledgement by one of several personal representatives of any claim to the personal estate of a deceased person or to any share or interest in any such estate, or a payment by one of several personal representatives in respect of any such claim, shall bind the estate of the deceased person.

(9) In this section 'successor', in relation to any mortgagee or person liable in respect of any debt or claim, means his personal representatives and any other person on whom the rights under the mortgage or, as the case may be, the liability in respect of the debt or claim devolve (whether on death or bankruptcy or the disposition of property or the determination of a limited estate or interest in settled property or otherwise).

32   Postponement of limitation period in case of fraud, concealment or mistake

(1) Subject to subsection (3) and (4A) below, where in the case of any action for which a period of limitation is prescribed by this Act, either –

(a) the action is based upon the fraud of the defendant; or

(b) any fact relevant to the plaintiff's right of action has been deliberately concealed from him by the defendant; or

(c) the action is for relief from the consequences of a mistake;

the period of limitation shall not begin to run until the plaintiff has discovered the fraud, concealment or mistake (as the case may be) or could with reasonable diligence have discovered it.

References in this subsection to the defendant include references to the defendant's agent and to any person through whom the defendant claims and his agent.

(2) For the purposes of subsection (1) above, deliberate commission of a breach of duty in circumstances in which it is unlikely to be discovered for some time amounts to deliberate concealment of the facts involved in that breach of duty.

(3) Nothing in this section shall enable any action –

(a) to recover, or recover the value of, any property; or

(b) to enforce any charge against, or set aside any transaction affecting, any property;

to be brought against the purchaser of the property or any person claiming through him in any case where the property has been purchased for valuable consideration by an innocent third party since the fraud or concealment or (as the case may be) the transaction in which the mistake was made took place.

(4) A purchaser is an innocent third party for the purposes of this section –

(a) in the case of fraud or concealment of any fact relevant to the plaintiff's right of action, if he was not a party to the fraud or (as the case may be) to the concealment of that fact and did not at the time of the purchase know or have reason to believe that the fraud or concealment had taken place, and

(b) in the case of mistake, if he did not at the time of the purchase know or have reason to believe that the mistake had been made.

(4A) Subsection (1) above shall not apply in relation to the time limit prescribed by section 11A(3) of this Act or in relation to that time limit as applied by virtue of section 12(1) of this Act.

(5) Sections 14A and 14B of this Act shall not apply to any action to which subsection (1)(b) above applies (and accordingly the period of limitation referred to in that subsection, in any cae to which either of those sections would otherwise apply, is the period applicable under section 2 of this Act).

32A Discretionary extension of time limit for actions for defamation or malicious falsehood

(1) If it appears to the court that it would be equitable to allow an action to proceed having regard to the degree to which –

(a) the operation of section 4A of this Act prejudices the plaintiff or any person whom he represents, and

(b) any decision of the court under this subsection would prejudice the defendant or any person whom he represents,

the court may direct that that section shall not apply to the action or shall not apply to any specified cause of action to which the action relates.

(2) In acting under this section the court shall have regard to all the circumstances of the case and in particular to –

(a) the length of, and the reasons for, the delay on the part of the plaintiff;

(b) where the reason or one of the reasons for the delay was that all or any of the facts relevant to the cause of action did not become known to the plaintiff until after the end of the period mentioned in section 4A –

(i) the date on which any such facts did become known to him, and

(ii) the extent to which he acted promptly and reasonably once he knew whether or not the facts in question might be capable of giving rise to an action; and

(c) the extent to which, having regard to the delay, relevant evidence is likely –

(i) to be unavailable, or

(ii) to be less cogent than if the action had been brought within the period mentioned in section 4A.

(3) In the case of an action for slander of title, slander of goods or other malicious falsehood brought by a personal representative –

(a) the references in subsection (2) above to the plaintiff shall be construed as including the deceased person to whom the cause of action accrued and any previous personal representative of that person; and

(b) nothing in section 28(3) of this Act shall be construed as affecting the court's discretion under this section.

(4) In this section 'the court' means the court in which the action has been brought.

33 Discretionary exclusion of time limit for actions in respect of personal injuries or death

(1) If it appears to the court that it would be equitable to allow an action to proceed having regard to the degree to which –

(a) the provisions of section 11 or 11A or 12 of this Act prejudice the plaintiff or any person whom he represents; and

(b) any decision of the court under this subsection would prejudice the defendant or any person whom he represents;

the court may direct that those provisions shall not apply to the action, or shall not apply to any specified cause of action to which the action relates.

(1A) The court shall not under this section disapply –

(a) subsection (3) of section 11A; or

(b) where the damages claimed by the plaintiff are confined to damages for loss of or damage to any property, any other provision in its application to an action by virtue of Part I of the Consumer Protection Act 1987.

(2) The court shall not under this section disapply section 12(1) except where the reason why the person injured could no longer maintain an action was because of the time limit in section 11 or subsection (4) of section 11A.

If, for example, the person injured could at his death no longer maintain an action under the Fatal Accidents Act 1976 because of the time limit in Article 29 in Schedule 1 to the Carriage by Air Act 1961, the court has no power to direct that section 12(1) shall not apply.

(3) In acting under this section the court shall have regard to all the circumstances of the case and in particular to –

(a) the length of, and the reasons for, the delay on the part of the plaintiff;

(b) the extent to which, having regard to the delay, the evidence adduced or likely to be adduced by the plaintiff or the defendant is or is likely to be less cogent than if the action had been brought within the time allowed by section 11, by section 11A or (as the case may be) by section 12;

(c) the conduct of the defendant after the cause of action arose, including the extent (if any) to which he responded to requests reasonably made by the plaintiff for information or inspection for the purpose of ascertaining facts which were or might be relevant to the plaintiff's cause of action against the defendant;

(d) the duration of any disability of the plaintiff arising after the date of the accrual of the cause of action;

(e) the extent to which the plaintiff acted promptly and reasonably once he knew whether or not the act or omission of the defendant, to which the injury was attributable, might be capable at that time of giving rise to an action for damages;

(f) the steps, if any, taken by the plaintiff to obtain medical, legal or other expert advice and the nature of any such advice he may have received.

(4) In a case where the person injured died where, because of section 11 or subsection (4) of section 11A, he could no longer maintain an action and recover damages in respect of the injury, the court shall have regard in particular to the length of, and the reasons for, the delay on the part of the deceased.

(5) In a case under subsection (4) above, or any other case where the time limit, or one of the time limits, depends on the date of knowledge of a person other than the plaintiff, subsection (3) above shall have effect with appropriate modifications, and shall have effect in particular as if references to the plaintiff included references to any person whose date of knowledge is or was relevant in determining a time limit.

(6) A direction by the court disapplying the provisions of section 12(1) shall operate to disapply the provisions to the same effect in section 1(1) of the Fatal Accidents Act 1976.

(7) In this section 'the court' means the court in which the action has been brought.

(8) References in this section to section 11 or 11A include references to that section as extended by any of the preceding provisions of this Part of this Act or by any provision of Part III of this Act.

PART III

MISCELLANEOUS AND GENERAL

36   Equitable jurisdiction and remedies

(1) The following time limits under this Act, that is to say –

(a) the time limit under section 2 for actions founded on tort;

(aa) the time limt under section 4A for actions for libel or slander, or for slander of title, slander of goods or other malicious falsehood;

(b) the time limit under section 5 for actions founded on simple contract;

(c) the time limit under section 7 for actions to enforce awards where the submission is not by an instrument under seal;

(d) the time limit under section 8 for actions on a specialty;

(e) the time limit under section 9 for actions to recover a sum recoverable by virtue of any enactment; and

(f) the time limit under section 24 for actions to enforce a judgment;

shall not apply to any claim for specific performance of a contract or for an injunction or for other equitable relief; except in so far as any such time limit may be applied by the court by analogy in like manner as the corresponding time limit under any enactment repealed by the Limitation Act 1939 was applied before 1 July 1940.

(2) Nothing in this Act shall affect any equitable jurisdiction to refuse relief on the ground of acquiescence or otherwise.

38   Interpretation

(1) In this Act, unless the context otherwise requires –

'action' includes any proceeding in a court of law, including an ecclesiastical court;

'land' includes corporeal hereditaments, tithes and rentcharges and any legal or equitable estate or interest therein, but except as provided above in this definition does not include any incorporeal hereditament;

'personal estate' and 'personal property' do not include chattels real;

'personal injuries' includes any disease and any impairment of a person's physical or mental condition, and 'injury' and cognate expressions shall be construed accordingly;

'rent' includes a rentcharge and a rentservice;

'rentcharge' means any annuity or periodical sum of money charged upon or payable out of land, except a rent service or interest on a mortgage on land;

'settled land', 'statutory owner' and 'tenant for life' have the same meanings respectively as in the Settled Land Act 1925;

'trust' and 'trustee' have the same meanings respectively as in the Trustee Act 1925.

(2) For the purposes of this Act a person shall be treated as under a disability while he is an infant, or of unsound mind.

(3) For the purposes of subsection (2) above a person is of unsound mind if he is a person who, by reason of mental disorder is incapable of managing and administering his property and affairs; and in this section 'mental disorder' has the same meaning as in the Mental Health Act 1983.

(4) Without prejudice to the generality of subsection (3) above, a person shall be conclusively presumed for the purposes of subsection (2) above to be of unsound mind –

(a) while he is liable to be detained or subject to guardianship under the Mental Health Act 1983 (otherwise than by virtue of section 35 or 89); and

(b) while he is receiving treatment for mental disorder as an in-patient in any hospital within the meaning of the Mental Health Act 1983 or independent hospital or care home within the meaning of the Care Standards Act 2000 without being liable to be detained under the said Act of 1983 (otherwise than by virtue of section 35 or 89), being treatment which follows without any interval a period during which he was liable to be detained or subject to guardianship under the Mental Health Act 1959, or the said Act of 1983 (otherwise than by virtue of section 35 or 89) or by virtue of any enactment repealed or excluded by the Mental Health Act 1959.

(5) Subject to subsection (6) below, a person shall be treated as claiming through another person if he became entitled by, through, under, or by the act of that other person to the right claimed, and any person whose estate or interest might have been barred by a person entitled to an entailed interest in possession shall be treated as claiming through the person so entitled.

(6) A person becoming entitled to any estate or interest by virtue of a special power of appointment shall not be treated as claiming through the appointor.

(7) References in this Act to a right of action to recover land shall include references to a right to enter into possession of the land or, in the case of rentcharges and tithes, to distrain for arrears of rent or tithe, and references to the bringing of such an action shall include references to the making of such an entry or distress.

(8) References in this Act to the possession of land shall, in the case of tithes and rentcharges, be construed as references to the receipt of the tithe or rent, and references to the date of dispossession or discontinuance of possession of land shall, in the case of rentcharges, be construed as references to the date of the last receipt of rent.

(9) References in Part II of this Act to a right of action shall include references to –

(a) a cause of action;

(b) a right to receive money secured by a mortgage or charge on any property;

(c) a right to recover proceeds of the sale of land; and

(d) a right to receive a share or interest in the personal estate of a deceased person.

(10) References in Part II to the date of the accrual of a right of action shall be construed –

(a) in the case of an action upon a judgment, as references to the date on which the judgment became enforceable; and

(b) in the case of an action to recover arrears of rent or interest, or damages in respect of arrears of rent or interest, as references to the date on which the rent or interest became due.

39   Saving for other limitation enactments

This Act shall not apply to any action or arbitration for which a period of limitation is prescribed by or under any other enactment (whether passed before after the passing of this Act), or to any action or arbitration to which the Crown is a party and for which, if it were between subjects, a period of limitation would be prescribed by or under any such other enactment.

As amended by the Mental Health Act 1983, s148, Schedule 4, para 55; Administration of Justice Act 1985, s57(2), (3), (4), (5); Latent Damage Act 1986, ss1, 2(1), (2); Consumer Protection Act 1987, s6(6), Schedule 1, paras 1–6; Defamation Act 1996, s5; Trusts of Land and Appointment of Trustees Act 1996, s25(2), Schedule 4; Protection from Harassment Act 1997, s6; Care Standards Act 2000, s116, Schedule 4, para 8.

HIGHWAYS ACT 1980
(1980 c 66)

41   Duty to maintain highways maintainable at public expense

(1) The authority who are for the time being the highway authority for a highway maintainable at the public expense are under a duty, subject to subsections (2) and (4) below [proposed trunk road], to maintain the highway.

(1A) In particular, a highway authority are under a duty to ensure, so far as is reasonably practicable, that safe passage along a highway is not endangered by snow or ice. ...

58   Special defence in action against a highway authority for damages for non-repair of highway

(1) In an action against a highway authority in respect of damage resulting from their failure to maintain a highway maintainable at the public expense it is a defence (without prejudice to any other defence or the application of the law relating to contributory negligence) to prove that the authority had taken such care as in all the circumstances was reasonably required to secure that the part of the highway to which the action relates was not dangerous for traffic.

(2) For the purposes of a defence under subsection (1) above, the court shall in particular have regard to the following matters –

(a) the character of the highway, and the traffic which was reasonably to be expected to use it;

(b) the standard of maintenance appropriate for a highway of that character and used by such traffic;

(c) the state of repair in which a reasonable person would have expected to find the highway;

(d) whether the highway authority knew, or could reasonably have been expected to know, that the condition of the part of the highway to which the action relates was likely to cause danger to users of the highway;

(e) where the highway authority could not reasonably have been expected to repair that part of the highway before the cause of action arose, what warning notices of its condition had been displayed;

but for the purposes of such a defence it is not relevant to prove that the highway authority had arranged for a competent person to carry out or supervise the maintenance of the part of the highway to which the action relates unless it is also proved that the authority had given him proper instructions with regard to the maintenance of the highway and that he had carried out the instructions.

(3) This sections binds the Crown.

328 Meaning of 'highway'

(1) In this Act, except where the context otherwise requires, 'highway' means the whole or a part of a highway other than a ferry or waterway.

(2) Where a highway passes over a bridge or through a tunnel, that bridge or tunnel is to be taken for the purposes of this Act to be a part of the highway.

(3) In this Act, 'highway maintainable at the public expense' and any other expression defined by references to a highway is to be construed in accordance with the foregoing provisions of this section.

329 Further provision as to interpretation

(1) In this Act, except where the context otherwise requires – ...

'maintenance' includes repair, and 'maintain' and 'maintainable' are to be construed accordingly; ...

'traffic' includes pedestrians and animals; ...

As amended by the New Roads and Street Works Act 1991, s168(2), Schedule 9; Railways and Transport Safety Act 2003, s111.

PUBLIC PASSENGER VEHICLES
ACT 1981
(1981 c 14)

29   Avoidance of contracts so far as restrictive of liability in respect of death of or injury to passengers in public service vehicles

A contract for the conveyance of a passenger in a public service vehicle shall, so far as it purports to negative or to restrict the liability of a person in respect of a claim which may be made against him in respect of the death of, or bodily injury to, the passenger while being carried in, entering or alighting from the vehicle, or purports to impose any conditions with respect to the enforcement of any such liability, be void.

SUPREME COURT ACT 1981
(1981 c 54)

32 Orders for interim payment

(1) As regards proceedings pending in the High Court, provision may be made by rules of court for enabling the court, in such circumstances as may be prescribed, to make an order requiring a party to the proceedings to make an interim payment of such amount as may be specified in the order, with provision for the payment to be made to such other party to the proceedings as may be so specified or, if the order so provides, by paying it into court.

(2) Any rules of court which make provision in accordance with subsection (1) may include provision for enabling a party to any proceedings who, in pursuance of such an order, has made an interim payment to recover the whole or part of the amount of the payment in such circumstances, and from such other party to the proceedings, as may be determined in accordance with the rules.

(3) Any rules made by virtue of this section may include such incidental, supplementary and consequential provisions as the rule-making authority may consider necessary or expedient.

(4) Nothing in this section shall be construed as affecting the exercise of any power relating to costs, including any power to make rules of court relating to costs.

(5) In this section 'interim payment', in relation to a party to any proceedings, means a payment on account of any damages, debt or other sum (excluding any costs) which that party may be held liable to pay to or for the benefit of another party to the proceedings if a final judgment or order of the court in the proceedings is given or made in favour of that other party.

32A Orders for provisional damages for personal injuries

(1) This section applies to an action for damages for personal injuries in which there is proved or admitted to be a chance that at some definite or indefinite time in the future the injured person will, as a result of the act or omission which gave rise to the cause of action, develop some serious disease or suffer some serious deterioration in his physical or mental condition.

(2) Subject to subsection (4) below, as regards any action for damages to which this section applies in which a judgment is given in the High Court, provision may be made by rules of court for enabling the court, in such circumstances as may be prescribed, to award the injured person –

(a) damages assessed on the assumption that the injured person will not develop the disease or suffer the deterioration in his condition; and

(b) further damages at a future date if he develops the disease or suffers the deterioration.

(3) Any rules made by virtue of this section may include such incidental, supplementary and consequential provisions as the rule-making authority may consider necessary or expedient.

(4) Nothing in this section shall be construed –

(a) as affecting the exercise of any power relating to costs, including any power to make rules of court relating to costs; or

(b) as prejudicing any duty of the court under any enactment or rule of law to reduce or limit the total damages which would have been recoverable apart from any such duty.

35A Power of High Court to award interest on debts and damages

(1) Subject to rules of court, in proceedings (whenever instituted) before the High Court for the recovery of a debt or damages there may be included in any sum for which judgment is given simple interest, at such rate as the court thinks fit or as rules of court may provide, on all or any part of the debt or damages in respect of which judgment is given, or payment is made before judgment, for all or any part of the period between the date when the cause of action arose and –

(a) in the case of any sum paid before judgment, the date of the payment; and

(b) in the case of the sum for which judgment is given, the date of the judgment.

(2) In relation to a judgment given for damages for personal injuries or death which exceed £200 subsection (1) shall have effect –

(a) with the substitution of 'shall be included' for 'may be included'; and

(b) with the addition of 'unless the court is satisfied that there are special reasons to the contrary' after 'given', where first occurring.

(3) Subject to rules of court, where –

(a) there are proceedings (whenever instituted) before the High Court for the recovery of a debt; and

(b) the defendant pays the whole debt to the plaintiff (otherwise than in pursuance of a judgment in the proceedings),

the defendant shall be liable to pay the plaintiff simple interest at such rate as the court thinks fit or as rules of court may provide on all or any part of the debt for all or any part of the period between the date when the cause of action arose and the date of the payment.

(4) Interest in respect of a debt shall not be awarded under this section for a period during which, for whatever reason, interest on the debt already runs.

(5) Without prejudice to the generality of section 84, rules of court may provide for

a rate of interest by reference to the rate specified in section 17 of the Judgments Act 1838 as that section has effect from time to time or by reference to a rate for which any other enactment provides.

(6) Interest under this section may be calculated at different rates in respect of different periods.

(7) In this section 'plaintiff' means the person seeking the debt or damages and 'defendant' means the person from whom the plaintiff seeks the debt or damages and 'personal injuries' includes any disease and any impairment of a person's physical or mental condition.

(8) Nothing in this section affects the damages recoverable for the dishonour of a bill of exchange.

37   Powers of High Court with respect to injunctions and receivers

(1) The High Court may by order (whether interlocutory or final) grant an injunction or appoint a receiver in all cases in which it appears to the court to be just and convenient to do so.

(2) Any such order may be made either unconditionally or on such terms and conditions as the court thinks just.

(3) The power of the High Court under subsection (1) to grant an interlocutory injunction restraining a party to any proceedings from removing from the jurisdiction of the High Court, or otherwise dealing with, assets located within that jurisdiction shall be exercisable in cases where that party is, as well as in cases where he is not, domiciled resident or present within that jurisdiction.

(4) The power of the High Court to appoint a receiver by way of equitable execution shall operate in relation to all legal estates and interests in land; and that power –

(a) may be exercised in relation to an estate or interest in land whether or not a charge has been imposed on that land under section 1 of the Charging Orders Act 1979 for the purpose of enforcing the judgment, order or award in question; and

(b) shall be in addition to, and not in derogation of, any power of any court to appoint a receiver in proceedings for enforcing such a charge.

(5) Where an order under the said section 1 imposing a charge for the purpose of enforcing a judgment, order or award has been, or has effect as if, registered under section 6 of the Land Charges Act 1972, subsection (4) of the said section 6 (effect of non-registration of writs and orders registrable under that section) shall not apply to an order appointing a receiver made either –

(a) in proceedings for enforcing the charge; or

(b) by way of equitable execution of the judgment, order or award or, as the case may be, of so much of it as requires payment of moneys secured by the charge.

49   Concurrent administration of law and equity

(1) Subject to the provisions of this or any other Act, every court exercising jurisdiction in England or Wales in any civil cause or matter shall continue to administer law and equity on the basis that, wherever there is any conflict or variance between the rules of equity and the rules of the common law with reference to the same matter, the rules of equity shall prevail.

(2) Every such court shall give the same effect as hitherto –

(a) to all equitable estates, titles, rights, reliefs, defences and counterclaims, and to all equitable duties and liabilities; and

(b) subject thereto, to all legal claims and demands and all estates, titles, rights, duties, obligations and liabilties existing by the common law or by any custom or created by any statute,

and, subject to the provisions of this or any other Act, shall so exercise its jurisdiction in every cause or matter before it as to secure that, as far as possible, all matters in dispute between the parties are completely and finally determined, and all multiplicity of legal proceedings with respect to any of these matters is avoided.

50   Power to award damages as well as, or in substitution for, injunction or specific performance

Where the Court of Appeal or the High Court has jurisdiction to entertain an application for an injunction for specific performance, it may award damages in addition to or in substitution for an injunction for specific performance.

69   Trial by jury

(1) Where, on the application of any party to an action to be tried in the Queen's Bench Division, the court is satisfied that there is in issue –

(a) a charge of fraud against that party; or

(b) a claim in respect of libel, slander, malicious prosecution or false imprisonment; or

(c) any question or issue of a kind prescribed for the purposes of this paragraph,

the action shall be tried with a jury, unless the court is of opinion that the trial requires any prolonged examination of documents or accounts or any scientific or local investigation which cannot conveniently be made with a jury.

(2) An application under subsection (1) must be made not later than such time before the trial as may be prescribed.

(3) An action to be tried in the Queen's Bench Division which does not by virtue of subsection (1) fall to be tried with a jury shall be tried without a jury unless the court in its discretion orders it to be tried with a jury.

(4) Nothing in subsections (1) to (3) shall affect the power of the court to order, in accordance with rules of court, that different questions of fact arising in any action

be tried by different modes of trial; and where any such order is made, subsection (1) shall have effect only as respects questions relating to any such charge, claim, question or issue as is mentioned in that subsection.

(5) Where for the purpose of disposing of any action or other matter which is being tried in the High Court by a judge with a jury it is necessary to ascertain the law of any other country which is applicable to the facts of the case, any question as to the effect of the evidence given with respect to that law shall, instead of being submitted to the jury, be decided by the judge alone.

Sections 32A and 35A were inserted by the Administration of Justice Act 1982, ss6(1) and 15(1) respectively.

SUPPLY OF GOODS AND SERVICES ACT 1982

(1982 c 29)

PART I

SUPPLY OF GOODS

1   The contracts concerned

(1) In this Act in its application to England and Wales and Northern Ireland a 'contract for the transfer of goods' means a contract under which one person transfers or agrees to transfer to another the property in goods, other than an excepted contract.

(2) For the purposes of this section an excepted contract means any of the following –

(a) a contract of sale of goods;

(b) a hire-purchase agreement;

(c) a contract under which the property in goods is (or is to be) transferred in exchange for trading stamps on their redemption;

(d) a transfer or agreement to transfer which is made by deed and for which there is no consideration other than the presumed consideration imported by the deed;

(e) a contract intended to operate by way of mortgage, pledge, charge or other security.

(3) For the purposes of this Act in its application to England and Wales and Northern Ireland a contract is a contract for the transfer of goods whether or not services are also provided or to be provided under the contract, and (subject to subsection (2) above) whatever is the nature of the consideration for the transfer or agreement to transfer.

2   Implied terms about title, etc

(1) In a contract for the transfer of goods, other than one to which subsection (3) below applies, there is an implied condition on the part of the transferor that in the case of a transfer of the property in the goods he has a right to transfer the

property and in the case of an agreement to transfer the property in the goods he will have such a right at the time when the property is to be transferred.

(2) In a contract for the transfer of goods, other than one to which subsection (3) below applies, there is also an implied warranty that –

(a) the goods are free, and will remain free until the time when the property is to be transferred, from any charge or encumbrance not disclosed or known to the transferee before the contract is made, and

(b) the transferee will enjoy quiet possession of the goods except so far as it may be disturbed by the owner or other person entitled to the benefit of any charge or encumbrance so disclosed or known.

(3) This subsection applies to a contract for the transfer of goods in the case of which there appears from the contract or is to be inferred from its circumstances an intention that the transferor should transfer only such title as he or a third person may have.

(4) In a contract to which subsection (3) above applies there is an implied warranty that all charges or encumbrances known to the transferor and not known to the transferee have been disclosed to the transferee before the contract is made.

(5) In a contract to which subsection (3) above applies there is also an implied warranty that none of the following will disturb the transferee's quiet possession of the goods, namely –

(a) the transferor;

(b) in a case where the parties to the contract intend that the transferor should transfer only such title as a third person may have, that person;

(c) anyone claiming through or under the transferor or that third person otherwise than under a charge or encumbrance disclosed or known to the transferee before the contract is made.

3   Implied terms where transfer is by description

(1) This section applies where, under a contract for the transfer of goods, the transferor transfers or agrees to transfer the property in the goods by description.

(2) In such a case there is an implied condition that the goods will correspond with the description.

(3) If the transferor transfers or agrees to transfer the property in the goods by sample as well as by description it is not sufficient that the bulk of the goods corresponds with the sample if the goods do not also correspond with the description.

(4) A contract is not prevented from falling within subsection (1) above by reason only that, being exposed for supply, the goods are selected by the transferee.

4 Contracts for transfer: quality or fitness

(1) Except as provided by this section and section 5 below and subject to the provisions of any other enactment, there is no implied condition or warranty about the quality or fitness for any particular purpose of goods supplied under a contract for the transfer of goods.

(2) Where, under such a contract, the transferor transfers the property in goods in the course of a business, there is an implied condition that the goods supplied under the contract are of satisfactory quality.

(2A) For the purposes of this section and section 5 below, goods are of satisfactory quality if they meet the standard that a reasonable person would regard as satisfactory, taking account of any description of the goods, the price (if relevant) and all the other relevant circumstances.

(2B) If the transferee deals as consumer, the relevant circumstances mentioned in subsection (2A) above include any public statements on the specific characteristics of the goods made about them by the transferor, the producer or his representative, particularly in advertising or on labelling.

(2C) A public statement is not by virtue of subsection (2B) above a relevant circumstance for the purposes of subsection (2A) above in the case of a contract for the transfer of goods, if the transferor shows that –

(a) at the time the contract was made, he was not, and could not reasonably have been, aware of the statement,

(b) before the contract was made, the statement had been withdrawn in public or, to the extent that it contained anything which was incorrect or misleading, it had been corrected in public, or

(c) the decision to acquire the goods could not have been influenced by the statement.

(2D) Subsections (2B) and (2C) above do not prevent any public statement from being a relevant circumstance for the purposes of subsection (2A) above (whether or not the the transferee deals as consumer) if the statement would have been such a circumstance apart from those subsections.

(3) The condition implied by subsection (2) above does not extend to any matter making the quality of goods unsatisfactory –

(a) which is specifically drawn to the transferee's attention before the contract is made,

(b) where the transferee examines the goods before the contract is made, which that examinatiion ought to reveal, or

(c) where the property in the goods is transferred by reference to a sample, which would have been apparent on a reasonable examination of the sample.

(4) Subsection (5) below applies where, under a contract for the transfer of goods, the transferor transfers the property in goods in the course of a business and the transferee, expressly or by implication, makes known –

(a) to the transferor, or

(b) where the consideration or part of the consideration for the transfer is a sum payable by instalments and the goods were previously sold by a credit-broker to the transferor, to that credit-broker

any particular purpose for which the goods are being acquired.

(5) In that case there is (subject to subsection (6) below) an implied condition that the goods supplied under the contract are reasonably fit for that purpose, whether or not that is a purpose for which such goods are commonly supplied.

(6) Subsection (5) above does not apply where the circumstances show that the transferee does not rely, or that it is unreasonable for him to rely, on the skill or judgment of the transferor or credit-broker.

(7) An implied condition or warranty about quality or fitness for a particular purpose may be annexed by usage to a contract for the transfer of goods.

(8) The preceding provisions of this section apply to a transfer by a person who in the course of a business is acting as agent for another as they apply to a transfer by a principal in the course of a business, except where that other is not transferring in the course of a business and either the transferee knows that fact or reasonable steps are taken to bring it to the transferee's notice before the contract concerned is made.

5   Transfer by sample

(1) This section applies where, under a contract for the transfer of goods, the transferor transfers or agrees to transfer the property in the goods by reference to a sample.

(2) In such a case there is an implied condition

(a) that the bulk will correspond with the sample in quality; and

(b) that the transferee will have a reasonable opportunity of comparing the bulk with the sample; and

(c) that the goods will be free from any defect, making their quality unsatisfactory, which would not be apparent on reasonable examination of the sample.

(4) For the purposes of this section a transferor transfers or agrees to transfer the property in goods by reference to a sample where there is an express or implied term to that effect in the contract concerned.

5A   Modification of remedies for breach of statutory condition in non-consumer cases

(1) Where in the case of a contract for the transfer of goods –

(a) the transferee would, apart from this subsection, have the right to treat the contract as repudiated by reason of a breach on the part of the transferor of a term implied by sections 3, 4 or 5(2)(a) or (c) above, but

(b) the breach is so slight that it would be unreasonable for him to do so,

then, if the transferee does not deal as consumer, the breach is not to be treated as a breach of condition but may be treated as a breach of warranty.

(2) This section applies unless a contrary intention appears in, or is to be implied from, the contract.

(3) It is for the transferor to show that a breach fell within subsection (1)(b) above.

6   The contracts concerned

(1) In this Act in its application to England and Wales and Northern Ireland a 'contract for the hire of goods' means a contract under which one person bails or agrees to bail goods to another by way of hire, other than an excepted contract.

(2) For the purposes of this section an excepted contract means any of the following –

(a) a hire-purchase agreement;
(b) a contract under which goods are (or are to be) bailed in exchange for trading stamps on their redemption.

(3) For the purposes of this Act in its application to England and Wales and Northern Ireland a contract is a contract for the hire of goods whether or not services are also provided or to be provided under the contract, and (subject to subsection (2) above) whatever is the nature of the consideration for the bailment or agreement to bail by way of hire.

7   Implied terms about right to transfer possession, etc

(1) In a contract for the hire of goods there is an implied condition on the part of the bailor that in the case of a bailment he has a right to transfer possession of the goods by way of hire for the period of the bailment and in the case of an agreement to bail he will have such a right at the time of the bailment.

(2) In a contract for the hire of goods there is also an implied warranty that the bailee will enjoy quiet possession of the goods for the period of the bailment except so far as the possession may be disturbed by the owner or other person entitled to the benefit of any charge or encumbrance disclosed or known to the bailee before the contract is made.

(3) The preceding provisions of this section do not affect the right of the bailor to repossess the goods under an express or implied term of the contract.

8   Implied terms where hire is by description

(1) This section applies where, under a contract for the hire of goods, the bailor bails or agrees to bail the goods by description.

(2) In such a case there is an implied condition that the goods will correspond with the description.

(3) If under the contract the bailor bails or agrees to bail the goods by reference to a sample as well as a description it is not sufficient that the bulk of the goods corresponds with the sample if the goods do not also correspond with the description.

(4) A contract is not prevented from falling within subsection (1) above by reason only that, being exposed for supply, the goods are selected by the bailee.

9 Contracts for hire: quality or fitness

(1) Except as provided by this section and section 10 below and subject to the provisions of any other enactment, there is no implied condition or warranty about the quality or fitness for any particular purpose of goods bailed under a contract for the hire of goods.

(2) Where, under such a contract, the bailor bails goods in the course of a business, there is an implied condition that the goods supplied under the contract are of satisfactory quality.

(2A) For the purposes of this section and section 10 below, goods are of satisfactory quality if they meet the standard that a reasonable person would regard as satisfactory, taking account of any description of the goods, the consideration for the bailment (if relevant) and all the other relevant circumstances.

(2B) If the bailee deals as consumer, the relevant circumstances mentioned in subsection (2A) above include any public statements on the specific characteristics of the goods made about them by the bailor, the producer or his representative, particularly in advertising or on labelling.

(2C) A public statement is not by virtue of subsection (2B) above a relevant circumstance for the purposes of subsection (2A) above in the case of a contract for the hire of goods, if the bailor shows that –

(a) at the time the contract was made, he was not, and could not reasonably have been, aware of the statement,

(b) before the contract was made, the statement had been withdrawn in public or, to the extent that it contained anything which was incorrect or misleading, it had been corrected in public, or

(c) the decision to acquire the goods could not have been influenced by the statement.

(2D) Subsections (2B) and (2C) above do not prevent any public statement from being a relevant circumstance for the purposes of subsection (2A) above (whether or not the bailee deals as consumer) if the statement would have been such a circumstance apart from those subsections.

(3) The condition implied by subsection (2) above does not extend to any matter making the quality of goods unsatisfactory –

(a) which is specifically drawn to the bailee's attention before the contract is made,

(b) where the bailee examines the goods before the contract is made, which that examination ought to reveal, or

(c) where the goods are bailed by reference to a sample, which would have been apparent on a reasonable examination of the sample.

(4) Subsection (5) below applies where, under a contract for the hire of goods, the bailor bails goods in the course of a business and the bailee, expressly or by implication, makes known –

(a) to the bailor in the course of negotiations conducted by him in relation to the making of the contract, or

(b) to a credit-broker in the course of negotiations conducted by that broker in relation to goods sold by him to the bailor before forming the subject matter of the contract,

any particular purpose for which the goods are being bailed.

(5) In that case there is (subject to subsection (6) below) an implied condition that the goods supplied under the contract are reasonably fit for that purpose, whether or not that is a purpose for which such goods are commonly supplied.

(6) Subsection (5) above does not apply where the circumstances show that the bailee does not rely, or that it is unreasonable for him to rely, on the skill or judgment of the bailor or credit-broker.

(7) An implied condition or warranty about quality or fitness for a particular purpose may be annexed by usage to a contract for the hire of goods.

(8) The preceding provisions of this section apply to a bailment by a person who in the course of a business is acting as agent for another as they apply to a bailment by a principal in the course of a business, except where that other is not bailing in the course of a business and either the bailee knows that fact or reasonable steps are taken to bring it to the bailer's notice before the contract concerned is made.

10   Implied terms where hire is by sample

(1) This section applies where, under a contract for the hire of goods, the bailor bails or agrees to bail the goods by reference to a sample.

(2) In such a case there is an implied condition –

(a) that the bulk will correspond with the sample in quality; and

(b) that the bailee will have a reasonable opportunity of comparing the bulk with the sample; and

(c) that the goods will be free from any defect, making their quality unsatisfactory, which would not be apparent on reasonable examination of the sample.

(4) For the purposes of this section a bailor bails or agrees to bail goods by reference to a sample where there is an express or implied term to that effect in the contract concerned.

10A Modification of remedies for breach of statutory condition in non-consumer cases

(1) Where in the case of a contract for the hire of goods –

(a) the bailee would, apart from this subsection, have the right to treat the contract as repudiated by reason of a breach on the part of the bailor of a term implied by sections 8, 9 or 10(2)(a) or (c) above, but

(b) the breach is so slight that it would be unreasonable for him to do so,

then, if the bailee does not deal as consumer, the breach is not to be treated as a breach of condition but may be treated as a breach of warranty.

(2) This section applies unless a contrary intention appears in, or is to be implied from, the contract.

(3) It is for the bailor to show that a breach fell within subsection (1)(b) above.

11 Exclusion of implied terms, etc

(1) Where a right, duty or liability would arise under a contract for the transfer of goods or a contract for the hire of goods by implication of law, it may (subject to subsection (2) below and the 1977 Act) be negatived or varied by express agreement, or by the course of dealing between the parties, or by such usage as binds both parties to the contract.

(2) An express condition or warranty does not negative a condition or warranty implied by the preceding provisions of this Act unless inconsistent with it.

(3) Nothing in the preceding provisions of this Act prejudices the operation of any other enactment or any rule of law whereby any condition or warranty (other than one related to quality or fitness) is to be implied in a contract for the transfer of goods or a contract for the hire of goods.

PART 1B

ADDITIONAL RIGHTS OF TRANSFEREE IN CONSUMER CASES

11M Introductory

(1) This section applies if –

(a) the transferee deals as consumer ... and

(b) the goods do not conform to the contract for the transfer of goods at the time of delivery.

(2) If this section applies, the transferee has the right –

(a) under and in accordance with section 11N below, to require the transferor to repair or replace the goods, or

(b) under and in accordance with section 11P below –

(i) to require the transferor to reduce the amount to be paid for the transfer by the transferee by an appropriate amount, or

(ii) to rescind the contract with regard to the goods in question.

(3) For the purposes of subsection (1)(b) above, goods which do not conform to the contract for the transfer of goods at any time within the period of six months starting with the date on which the goods were delivered to the transferee must be taken not to have so conformed at that date.

(4) Subsection (3) above does not apply if –

(a) it is established that the goods did so conform at that date;

(b) its application is incompatible with the nature of the goods or the nature of the lack of conformity.

(5) For the purposes of this section, 'consumer contract' has the same meaning as in section 11F(3) above.

11N Repair or replacement of the goods

(1) If section 11M above applies, the transferee may require the transferor –

(a) to repair the goods, or

(b) to replace the goods.

(2) If the transferee requires the transferor to repair or replace the goods, the transferor must –

(a) repair or, as the case may be, replace the goods within a reasonable time but without causing significant inconvenience to the transferee;

(b) bear any necessary costs incurred in doing so (including in particular the cost of any labour, materials or postage).

(3) The transferee must not require the transferor to repair or, as the case may be, replace the goods if that remedy is –

(a) impossible,

(b) disproportionate in comparison to the other of those remedies, or

(c) disproportionate in comparison to an appropriate reduction in the purchase price under paragraph (a), or rescission under paragraph (b), of section 11P(1) below.

(4) One remedy is disproportionate in comparison to the other if the one imposes costs on the transferor which, in comparison to those imposed on him by the other, are unreasonable, taking into account –

(a) the value which the goods would have if they conformed to the contract for the transfer of goods,

(b) the significance of the lack of conformity to the contract for the transfer of goods, and

(c) whether the other remedy could be effected without significant inconvenience to the transferee.

(5) Any question as to what is a reasonable time or significant inconvenience is to be determined by reference to –

(a) the nature of the goods, and

(b) the purpose for which the goods were acquired.

11P Reduction of purchase price or rescission of contract

(1) If section 11M above applies, the transferee may –

(a) require the transferor to reduce the purchase price of the goods in question to the transferee by an appropriate amount, or

(b) rescind the contract with regard to those goods,

if the condition in subsection (2) below is satisfied.

(2) The condition is that –

(a) by virtue of section 11N(3) above the transferee may require neither repair nor replacement of the goods, or

(b) the transferee has required the transferor to repair or replace the goods, but the transferor is in breach of the requirement of section 11N(2)(a) above to do so within a reasonable time and without significant inconvenience to the transferee.

(3) If the transferee rescinds the contract, any reimbursement to the transferee may be reduced to take account of the use he has had of the goods since they were delivered to him.

11Q Relation to other remedies, etc

(1) If the transferee requires the transferor to repair or replace the goods the transferee must not act under subsection (2) until he has given the transferor a reasonable time in which to repair or replace (as the case may be) the goods.

(2) The transferee acts under this subsection if –

(a) in England and Wales or Northern Ireland he rejects the goods and terminates the contract for breach of condition; ... or

(c) he requires the goods to be replaced or repaired (as the case may be).

11R Powers of the court

(1) In any proceedings in which a remedy is sought by virtue of this Part the court, in addition to any other power it has, may act under this section.

(2) On the application of the transferee the court may make an order requiring specific performance ... by the transferor of any obligation imposed on him by virtue of section 11N above.

(3) Subsection (4) applies if –

(a) the transferee requires the transferor to give effect to a remedy under section 11N or 11P above or has claims to rescind under section 11P, but

(b) the court decides that another remedy under section 11N or 11P is appropriate.

(4) The court may proceed –

(a) as if the transferee had required the transferor to give effect to the other remedy, or if the other remedy is rescission under section 11P,

(b) as if the transferee had claimed to rescind the contract under that section.

(5) If the transferee has claimed to rescind the contract the court may order that any reimbursement to the transferee is reduced to take account of the use he has had of the goods since they were delivered to him.

(6) The court may make an order under this section unconditionally or on such terms and conditions as to damages, payment of the price and otherwise as it thinks just.

11S   Conformity with the contract

(1) Goods do not conform to a contract for the supply or transfer of goods if –

(a) there is, in relation to the goods, a breach of an express term of the contract or a term implied by section 3, 4 or 5 above ..., or

(b) installation of the goods forms part of the contract for the transfer of goods, and the goods were installed by the transferor, or under his responsibility, in breach of the term implied by section 13 below ... as to the manner in which the installation is carried out.

PART II

SUPPLY OF SERVICES

12   The contracts concerned

(1) In this Act a 'contract for the supply of a service' means, subject to subsection (2) below, a contract under which a person ('the supplier') agrees to carry out a service.

(2) For the purposes of this Act, a contract of service or apprenticeship is not a contract for the supply of a service.

(3) Subject to subsection (2) above, a contract is a contract for the supply of a service for the purposes of this Act whether or not goods are also

(a) transferred or to be transferred, or

(b) bailed or to be bailed by way of hire,

under the contract, and whatever is the nature of the consideration for which the service is to be carried out.

(4) The Secretary of State may by order provide that one or more of sections 13 to 15 below shall not apply to services of a description specified in the order, and such an order may make different provision for different circumstances.

(5) The power to make an order under subsection (4) above shall be exercisable by statutory instrument subject to annulment in pursuance of a resolution of either House of Parliament.

13   Implied term about care and skill

In a contract for the supply of a service where the supplier is acting in the course of a business, there is an implied term that the supplier will carry out the service with reasonable care and skill.

14   Implied term about time for performance

(1) Where, under a contract for the supply of a service by a supplier acting in the course of a business, the time for the service to be carried out is not fixed by the contract, left to be fixed in a manner agreed by the contract or determined by the course of dealing between the parties, there is an implied term that the supplier will carry out the service within a reasonable time.

(2) What is a reasonable time is a question of fact.

15   Implied term about consideration

(1) Where, under a contract for the supply of a service, the consideration for the service is not determined by the contract, left to be determined in a manner agreed by the contract or determined by the course of dealing between the parties, there is an implied term that the party contracting with the supplier will pay a reasonable charge.

(2) What is a reasonable charge is a question of fact.

16   Exclusion of implied terms, etc

(1) Where a right, duty or liability would arise under a contract for the supply of a service by virtue of this Part of this Act, it may (subject to subsection (2) below and the 1977 Act) be negatived or varied by express agreement, or by the course of dealing between the parties, or by such usage as binds both parties to the contract.

(2) An express term does not negative a term implied by this Part of this Act unless inconsistent with it.

(3) Nothing in this Part of this Act prejudices –

(a) any rule of law which imposes on the supplier a duty stricter than that imposed by section 13 or 14 above; or

(b) subject to paragraph (a) above, any rule of law whereby any term not inconsistent with this Part of this Act is to be implied in a contract for the supply of a service.

(4) This Part of this Act has effect subject to any other enactment which defines or restricts the rights, duties or liabilities arising in connection with a service of any description.

PART III

SUPPLEMENTARY

18   Interpretation: general

(1) In the preceding provisions of this Act and this section –

'bailee', in relation to a contract for the hire of goods means (depending on the context) a person to whom the goods are bailed under the contract, or a person to whom they are to be so bailed, or a person to whom the rights under the contract of either of those persons have passed;

'bailor', in relation to a contract for the hire of goods, means (depending on the context) a person who bails the goods under the contract, or a person who agrees to do so, or a person to whom the duties under the contract of either of those persons have passed;

'business' includes a profession and the activities of any government department or local or public authority;

'credit-broker' means a person acting in the course of a business of credit brokerage carried on by him;

'credit brokerage' means the effecting of introductions –

(a) of individuals desiring to obtain credit to persons carrying on any business so far as it relates to the provision of credit; or

(b) of individuals desiring to obtain goods on hire to persons carrying on a business which comprises or relates to the bailment ... of goods under a contract for the hire of goods; or

(c) of individuals desiring to obtain credit, or to obtain goods on hire, to other credit-brokers;

'enactment' means any legislation (including subordinate legislation) of the United Kingdom or Northern Ireland;

'goods' include all personal chattels (including emblements, industrial growing crops, and things attached to or forming part of the land which are agreed to be severed before the transfer or bailment concerned or under the contract concerned), other than things in action and money;

'hire-purchase agreement' has the same meaning as in the 1974 Act;

'producer' means the manufacturer of goods, the importer of goods into the European Economic Area or any person purporting to be a producer by placig his name, trade mark or other distinctive sign on the goods;

'property', in relation to goods, means the general property in them and not merely a special property;

'redemption', in relation to trading stamps, has the same meaning as in the Trading Stamps Act 1964 or, as respects Northern Ireland, the Trading Stamps Act (Northern Ireland) 1965;

'repair' means, in cases where there is a lack of conformity in goods for the purposes of this Act, to bring the goods into conformity with the contract;

'trading stamps' has the same meaning as in the said Act of 1964 or, as respects Northern Ireland, the said Act of 1965;

'transferee', in relation to a contract for the transfer of goods, means (depending on the context) a person to whom the property in the goods is transferred under the contract, or a person to whom the property is to be so transferred, or a person to whom the rights under the contract of either of those persons have passed;

'transferor', in relation to a contract for the transfer of goods, means (depending on the context) a person who transfers the property in the goods under the contract, or a person who agrees to do so, or a person to whom the duties under the contract of either of those persons have passed.

(2) In subsection (1) above, in the definitions of bailee, bailor, transferee and transferor, a reference to rights or duties passing is to their passing by assignment, ... operation of law or otherwise.

(3) For the purposes of this Act, the quality of goods includes their state and condition and the following (among others) are in appropriate cases aspects of the quality of goods –

    (a) fitness for all the purposes for which goods of the kind in question are commonly supplied;

    (b) appearance and finish;

    (c) freedom from minor defects,

    (d) safety, and

    (e) durability.

(4) References in this Act to dealing as consumer are to be construed in accordance with Part I of the Unfair Contract Terms Act 1977; and, for the purposes of this Act, it is for the transferor or bailor claiming that the transferee or bailee does not deal as consumer to show that he does not.

19   Interpretation: references to Acts

In this Act –

'the 1973 Act' means the Supply of Goods (Implied Terms) Act 1973;

'the 1974 Act' means the Consumer Credit Act 1974;

'the 1977 Act' means the Unfair Contract Terms Act 1977; and 'the 1979 Act' means the Sale of Goods Act 1979.

As amended by the Sale and Supply of Goods Act 1994, s7, Schedule 2, para 6, Schedule 3 (with effect from 3 January 1995); Sale and Supply of Goods to Consumers Regulations 2002, regs 7–10, 12.

ADMINISTRATION OF JUSTICE ACT 1982
(1982 c 53)

1   Abolition of right of damages for loss of expectation of life

(1) In an action under the law of England and Wales or the law of Northern Ireland for damages for personal injuries –

(a) no damages shall be recoverable in respect of any loss of expectation of life caused to the injured person by the injuries; but

(b) if the injured person's expectation of life has been reduced by the injuries, the court, in assessing damages in respect of pain and suffering caused by the injuries, shall take account of any suffering caused or likely to be caused to him by awareness that his expectation of life has been so reduced.

(2) The reference in subsection (1)(a) above to damages in respect of loss of expectation of life does not include damages in respect of loss of income.

2   Abolition of actions for loss of services, etc

No person shall be liable in tort under the law of England and Wales or the law of Northern Ireland –

(a) to a husband on the ground only of his having deprived him of the services or society of his wife;

(b) to a parent (or person standing in the place of a parent) on the ground only of his having deprived him of the services of a child; or

(c) on the ground only –

(i) of having deprived another of the services of his menial servant;

(ii) of having deprived another of the services of his female servant by raping or seducing her; or

(iii) of enticement of a servant or harbouring a servant.

5   Maintenance at public expense to be taken into account in assessment of damages

In an action under the law of England and Wales or the law of Northern Ireland for damages for personal injuries (including any such action arising out of a contract) any saving to the injured person which is attributable to his maintenance wholly or partly at public expense in a hospital, nursing home or other institution shall be set off against any income lost by him as a result of his injuries.

OCCUPIERS' LIABILITY ACT 1984
(1984 c 3)

1　Duty of occupier to persons other than his visitors

(1) The rules enacted by this section shall have effect, in place of the rules of the common law, to determine –

    (a) whether any duty is owed by a person as occupier of premises to persons other than his visitors in respect of any risk of their suffering injury on the premises by reason of any danger due to the state of the premises or to things done or omitted to be done on them; and

    (b) if so, what that duty is.

(2) For the purposes of this section, the persons who are to be treated respectively as an occupier of any premises (which, for those purposes, include any fixed or movable structure) and as his visitors are –

    (a) any person who owes in relation to the premises the duty referred to in section 2 of the Occupiers' Liability Act 1957 (the common duty of care), and

    (b) those who are his visitors for the purposes of that duty.

(3) An occupier of premises owes a duty to another (not being his visitor) in respect of any such risk as is referred to in subsection (1) above if –

    (a) he is aware of the danger or has reasonable grounds to believe that it exists;

    (b) he knows or has reasonable grounds to believe that the other is in the vicinity of the danger concerned or that he may come into the vicinity of the danger (in either case, whether the other has lawful authority for being in that vicinity or not); and

    (c) the risk is one against which, in all the circumstances of the case, he may reasonably be expected to offer the other some protection.

(4) Where, by virtue of this section, an occupier of premises owes a duty to another in respect of such a risk, the duty is to take such care as is reasonable in all the circumstances of the case to see that he does not suffer injury on the premises by reason of the danger concerned.

(5) Any duty owed by virtue of this section in respect of a risk may, in an appropriate case, be discharged by taking such steps as are reasonable in all the circumstances of the case to give warning of the danger concerned or to discourage persons from incurring the risk.

(6) No duty is owed by virtue of this section to any person in respect of risks willingly accepted as his by that person (the question whether a risk was so accepted to be decided on the same principles as in other cases in which one person owes a duty of care to another).

(6A) At any time when the right conferred by section 2(1) of the Countryside and Rights of Way Act 2000 is exercisable in relation to land which is access land for the purposes of Part I of that Act, an occupier of the land owes (subject to subsection (6C) below) no duty by virtue of this section to any person in respect of –

(a) a risk resulting from the existence of any natural feature of the landscape, or any river, stream, ditch or pond whether or not a natural feature, or

(b) a risk of that person suffering injury when passing over, under or through any wall, fence or gate, except by proper use of the gate or of a stile.

(6B) For the purposes of subsection (6A) above, any plant, shrub or tree, of whatever origin, is to be regarded as a natural feature of the landscape.

(6C) Subsection (6A) does not prevent an occupier from owing a duty by virtue of this section in respect of any risk where the danger concerned is due to anything done by the occupier –

(a) with the intention of creating that risk, or

(b) being reckless as to whether that risk is created.

(7) No duty is owed by virtue of this section to persons using the highway, and this section does not affect any duty owed to such persons.

(8) Where a person owes a duty by virtue of this section, he does not, by reason of any breach of the duty, incur any liability in respect of any loss of or damage to property.

(9) In this section –

'highway' means any part of a highway other than a ferry or waterway;

'injury' means anything resulting in death or personal injury, including any disease and any impairment of physical or mental condition; and

'movable structure' includes any vessel, vehicle or aircraft.

1A   Special considerations relating to access land

In determining whether any, and if so what, duty is owed by virtue of section 1 by an occupier of land at any time when the right conferred by section 2(1) of the Countryside and Rights of Way Act 2000 is exercisable in relation to the land, regard is to be had, in particular, to –

(a) the fact that the existence of that right ought not to place an undue burden (whether financial or otherwise) on the occupier,

(b) the importance of maintaining the character of the countryside, including features of historic, traditional or archaeological interest, and

(c) any relevant guidance given under section 20 of that Act.

3 Application to Crown

Section 1 of this Act shall bind the Crown, but as regards the Crown's liability in tort shall not bind the Crown further than the Crown is made liable in tort by the Crown Proceedings Act 1947.

As amended by the Countryside and Rights of Way Act 2000, s13(2), (3).

POLICE AND CRIMINAL EVIDENCE ACT 1984

(1984 c 60)

117 Power of constable to use reasonable force

Where any provision of this Act –

(a) confers a power on a constable; and

(b) does not provide that the power may only be exercised with the consent of some person, other than a police officer,

the officer may use reasonable force, if necessary, in the exercise of the power.

COMPANIES ACT 1985
(1985 c 6)

1   Mode of forming incorporated company

(1) Any two or more persons associated for a lawful purpose may, by subscribing their names to a memorandum of association and otherwise complying with the requirements of this Act in respect of registration, form an incorporated company, with or without limited liability.

(2) A company so formed may be either –

(a) a company having the liability of its members limited by the memorandum to the amount, if any, unpaid on the shares respectively held by them ('a company limited by shares');

(b) a company having the liability of its members limited by the memorandum to such amount as the members may respectively thereby undertake to contribute to the assets of the company in the event of its being wound up ('a company limited by guarantee'); or

(c) a company not having any limit on the liability of its members ('an unlimited company').

(3) A 'public company' is a company limited by shares or limited by guarantee and having a share capital, being a company –

(a) the memorandum of which states that it is to be a public company, and

(b) in relation to which the provisions of this Act or the former Companies Acts as to the registration or re-registration of a company as a public company have been complied with on or after 22 December 1980;

and a 'private company' is a company that is not a public company.

(3A) Notwithstanding subsection (1), one person may, for a lawful purpose, by subscribing his name to a memorandum of association and otherwise complying with the requirements of this Act in respect of registration, form an incorporated company being a private company limited by shares or by guarantee.

(4) With effect from 22 December 1980, a company cannot be formed as, or become, a company limited by guarantee with a share capital.

3A   Statement of company's objects: general commercial company

Where the company's memorandum states that the object of the company is to carry on business as a general commercial company –

(a) the object of the company is to carry on any trade or business whatsoever, and

(b) the company has power to do all such things as are incidental or conducive to the carrying on of any trade or business by it.

14 Effect of memorandum and articles

(1) Subject to the provisions of this Act, the memorandum and articles, when registered, bind the company and its members to the same extent as if they respectively had been signed and sealed by each member, and contained covenants on the part of each member to observe all the provisions of the memorandum and of the articles.

(2) Money payable by a member to the company under the memorandum or articles is a debt due from him to the company, and in England and Wales is of the nature of a specialty debt.

35 A company's capacity not limited by its memorandum

(1) The validity of an act done by a company shall not be called into question on the ground of lack of capacity by reason of anything in the company's memorandum.

(2) A member of a company may bring proceedings to restrain the doing of an act which but for subsection (1) would be beyond the company's capacity; but no such proceedings shall lie in respect of an act to be done in fulfilment of a legal obligation arising from a previous act of the company.

(3) It remains the duty of the directors to observe any limitations on their powers flowing from the company's memorandum; and action by the directors which but for subsection (1) would be beyond the company's capacity may only be ratified by the company by special resolution.

A resolution ratifying such action shall not affect any liability incurred by the directors or any other person; relief from any such liability must be agreed to separately by special resolution ...

(4) The operation of this section is restricted by section 65(1) of the Charities Act 1993 and section 112(3) of the Companies Act 1989 in relation to companies which are charities; and section 322A below (invalidity of certain transactions to which directors or their associates are parties) has effect notwithstanding this section.

35A Power of directors to bind the company

(1) In favour of a person dealing with a company in good faith, the power of the board of directors to bind the company, or authorise others to do so, shall be deemed to be free of any limitation under the company's constitution.

(2) For this purpose –

(a) a person 'deals with' a company if he is a party to any transaction or other act to which the company is a party;

(b) a person shall not be regarded as acting in bad faith by reason only of his knowing that an act is beyond the powers of the directors under the company's constitution; and

(c) a person shall be presumed to have acted in good faith unless the contrary is proved.

(3) The references above to limitations on the directors' powers under the company's constitution include limitations deriving –

(a) from a resolution of the company in general meeting or a meeting of any class of shareholders, or

(b) from any agreement between the members of the company or of any class of shareholders.

(4) Subsection (1) does not affect any right of a member of the company to bring proceedings to restrain the doing of an act which is beyond the powers of the directors; but no such proceedings shall lie in respect of an act to be done in fulfilment of a legal obligation arising from a previous act of the company.

(5) Nor does that subsection affect any liability incurred by the directors, or any other person, by reason of the directors' exceeding their powers ...

(6) The operation of this section is restricted by section 65(1) of the Charities Act 1993 and section 112(3) of the Companies Act 1989 in relation to companies which are charities; and section 322A below (invalidity of certain transactions to which directors or their associates are parties) has effect notwithstanding this section.

35B No duty to enquire as to capacity of company or authority of directors

A party to a transaction with a company is not bound to enquire as to whether it is permitted by the company's memorandum or as to any limitation on the powers of the board of directors to bind the company or authorise others to do so.

36 Company contracts: England and Wales

Under the law of England and Wales a contract may be made –

(a) by a company, by writing under its common seal, or

(b) on behalf of a company, by any person acting under its authority, express or implied;

and any formalities required by law in the case of a contract made by an individual also apply, unless a contrary intention appears, to a contract made by or on behalf of a company.

36A Execution of documents: England and Wales

(1) Under the law of England and Wales the following provisions have effect with respect to the execution of documents by a company.

(2) A document is executed by a company by the affixing of its common seal.

(3) A company need not have a common seal, however, and the following subsections apply whether it does or not.

(4) A document signed by a director and the secretary of a company, or by two directors of a company, and expressed (in whatever form of words) to be executed by the company has the same effect as if executed under the common seal of the company.

(5) A document executed by a company which makes it clear on its face that it is intended by the person or persons making it to be a deed has effect, upon delivery, as a deed; and it shall be presumed, unless a contrary intention is proved, to be delivered upon its being so executed.

(6) In favour of a purchaser a document shall be deemed to have been duly executed by a company if it purports to be signed by a director and the secretary of the company, or by two directors of the company, and, where it makes it clear on its face that it is intended by the person or persons making it to be a deed, to have been delivered upon its being executed.

A 'purchaser' means a purchaser in good faith for valuable consideration and includes a lessee, mortgagee or other person who for valuable consideration acquires an interest in property.

36C Pre-incorporation contracts, deeds and obligations

(1) A contract which purports to be made by or on behalf of a company at a time when the company has not been formed has effect, subject to any agreement to the contrary, as one made with the person purporting to act for the company or as agent for it, and he is personally liable on the contract accordingly.

(2) Subsection (1) applies –

(a) to the making of a deed under the law of England and Wales ...

as it applies to the making of a contract.

As amended by the Companies Act 1989, ss108(1), 110(1), 130(1), (2), (4); Companies (Single Member Private Limited Companies) Regulations 1992, art 2(1)(b), Schedule, para 1; Charities Act 1993, s98(1), Schedule 6, para 20(1), (2).

LATENT DAMAGE ACT 1986
(1986 c 37)

3   Accrual of cause of action to successive owners in respect of latent damage to property

(1) Subject to the following provisions of this section, where –

(a) a cause of action ('the original cause of action') has accrued to any person in respect of any negligence to which damage to any property in which he has an interest is attributable (in whole or in part); and

(b) another person acquires an interest in that property after the date on which the original cause of action occurred but before the material facts about the damage have become known to any person who, at the time when he first has knowledge of those facts, has any interest in the property;

a fresh cause of action in respect of that negligence shall accrue to that other person on the date on which he acquires his interest in the property.

(2) A cause of action accruing to any person by virtue of subsection (1) above –

(a) shall be treated as if based on breach of a duty of care at common law owed to the person to whom it accrues; and

(b) shall be treated for the purposes of section 14A of the 1980 Act (special time limit for negligence actions where facts relevant to cause of action are not known at date of accrual) as having accrued on the date on which the original cause of action accrued.

(3) Section 28 of the 1980 Act (extension of limitation period in case of disability) shall not apply in relation to any such cause of action.

(4) Subsection (1) above shall not apply in any case where the person acquiring an interest in the damaged property is either –

(a) a person in whom the original cause of action vests by operation of law; or

(b) a person in whom the interest in that property vests by virtue of any order made by a court under section 538 of the Companies Act 1985 (vesting of company property in liquidator).

(5) For the purposes of subsection (1)(b) above, the material facts about the damage are such facts about the damage as would lead a reasonable person who has an interest in the damaged property at the time when those facts became known to him to consider it sufficiently serious to justify his instituting proceedings for damages

against a defendant who did not dispute liability and was able to satisfy a judgment.

(6) For the purposes of this section a person's knowledge includes knowledge which he might reasonably have been expected to acquire –

(a) from facts observable or ascertainable by him; or

(b) from facts ascertainable by him with the help of appropriate expert advice which it is reasonable for him to seek;

but a person shall not be taken by virtue of this subsection to have knowledge of a fact ascertainable by him only with the help of expert advice so long as he has taken all reasonable steps to obtain (and, where appropriate, to act on) that advice.

(7) This section shall bind the Crown, but as regards the Crown's liability in tort shall not bind the Crown further than the Crown is made liable in tort by the Crown Proceedings Act 1947.

4 Transitional provisions

(1) Nothing in section 1 or 2 of this Act [these sections inserted ss14A, 14B and 28A, 32(5) of the Limitation Act 1980 respectively] shall –

(a) enable any action to be brought which was barred by the 1980 Act or (as the case may be) by the Limitation Act 1939 before this Act comes into force; or

(b) affect any action commenced before this Act comes into force.

(2) Subject to subsection (1) above, sections 1 and 2 of this Act shall have effect in relation to causes of action accruing before, as well as in relation to causes of action accruing after, this Act comes into force.

(3) Section 3 of this Act shall only apply in cases where an interest in damaged property is acquired after this Act comes into force but shall so apply, subject to subsection (4) below, irrespective of whether the original cause of action accrued before or after this Act comes into force.

(4) Where –

(a) a person acquires an interest in damaged property in circumstances to which section 3 would apart from this subsection apply; but

(b) the original cause of action accrued more than six years before this Act comes into force;

a cause of action shall not accrue to that person by virtue of subsection (1) of that section unless section 32(1)(b) of the 1980 Act (postponement of limitation period in case of deliberate concealment of relevant facts) would apply to any action founded on the original cause of action.

5 Citation, interpretation, commencement and extent ...

(2) In this Act –

'the 1980 Act' has the meaning given by section 1; and

'action' includes any proceeding in a court of law, an arbitration and any new claim within the meaning of section 35 of 1980 Act (new claims in pending actions).

(3) This act shall come into force at the end of the period of two months beginning with the date on which it is passed. ...

INSOLVENCY ACT 1986
(1986 c 45)

345 Contracts to which bankrupt is a party

(1) The following applies where a contract has been made with a person who is subsequently adjudged bankrupt.

(2) The court may, on the application of any other party to the contract, make an order discharging obligations under the contract on such terms as to payment by the applicant or the bankrupt of damages for non-performance or otherwise as appear to the court to be equitable.

(3) Any damages payable by the bankrupt by virtue of an order of the court under this section are provable as a bankruptcy debt.

(4) Where an undischarged bankrupt is a contractor in respect of any contract jointly with any person, that person may sue or be sued in respect of the contract without the joinder of the bankrupt.

MINORS' CONTRACTS ACT 1987
(1987 c 13)

1   Disapplication of Infants Relief Act 1874, etc

The following enactments shall not apply to any contract made by a minor after the commencement of this Act –

(a) the Infants Relief Act 1874 (which invalidates certain contracts made by minors and prohibits actions to enforce contracts ratified after majority); and

(b) section 5 of the Betting and Loans (Infants) Act 1892 (which invalidates contracts to repay loans advanced during minority).

2   Guarantees

Where –

(a) a guarantee is given in respect of an obligation of a party to a contract made after the commencement of this Act, and

(b) the obligation is unenforceable against him (or he repudiates the contract) because he was a minor when the contract was made,

the guarantee shall not for that reason alone be unenforceable against the guarantor.

3   Restitution

(1) Where –

(a) a person ('the plaintiff') has after the commencement of this Act entered into a contract with another ('the defendant'), and

(b) the contract is unenforceable against the defendant (or he repudiates it) because he was a minor when the contract was made,

the court may, if it is just and equitable to do so, require the defendant to transfer to the plaintiff any property acquired by the defendant under the contract or any property representing it.

(2) Nothing in this section shall be taken to prejudice any other remedy available to the plaintiff.

4 Consequential amendment and repeals

(2) The Infants Relief Act 1874 and the Betting and Loans (Infants) Act 1892 are hereby repealed (in accordance with section 1 of this Act).

CONSUMER PROTECTION ACT 1987
(1987 c 43)

PART I

PRODUCT LIABILITY

1 Purpose and construction of Part I

(1) This part shall have effect for the purpose of making such provision as is necessary in order to comply with the product liability Directive and shall be construed accordingly.

(2) In this Part, except in so far as the context otherwise requires –

'dependant' and 'relative' have the same meaning as they have in, respectively, the Fatal Accidents Act 1976 and the Damages (Scotland) Act 1976;

'producer', in relation to a product, means –

(a) the person who manufactured it;

(b) in the case of a substance which has not been manufactured but has been won or abstracted, the person who won or abstracted it;

(c) in the case of a product, which has not been manufactured, won or abstracted but essential characteristics of which are attributable to an industrial or other process having been carried out (for example, in relation to agricultural produce), the person who carried out that process;

'product' means any goods or electricity and (subject to subsection (3) below) includes a product which is comprised in another product, whether by virtue of being a component part or raw material or otherwise; and

'the product liability Directive' means the Directive of the Council of the European Communities, dated 25 July 1985, (No 85/374/EEC) on the approximation of the laws, regulations and administrative provisions of the member States concerning liability for defective products.

(3) For the purposes of this Part a person who supplies any product in which products are comprised, whether by virtue of being component parts or raw materials or otherwise, shall not be treated by reason only of his supply of that product as supplying any of the products so comprised.

2 Liability for defective products

(1) Subject to the following provisions of this Part, where any damage is caused wholly or partly by a defect in a product, every person to whom subsection (2) below applies shall be liable for the damage.

(2) This subsection applies to –

(a) the producer of the product;

(b) any person who, by putting his name on the product or using a trade mark or other distinguishing mark in relation to the product, has held himself out to be the producer of the product;

(c) any person who has imported the product into a member State from a place outside the member States in order, in the course of any business of his, to supply it to another.

(3) Subject as aforesaid, where any damage is caused wholly or partly by a defect in a product, any person who supplied the product (whether to the person who suffered the damage, to the producer of any product in which the product in question is comprised or to any other person) shall be liable for the damage if –

(a) the person who suffered the damage requests the supplier to identify one or more of the persons (whether still in existence or not) to whom subsection (2) above applies in relation to the product;

(b) that request is made within a reasonable period after the damage occurs and at a time when it is not reasonably practicable for the person making the request to identify all those persons; and

(c) the supplier fails, within a reasonable period after receiving the request, either to comply with the request or to identify the person who supplied the product to him.

(5) Where two or more persons are liable by virtue of this Part for the same damage, their liability shall be joint and several.

(6) This section shall be without prejudice to any liability arising otherwise than by virtue of this Part.

3 Meaning of 'defect'

(1) Subject to the following provisions of this section, there is a defect in a product for the purposes of this Part if the safety of the product is not such as persons generally are entitled to expect; and for those purposes 'safety', in relation to a product, shall include safety with respect to products comprised in that product and safety in the context of risks of damage to property, as well as in the context of risks of death or personal injury.

(2) In determining for the purposes of subsection (1) above what persons generally are entitled to expect in relation to a product all the circumstances shall be taken into account, including –

(a) the manner in which, and purposes for which, the product has been marketed, its get-up, the use of any mark in relation to the product and any instructions for, or warnings with respect to, doing or refraining from doing anything with or in relation to the product;

(b) what might reasonably be expected to be done with or in relation to the product; and

(c) the time when the product was supplied by its producer to another;

and nothing in this section shall require a defect to be inferred from the fact alone that the safety of a product which is supplied after that time is greater than the safety of the product in question.

4   Defences

(1) In any civil proceedings by virtue of this Part against any person ('the person proceeded against') in respect of a defect in a product it shall be a defence for him to show –

(a) that the defect is attributable to compliance with any requirement imposed by or under any enactment or with any Community obligation; or

(b) that the person proceeded against did not at any time supply the products to another; or

(c) that the following conditions are satisfied, that is to say –

(i) that the only supply of the product to another by the person proceeded against was otherwise than in the course of a business of that person's;

(ii) that section 2(2) above does not apply to that person or applies to him by virtue only of things done otherwise than with a view to profit; or

(d) that the defect did not exist in the product at the relevant time; or

(e) that the state of scientific and technical knowledge at the relevant time was not such that a producer of products of the same description as the product in question might be expected to have discovered the defect if it had existed in his products while they were under his control; or

(f) that the defect –

(i) constituted a defect in a product ('the subsequent product') in which the product in question had been comprised; and

(ii) was wholly attributable to the design of the subsequent product or to compliance by the producer of the product in question with instructions given by the producer of the subsequent product.

(2) In this section 'the relevant time', in relation to electricity, means the time at which it was generated, being a time before it was transmitted or distributed, and in relation to any other product, means –

(a) if the person proceeded against is a person to whom subsection (2) of section 2 above applies in relation to the product, the time when he supplied the product to another;

(b) if that subsection does not apply to that person in relation to the product, the time when the product was last supplied by a person to whom that subsection does apply in relation to the product.

5   Damage giving rise to liability

(1) Subject to the following provisions of this section, in this Part 'damage' means death or personal injury or any loss of or damage to any property (including land).

(2) A person shall not be liable under section 2 above in respect of any defect in a product for the loss of or any damage to the product itself or for the loss of or any damage to the whole or any part of any product which has been supplied with the product in question comprised in it.

(3) A person shall not be liable under section 2 above for any loss of or damage to any property which, at the time it is lost or damaged, is not –

(a) of a description of property ordinarily intended for private use, occupation or consumption; and

(b) intended by the person suffering the loss or damage mainly for his own private use, occupation or consumption.

(4) No damages shall be awarded to any person by virtue of this Part in respect of any loss of or damage to any property if the amount which would fall to be so awarded to that person, apart from this subsection and any liability for interest, does not exceed £275.

(5) In determining for the purposes of this Part who has suffered any loss of or damage to property and when any such loss or damage occurred, the loss or damage shall be regarded as having occurred at the earliest time at which a person with an interest in the property had knowledge of the material facts about the loss or damage.

(6) For the purposes of subsection (5) above the material facts about any loss of or damage to any property are such facts about the loss or damage as would lead a reasonable person with an interest in the property to consider the loss or damage sufficiently serious to justify his instituting proceedings for damages against a defendant who did not dispute liability and was able to satisfy a judgment.

(7) For the purposes of subsection (5) above a person's knowledge includes knowledge which he might reasonably have been expected to acquire –

(a) from facts observable or ascertainable by him; or

(b) from facts ascertainable by him with the help of appropriate expert advice which it is reasonable for him to seek;

but a person shall not be taken by virtue of this subsection to have knowledge of a fact ascertainable by him only with the help of expert advice unless he has failed to take all reasonable steps to obtain (and, where appropriate, to act on) that advice.

6 Application of certain enactments

(1) Any damage for which a person is liable under section 2 above shall be deemed to have been caused –

(a) for the purposes of the Fatal Accidents Act 1976, by that person's wrongful act, neglect or default; ...

(2) Where –

(a) a person's death is caused wholly or partly by a defect in a product, or a person dies after suffering damage which has been so caused;

(b) a request such as mentioned in paragraph (a) of subsection (3) of section 2 above is made to a supplier of the product by that person's personal representatives or, in the case of a person whose death is caused wholly or partly by the defect, by any dependant or relative of that person; and

(c) the conditions specified in paragraphs (b) and (c) of that subsection are satisfied in relation to that request;

this Part shall have effect for the purposes of the Law Reform (Miscellaneous Provisions) Act 1934, the Fatal Accidents Act 1976 and the Damages (Scotland) Act 1976 as if liability of the supplier to that person under that subsection did not depend on that person having requested the supplier to identify certain persons or on the said conditions having been satisfied in relation to a request made by that person.

(3) Section 1 of the Congenital Disabilities (Civil Liability) Act 1976 shall have effect for the purposes of this Part as if –

(a) a person were answerable to a child in respect of an occurrence caused wholly or partly by a defect in a product if he is or has been liable under section 2 above in respect of any effect of the occurrence on a parent of the child, or would be so liable if the occurrence caused a parent of the child to suffer damage;

(b) the provisions of this Part relating to liability under section 2 above applied in relation to liability by virtue of paragraph (a) above under the said section 1; and

(c) subsection (6) of the said section 1 (exclusion of liability) were omitted.

(4) Where any damage is caused partly by a defect in a product and partly by the fault of the person suffering the damage, the Law Reform (Contributory Negligence) Act 1945 and section 5 of the Fatal Accidents Act 1976 (contributory negligence) shall have effect as if the defect were the fault of every person liable by virtue of this Part for the damage caused by the defect.

(5) In subsection (4) above 'fault' has the same meaning as in the said Act of 1945.

(6) Schedule 1 to this Act shall have effect for the purpose of amending the Limitation Act 1980 and the Prescription and Limitation (Scotland) Act 1973 in their application in relation to the bringing of actions by virtue of this Part.

(7) It is hereby declared that liability by virtue of this Part is to be treated as

liability in tort for the purposes of any enactment conferring jurisdiction on any court with respect to any matter.

(8) Nothing in this Part shall prejudice the operation of section 12 of the Nuclear Installations Act 1965 (rights to compensation for certain breaches of duties confined to rights under that Act).

7   Prohibition on exclusions from liability

The liability of a person by virtue of this Part to a person who has suffered damage caused wholly or partly by a defect in a product, or to a dependant or relative of such a person, shall not be limited or excluded by any contract term, by any notice or by any other provision.

8   Power to modify Part I

(1) Her Majesty may by Order in Council make such modifications of this Part and of another enactment (including an enactment contained in the following Parts of this Act, or in an Act passed after this Act) as appear to Her Majesty in Council to be necessary or expedient in consequence of any modification of the product liability Directive which is made at any time after the passing of this Act.

(2) An Order in Council under subsection (1) above shall not be submitted to Her Majesty in Council unless a draft of the Order has been laid before, and approved by a resolution of, each House of Parliament.

9   Application of Part I to Crown

(1) Subject to subsection (2) below, this Part shall bind the Crown.

(2) The Crown shall not, as regards the Crown's liability by virtue of this Part, be bound by this Part further than the Crown is made liable in tort or in reparation under the Crown Proceedings Act 1947, as that Act has effect from time to time.

PART V

MISCELLANEOUS AND SUPPLEMENTAL

45   Interpretation

(1) In this Act, except in so far as the context otherwise requires –

'aircraft' includes gliders, balloons and hovercraft;

'business' includes a trade or profession and the activities of a professional or trade association or of a local authority or other public authority;

'conditional sale agreement', 'credit-sale agreement' and 'hire-purchase agreement' have the same meanings as in the Consumer Credit Act 1974 but as if in the definitions of that Act 'goods' had the same meaning as in this Act; ...

'gas' has the same meaning as in Part I of the Gas Act 1986;

'goods' includes substances, growing crops and things comprised in land by virtue of being attached to it and any ship, aircraft or vehicle;

'information' includes accounts, estimates and returns; ...

'modifications' includes additions, alterations and omissions, and cognate expressions shall be construed accordingly;

'motor vehicle' has the same meaning as in the Road Traffic Act 1988;

'notice' means a notice in writing; ...

'personal injury' includes any disease and any other impairment of a person's physical or mental condition;

'premises' includes any place and any ship, aircraft or vehicle; ...

'records' includes any books or documents and any records in non-documentary form; ...

'ship' includes any boat and any other description of vessel used in navigation;

'substance' means any natural or artificial substance, whether in solid, liquid or gaseous form or in the form of a vapour, and includes substances that are comprised in or mixed with other goods;

'supply' and cognate expressions shall be construed in accordance with section 46 below; ...

(2) Except in so far as the context otherwise requires, reference in this Act to a contravention of a safety provision shall, in relation to any goods, include references to anything which would constitute such a contravention if the goods were supplied to any person.

(3) Reference in this Act to any goods in relation to which any safety provision has been or may have been contravened shall include references to any goods which it is not reasonably practicable to separate from any such goods.

46 Meaning of 'supply'

(1) Subject to the following provisions of this section, references in this Act to supplying goods shall be construed as references to doing any of the following, whether as principal or agent, that is to say –

   (a) selling, hiring out or lending the goods;
   (b) entering into a hire-purchase agreement to furnish the goods;
   (c) the performance of any contract for work and materials to furnish the goods;
   (d) providing the goods in exchange for any consideration (including trading stamps) other than money;
   (e) providing the goods in or in connection with the performance of any statutory function; or
   (f) giving the goods as a prize or otherwise making a gift of the goods;

and, in relation to gas or water, those references shall be construed as including references to providing the service by which the gas or water is made available for use.

(2) For the purposes of any reference in this Act to supplying goods, where a person ('the ostensible supplier') supplies goods to another person ('the customer') under a hire-purchase agreement, conditional sale agreement or credit-sale agreement or under an agreement for the hiring of goods (other than a hire-purchase agreement) and the ostensible supplier –

(a) carries on the business of financing the provision of goods for others by means of such agreements; and

(b) in the course of that business acquired his interest in the goods supplied to the customer as a means of financing the provision of them for the customer by a further person ('the effective supplier'), the effective supplier and not the ostensible supplier shall be treated as supplying the goods to the customer.

(3) Subject to subsection (4) below, the performance of any contract by the erection of any building or structure on any land or by the carrying out of any other building works shall be treated for the purposes of this Act as a supply of goods in so far as, but only in so far as, it involves the provision of any goods to any person by means of their incorporation into the building, structure or works.

(4) Except for the purposes of, and in relation to, notices to warn or any provision made by or under Part III of this Act, references in this Act to supplying goods shall not include references to supplying goods comprised in land where the supply is effected by the creation or disposal of an interest in the land.

(5) Except in Part I of this Act references in this Act to a person's supplying goods shall be confined to references to that person's supplying goods in the course of a business of his, but for the purposes of this subsection it shall be immaterial whether the business is a business of dealing in the goods.

(6) For the purposes of subsection (5) above goods shall not be treated as supplied in the course of a business if they are supplied, in pursuance of an obligation arising under or in connection with the insurance of the goods, to the person with whom they were insured.

(7) Except for the purposes of, and in relation to, prohibition notices or suspension notices, references in Parts II to IV of this Act to supplying goods shall not include –

(a) references to supplying goods where the person supplied carries on a business of buying goods of the same description as those goods and repairing or reconditioning them';

(b) references to supplying goods by a sale of articles as scrap (that is to say, for the value of materials included in the articles rather than for the value of the articles themselves).

(8) Where any goods have at any time been supplied by being hired out or lent to any person, neither a continuation or renewal of the hire or loan (whether on the same or different terms) nor any transaction for the transfer after that time of any

interest in the goods to the person to whom they were hired or lent shall be treated for the purposes of this Act as a further supply of the goods to that person.

(9) A ship, aircraft or motor vehicle shall not be treated for the purposes of this Act as supplied to any person by reason only that services consisting in the carriage of goods or passengers in that ship, aircraft or vehicle, or in its use for any other purpose, are provided to that person in pursuance of an agreement relating to the use of the ship, aircraft or vehicle for a particular period or for particular voyages, flights or journeys.

As amended by the Road Traffic (Consequential Provisions) Act 1988, s4, Schedule 3, para 35; Consumer Protection Act 1987 (Product Liability) (Modification) Order 2000, art 2.

ROAD TRAFFIC ACT 1988
(1988 c 52)

148 Avoidance of certain exceptions to policies or securities

(1) Where a certificate of insurance or certificate of security has been delivered under section 147 of this Act to the person by whom a policy has been effected or to whom a security has been given, so much of the policy or security as purports to restrict –

   (a) the insurance of the persons insured by the policy, or

   (b) the operation of the security,

(as the case may be) by reference to any of the matters mentioned in subsection (2) below shall, as respects such liabilities as are required to be covered by a policy under section 145 of this Act, be of no effect.

(2) Those matters are –

   (a) the age or physical or mental condition of persons driving the vehicle,

   (b) the condition of the vehicle,

   (c) the number of persons that the vehicle carries,

   (d) the weight or physical characteristics of the goods that the vehicle carries,

   (e) the time at which or the areas within which the vehicle is used,

   (f) the horsepower or cylinder capacity or value of the vehicle,

   (g) the carrying on the vehicle of any particular apparatus, or

   (h) the carrying on the vehicle of any particular means of identification other than any means of identification required to be carried by or under the Vehicle Excise and Registration Act 1994.

(3) Nothing in subsection (1) above requires an insurer or the giver of a security to pay any sum in respect of the liability of any person otherwise than in or towards the discharge of that liability.

(4) Any sum paid by an insurer or the giver of a security in or towards the discharge of any liability of any person which is covered by the policy or security by virtue only of subsection (1) above is recoverable by the insurer or giver of the security from that person.

(5) A condition in a policy or security issued or given for the purposes of this Part of this Act providing –

   (a) that no liability shall arise under the policy or security, or

(b) that any liability so arising shall cease,

in the event of some specified thing being done or omitted to be done after the happening of the event giving rise to a claim under the policy or security, shall be of no effect in connection with such liabilities as are required to be covered by a policy under section 145 of this Act.

(6) Nothing in subsection (5) above shall be taken to render void any provision in a policy or security requiring the person insured or secured to pay to the insurer or the giver of the security any sums which the latter may have become liable to pay under the policy or security and which have been applied to the satisfaction of the claims of third parties.

(7) Notwithstanding anything in any enactment, a person issuing a policy of insurance under section 145 of this Act shall be liable to indemnify the persons or classes of persons specified in the policy in respect of any liability which the policy purports to cover in the case of those persons or classes of persons.

149 Avoidance of certain agreements as to liability towards passengers

(1) This section applies where a person uses a motor vehicle in circumstances such that under section 143 of this Act there is required to be in force in relation to his use of it such a policy of insurance or such a security in respect of third-party risks as complies with the requirements of this Part of this Act.

(2) If any other person is carried in or upon the vehicle while the user is so using it, any antecedent agreement or understanding between them (whether intended to be legally binding or not) shall be of no effect so far as it purports or might be held –

(a) to negative or restrict any such liability of the user in respect of persons carried in or upon the vehicle as is required by section 145 of this Act to be covered by a policy of insurance, or

(b) to impose any conditions with respect to the enforcement of any such liability of the user.

(3) The fact that a person so carried has willingly accepted as his the risk of negligence on the part of the user shall not be treated as negativing any such liability of the user.

(4) For the purposes of this section –

(a) references to a person being carried in or upon a vehicle include references to a person entering or getting on to, or alighting from, the vehicle, and

(b) the reference to an antecedent agreement is to one made at any time before the liability arose.

As amended by the Vehicle Excise and Registration Act 1994, s63, Schedule 3, para 24(1).

LAW OF PROPERTY (MISCELLANEOUS PROVISIONS) ACT 1989
(1989 c 34)

1   Deeds and their execution

(1) Any rule of law which –

(a) restricts the substances on which a deed may be written;

(b) requires a seal for the valid execution of an instrument as a deed by an individual; or

(c) requires authority by one person to another to deliver an instrument as a deed on his behalf to be given a deed,

is abolished.

(2) An instrument shall not be a deed unless –

(a) it makes it clear on its face that it is intended to be a deed by the person making it or, as the case may be, by the parties to it (whether by describing itself as a deed or expressing itself to be executed or signed as a deed or otherwise); and

(b) it is validly executed as a deed by that person or, as the case may be, one or more of those parties.

(3) An instrument is validly executed as a deed by an individual if, and only if –

(a) it is signed –

(i) by him in the presence of a witness who attests the signature; or

(ii) at his direction and in his presence and the presence of two witnesses who each attest the signature; and

(b) it is delivered as a deed by him or a person authorised to do so on his behalf.

(4) In subsections (2) and (3) above 'sign', in relation to an instrument, includes making one's mark on the instrument and 'signature' is to be construed accordingly.

(5) Where a solicitor, duly certificated notary public or licensed conveyancer, or an agent or employee of a solicitor, duly certified notary public or licensed conveyancer, in the course of or in connection with a transaction involving the disposition or creation of an interest in land, purports to deliver an instrument as a deed on behalf of a party to the instrument, it shall be conclusively presumed in favour of a purchaser that he is authorised so to deliver the instrument.

(6) In subsection (5) above –

'disposition' and 'purchaser' have the same meanings as in the Law of Property Act 1925;

'duly certified notary public' has the same meaning as it has in the Solicitors Act 1974 by virtue of section 87 of that Act; and

'interest in land' means any estate, interest or charge in or over land.

(7) Where an instrument under seal that constitutes a deed is required for the purposes of an Act passed before this section comes into force, this section shall have effect as to signing, sealing or delivery of an instrument by an individual in place of any provision of that Act as to signing, sealing or delivery....

(9) Nothing in subsection (1)(b), (2), (3), (7) or (8) above applies in relation to deeds required or authorised to be made under –

(a) the seal of the county palatine of Lancaster;

(b) the seal of the Duchy of Lancaster; or

(c) the seal of the Duchy of Cornwall.

(10) The references in this section to the execution of a deed by an individual do not include execution by a corporation sole and the reference in subsection (7) above to signing, sealing or delivery by an individual does not include signing, sealing or delivery by such a corporation.

(11) Nothing in this section applies in relation to instruments delivered as deeds before this section comes into force.

2 Contracts for sale, etc of land to be made by signed writing

(1) A contract for the sale or other disposition of an interest in land can only be made in writing and only by incorporating all the terms which the parties have expressly agreed in one document or, where contracts are exchanged, in each.

(2) The terms may be incorporated in a document either by being set out in it or by reference to some other document.

(3) The document incorporating the terms or, where contracts are exchanged, one of the documents incorporating them (but not necessarily the same one) must be signed by or on behalf of each party to the contract.

(4) Where a contract for the sale or other disposition of an interest in land satisfies the conditions of this section by reason only of the rectification of one or more documents in pursuance of an order of a court, the contract shall come into being, or be deemed to have come into being, at such time as may be specified in the order.

(5) This section does not apply in relation to –

(a) a contract to grant such a lease as is mentioned in section 54(2) of the Law of Property Act 1925 (short leases);

(b) a contract made in the course of a public auction; or

(c) a contract regulated under the Financial Services and Markets Act 2000, other than a regulated mortgage contract;

and nothing in this section affects the creation or operation of resulting, implied or constructive trusts.

(6) In this section –

'disposition' has the same meaning as in the Law of Property Act 1925;
'interest in land' means any estate, interest or charge in or over land;
'regulated mortgage contract' must be read with –

(a) section 22 of the Financial Services and Markets Act 2000,
(b) any relevant order under that section, and
(c) Schedule 22 to that Act.

(7) Nothing in this section shall apply in relation to contracts made before this section comes into force.

(8) Section 40 of the Law of Property Act 1925 (which is superseded by this section) shall cease to have effect.

3   Abolition of rule in Bain v Fothergill

The rule of law known as the rule in Bain v Fothergill is abolished in relation to contracts made after this section comes into force.

NB Sections 2 and 3 of this Act came into force on 27 September 1989, s1 on 31 July 1990.

As amended by the Courts and Legal Services Act 1990, s125(2), Schedule 17, para 20(1), (2); Trusts of Land and Appointment of Trustees Act 1996, s25(2), Schedule 4; Financial Services and Markets Acts 2000 (Consequential Amendments and Repeals) Order 2001, art 317.

CHILDREN ACT 1989
(1989 c 41)

2   Parental responsibility for children

(1) Where a child's father and mother were married to each other at the time of his birth, they shall each have a parental responsibility for the child.

(2) Where a child's father and mother were not married to each other at the time of his birth –

(a) the mother shall have parental responsibility for the child;

(b) the father shall have parental responsibility for the child if he has acquired it (and has not ceased to have it).

(3) References in this Act to a child whose father and mother were, or (as the case may be) were not, married to each other at the time of his birth must be read with section 1 of the Family Law Reform Act 1987 (which extends their meaning).

(4) The rule of law that a father is the natural guardian of his legitimate child is abolished.

(5) More than one person may have parental responsibility for the same child at the same time.

(6) A person who has parental responsibility for a child at any time shall not cease to have that responsibility solely because some other person subsequently acquires parental responsibility for the child.

(7) Where more than one person has parental responsibility for a child, each of them may act alone and without the other (or others) in meeting that responsibility; but nothing in this Part shall be taken to affect the operation of any enactment which requires the consent of more than one person in a matter affecting the child.

(8) The fact that a person has parental responsibility for a child shall not entitle him to act in any way which would be incompatible with any order made with respect to the child under this Act.

(9) A person who has parental responsibility for a child may not surrender or transfer any part of that responsibility to another but may arrange for some or all of it to be met by one or more persons acting on his behalf.

(10) The person with whom any such arrangement is made may himself be a person who already has parental responsibility for the child concerned.

(11) The making of any such arrangement shall not affect any liability of the person

making it which may arise from any failure to meet any part of his parental responsibility for the child concerned.

3   Meaning of 'parental responsibility'

(1) In this Act 'parental responsibility' means all the rights, duties, powers, responsibilities and authority which by law a parent of a child has in relation to the child and his property.

(2) It also includes the rights, powers and duties which a guardian of the child's estate (appointed, before the commencement of section 5, to act generally) would have had in relation to the child and his property.

(3) The rights referred to in subsection (2) include, in particular, the right of the guardian to receive or recover in his own name, for the benefit of the child, property of whatever description and wherever situated which the child is entitled to receive or recover.

(4) The fact that a person has, or does not have, parental responsibility for a child shall not affect –

  (a) any obligation which he may have in relation to the child (such as a statutory duty to maintain the child); or

  (b) any rights which, in the event of the child's death, he (or any other person) may have in relation to the child's property.

(5) A person who –

  (a) does not have parental responsibility for a particular child; but

  (b) has care of the child,

may (subject to the provisions of this Act) do what is reasonable in all the circumstances of the case for the purpose of safeguarding or promoting the child's welfare.

As amended by the Adoption and Children Act 2002, s111(5).

CONTRACTS (APPLICABLE LAW)
ACT 1990
(1990 c 36)

1   Meaning of 'the Conventions'

In this Act –

(a) 'the Rome Convention' means the Convention on the law applicable to contractual obligations opened for signature in Rome on 19th June 1980 and signed by the United Kingdom on 7th December 1981;

(b) 'the Luxembourg Convention' means the Convention on the accession of the Hellenic Republic to the Rome Convention signed by the United Kingdom in Luxembourg on 10th April 1984; and

(c) 'the Brussels Protocol' means the first Protocol on the interpretation of the Rome Convention by the European Court signed by the United Kingdom in Brussels on 19th December 1988;

(d) 'the Funchal Convention' means the Convention on the accession of the Kingdom of Spain and the Portuguese Republic to the Rome Convention and the Brussels Protocol, with adjustments made to the Rome Convention by the Luxembourg Convention, signed by the United Kingdom in Funchal on 18th May 1992;

(e) 'the 1996 Accession Convention' means the Convention on the accession of the Republic of Austria, the Republic of Finland and the Kingdom of Sweden to the Rome Convention and the Brussels Protocol, with the adjustments made to the Rome Convention by the Luxembourg Convention and the Funchal Convention, signed by the United Kingdom in Brussels on 29th November 1996;

and these Conventions and the Protocol are together referred to as 'the Conventions'.

2   Conventions to have force of law

(1) Subject to subsections (2) and (3) below, the Conventions shall have the force of law in the United Kingdom.

(1A) The internal law for the purposes of Article 1(3) of the Rome Convention is the provisions of the regulations for the time being in force under section 424(3) of the Financial Services and Markets Act 2000.

(2) Articles 7(1) and 10(1)(e) of the Rome Convention shall not have the force of law in the United Kingdom.

(3) Notwithstanding Article 19(2) of the Rome Convention, the Conventions shall apply in the case of conflicts between the laws of different parts of the United Kingdom.

(4) For ease of reference there are set out in Schedules 1, 2, 3, 3A and 3B to this Act respectively the English texts of –

> (a) the Rome Convention;
> (b) the Luxembourg Convention;
> (c) the Brussels Protocol;
> (d) the Funchal Convention; and
> (e) the 1996 Accession Convention.

3 Interpretation of Conventions

(1) Any question as to the meaning or effect of any provision of the Conventions shall, if not referred to the European Court in accordance with the Brussels Protocol, be determined in accordance with the principles laid down by, and any relevant decision of, the European Court.

(2) Judicial notice shall be taken of any decision of, or expression of opinion by, the European Court on any such question.

(3) Without prejudice to any practice of the courts as to the matters which may be considered apart from this subsection –

> (a) the report on the Rome Convention by Professor Mario Giuliano and Professor Paul Lagarde which is reproduced in the Official Journal of the Communities of 31st October 1980 may be considered in ascertaining the meaning or effect of any provision of that Convention; and
> (b) any report on the Brussels Protocol which is reproduced in the Official Journal of the Communities may be considered in ascertaining the meaning or effect of any provision of that Protocol.

As amended by the Friendly Societies (Amendment) Regulations 1993, reg 6(5); Contracts (Applicable Law) Act 1990 (Amendment) Order 1994, arts 3–6; Contracts (Applicable Law) Act 1990 (Amendment) Order 2000, arts 3, 4; Financial Services and Markets Act 2000 (Consequential Amendments and Repeals) Order 2001, art 320.

HUMAN FERTILISATION AND EMBRYOLOGY ACT 1990

(1990 c 37)

35   Disclosure in interests of justice: congenital disabilities, etc

(1) Where for the purpose of instituting proceedings under section 1 of the Congenital Disabilities (Civil Liability) Act 1976 (civil liability to child born disabled) it is necessary to identify a person who would or might be the parent of a child but for sections 27 to 29 of this Act, the court may, on the application of the child, make an order requiring the Authority to disclose any information contained in the register kept in pursuance of section 31 of this Act identifying that person. ...

COURTS AND LEGAL SERVICES ACT 1990

(1990 c 41)

61 Right of barrister to enter into contract for the provision of his services

(1) Any rule of law which prevents a barrister from entering into a contract for the provision of his services as a barrister is hereby abolished.

(2) Nothing in subsection (1) prevents the General Council of the Bar from making rules (however described) which prohibit barristers from entering into contracts or restricts their right to do so.

69 Exemption from liability for damages, etc

(1) Neither the Secretary of State nor any of the designated judges shall be liable in damages for anything done or omitted in the discharge or purported discharge of any of their functions under this Part [legal services].

(2) For the purposes of the law of defamation, the publication by the Secretary of State, a designated judge or the OFT of any advice or reasons given by or to him or it in the exercise of functions under this Part shall be absolutely privileged.

119 Interpretation

(1) In this Act – ...

'designated judge' means the Lord Chief Justice, the Master of the Rolls, the President of the Family Division or the Vice-Chancellor; ...

'the OFT' means the Office of Fair Trading; ...

As amended by the Enterprise Act 2002, s278, Schedule 25, para 23(1), (6), (9); Secretary of State for Constitutional Affairs Order 2003, art 9, Schedule 2, para 8(1)(c).

BROADCASTING ACT 1990
(1990 c 42)

166 Defamatory material

(1) For the purposes of the law of libel and slander (including the law of criminal libel so far as it relates to the publication of defamatory matter) the publication of works in the course of any programme included in a programme service shall be treated as publication in permanent form.

(2) Subsection (1) above shall apply for the purposes of section 3 of each of the Defamation Acts (slander of title, etc) as it applies for the purposes of the law of libel and slander.

(4) In this section 'the Defamation Acts' means the Defamation Act 1952 and the Defamation Act (Northern Ireland) 1955.

201 Programme services

(1) In this Act 'programme service' means any of the following services whether or not it is, or it requires to be, licensed), namely –

> (aa) any service which is a programme service within the meaning of the Communications Act 2003;
>
> (c) any other service which consists in the sending, by means of an electronic communications network (within the meaning of the Communications Act 2003), of sounds or visual images or both either –
>
>> (i) for reception at two or more places in the United Kingdom (whether they are so sent for simultaneous reception or at different times in response to requests made by different users of the service); or
>>
>> (ii) for reception at a place in the United Kingdom for the purpose of being presented there to members of the public or to any group of persons.

(2A) Subsection (1)(c) does not apply to so much of a service consisting only of sound programmes as –

> (a) is a two-way service (within the meaning of section 248(4) of the Communications Act 2003);
>
> (b) satisfies the conditions in section 248(5) of that Act; or
>
> (c) is provided for the purpose only of being received by persons who have qualified as users of the service by reason of being persons who fall within paragraph (a) or (b) of section 248(7) of that Act.

(2B) Subsection (1)(c) does not apply to so much of a service not consisting only of sound programmes as –

(a) is a two-way service (within the meaning of section 232 of the Communications Act 2003);

(b) satisfies the conditions in section 233(5) of that Act; or

(c) is provided for the purpose only of being received by persons who have qualified as users of the service by reason of being persons who fall within paragraph (a) or (b) of section 233(7) of that Act.

202 General interpretation

(1) In this Act (unless the context otherwise requires) – ...

'programme' includes an advertisement and, in relation to any service, includes any item included in that service; ...

203 Consequential and transitional provisions

(1) The enactments mentioned in Schedule 20 to this Act shall have effect subject to the amendments there specified (being minor amendments or amendments consequential on the provisions of this Act).

(2) Unless the context otherwise requires, in any enactment amended by this Act –

'programme', in relation to a programme service, includes any items included in that service; and

'television programme' includes a teletext transmission. ...

SCHEDULE 20

MINOR AND CONSEQUENTIAL AMENDMENTS

Parliamentary Papers Act 1840 (c 9)

1. Section 3 (protection in respect of proceedings for printing extracts from or abstracts of parliamentary papers) shall have effect as if the reference to printing included a reference to including in a programme service. ...

As amended by the Broadcasting Act 1996, s148(1), Schedule 10, Pt I, para 11; Communications Act 2003, ss360, 406(7), Schedule 19(1).

ENVIRONMENTAL PROTECTION
ACT 1990
(1990 c 43)

33   Prohibition on unauthorised or harmful deposit, treatment or disposal, etc, of waste ...

(7) It shall be a defence for a person charged with an offence under this section to prove –

(a) that he took all reasonable precautions and exercised all due diligence to avoid the commission of the offence; or

(b) that he acted under instructions from his employer and neither knew nor had reason to suppose that the acts done by him constituted a contravention of subsection (1) above; or

(c) that the acts alleged to constitute the contravention were done in an emergency in order to avoid danger to human health in a case where –

(i) he took all such steps as were reasonably practicable in the circumstances for minimising pollution of the environment and harm to human health; and

(ii) particulars of the acts were furnished to the waste regulation authority as soon as reasonably practicable after they were done. ...

73   Appeals and other provisions relating to legal proceedings and civil liability ...

(6) Where any damage is caused by waste which has been deposited in or on land, any person who deposited it, or knowingly caused or knowingly permitted it to be deposited, in either case so as to commit an offence under section 33(1) or 63(2) above, is liable for the damage except where the damage –

(a) was due wholly to the fault of the person who suffered it; or

(b) was suffered by a person who voluntarily accepted the risk of the damage being caused;

but without prejudice to any liability arising otherwise than under this subsection.

(7) The matters which may be proved by way of defence under section 33(7) above may be proved also by way of defence to an action brought under subsection (6) above.

(8) In subsection (6) above –

'damage' includes the death of, or injury to, any person (including any disease and any impairment of physical or mental condition); and

'fault' has the same meaning as in the Law Reform (Contributory Negligence) Act 1945.

(9) For the purposes of the following enactments –

(a) the Fatal Accidents Act 1976;

(b) the Law Reform (Contributory Negligence) Act 1945; and

(c) the Limitation Act 1980; ...

any damage for which a person is liable under subsection (6) above shall be treated as due to his fault.

75 Meaning of 'waste' and household, commercial and industrial waste and special waste ...

(2) 'Waste' means any substance or object in the categories set out in Schedule 2B to this Act which the holder discards or intends or is required to discard; and for the purposes of this definition –

'holder' means the producer of the waste or the person who is in possession of it; and

'producer' means any person whose activities produce waste or any person who carries out pre-processing, mixing or other operations resulting in a change in the nature or composition of this waste. ...

As amended by the Environment Act 1995, s 120(1), (3), Schedule 22, paras 64, 88, Schedule 24.

PROPERTY MISDESCRIPTIONS ACT 1991
(1991 c 29)

1   Offence of property misdescription

(1) Where a false or misleading statement about a prescribed matter is made in the course of an estate agency business or a property development business, otherwise than in providing conveyancing services, the person by whom the business is carried on shall be guilty of an offence under this section.

(2) Where the making of the statement is due to the act or default of an employee the employee shall be guilty of an offence under this section; and the employee may be proceeded against and punished whether or not proceedings are also taken against his employer.

(3) A person guilty of an offence under this section shall be liable –

    (a) on summary conviction, to a fine not exceeding the statutory maximum, and

    (b) on conviction on indictment, to a fine.

(4) No contract shall be void or unenforceable, and no right of action in civil proceedings in respect of any loss shall arise, by reason only of the commission of an offence under this section …

(5) For the purposes of this section –

    (a) 'false' means false to a material degree,

    (b) a statement is misleading if (though not false) what a reasonable person may be expected to infer from it, or from any omission from it, is false,

    (c) a statement may be made by pictures or any other method of signifying meaning as well as by words and, if made by words, may be made orally or in writing,

    (d) a prescribed matter is any matter relating to land which is specified in an order made by the Secretary of State,

    (e) a statement is made in the course of an estate agency business if (but only if) the making of the statement is a thing done as mentioned in subsection (1) of section 1 of the Estate Agents Act 1979 and that Act either applies to it or would apply to it but for subsection (2)(a) of that section (exception for things done in course of profession by practising solicitor or employee),

    (f) a statement is made in the course of a property development business if (but only if) it is made –

(i) in the course of a business (including a business in which the person making the statement is employed) concerned wholly or substantially with the development of land, and

(ii) for the purpose of, or with a view to, disposing of an interest in land consisting of or including a building, or a part of a building, constructed or renovated in the course of the business, and

(g) 'conveyancing services' means the preparation of any transfer, conveyance, writ, contract or other document in connection with the disposal or acquisition of an interest in land, and services ancillary to that, but does not include anything done as mentioned in section 1(1)(a) of the Estate Agents Act 1979.

(6) For the purposes of this section any reference in this section or section 1 of the Estate Agents Act 1979 to disposing of or acquiring an interest in land –

(a) in England and Wales and Northern Ireland shall be construed in accordance with section 2 of that Act ...

2   Due diligence defence

(1) In proceedings against a person for an offence under section 1 above it shall be a defence for him to show that he took all reasonable steps and exercised all due diligence to avoid committing the offence. ...

WATER RESOURCES ACT 1991
(1991 c 57)

208 Civil liability of the Agency for escapes of water, etc

(1) Where an escape of water, however caused, from a pipe vested in the Agency causes loss or damage, the Agency shall be liable, except as otherwise provided in this section, for the loss or damage.

(2) The Agency shall not incur any liability under subsection (1) above if the escape was due wholly to the fault of the person who sustained the loss or damage or of any servant, agent or contractor of his.

(3) The Agency shall not incur any liability under subsection (1) above in respect of any loss or damage for which the Agency would not be liable apart from that subsection and which is sustained –

> (a) by any water undertaker or sewerage undertaker or by any statutory undertakers, within the meaning of section 336(1) of the Town and Country Planning Act 1990;
>
> (b) by any gas transporter within the meaning of Part I of the Gas Act 1986 or the holder of a licence under section 6(1) of the Electricity Act 1989;
>
> (c) by any highway authority; or
>
> (d) by any person on whom a right to compensation is conferred by section 82 of the New Roads and Street Works Act 1991.

(4) The Law Reform (Contributory Negligence) Act 1945, the Fatal Accidents Act 1976 and the Limitation Act 1980 shall apply in relation to any loss or damage for which the Agency is liable under this section, but which is not due to the Agency's fault, as if it were due to its fault.

(5) Nothing in subsection (1) above affects any entitlement which the Agency may have to recover contribution under the Civil Liability (Contribution) Act 1978; and for the purposes of that Act, any loss for which the Agency is liable under that subsection shall be treated as if it were damage.

(6) Where the Agency is liable under any enactment or agreement passed or made before 1 April 1982 to make any payment in respect of any loss or damage the Agency shall not incur liability under subsection (1) above in respect of the same loss or damage.

(7) In this section 'fault' has the same meaning as in the Law Reform (Contributory Negligence) Act 1945. ...

221 General interpretation

(1) In this Act, except in so far as the context otherwise requires – ...

'the Agency' means the Environment Agency; ...

'damage', in relation to individuals, includes death and any personal injury (including any disease or impairment of physical or mental condition). ...

NB The civil liability of water undertakers for escapes of water, etc, is in similar terms: see s209 of the Water Industry Act 1991, as amended.

As amended by the Environment Act 1995, s120(1), (3), Schedule 22, paras 128, 177, Schedule 24; Utilities Act 2000, s76(7).

TRADE UNION AND LABOUR RELATIONS (CONSOLIDATION) ACT 1992
(1992 c 52)

1 Meaning of 'trade union'

In this Act a 'trade union' means an organisation (whether temporary or permanent) –

(a) which consists wholly or mainly or workers of one or more descriptions and whose principal purposes include the regulation of relations between workers of that description or those descriptions and employers or employers' associations; or

(b) which consists wholly or mainly of –

(i) constituent or affiliated organisations which fulfil the conditions in paragraph (a) (or themselves consist wholly or mainly of constituent or affiliated organisations which fulfil those conditions), or

(ii) representatives of such constituent or affiliated organisations,

and whose principal purposes include the regulation of relations between workers and employers or between workers and employers' associations, or the regulation of relations between its constituent or affiliated organisations.

10 Quasi-corporate status of trade unions

(1) A trade union is not a body corporate but –

(a) it is capable of making contracts;

(b) it is capable of suing and being sued in its own name, whether in proceedings relating to property or founded on contract or tort or any other cause of action; and

(c) proceedings for an offence alleged to have been committed by it or on its behalf may be brought against it in its own name.

(2) A trade union shall not be treated as if it were a body corporate except to the extent authorised by the provisions of this Part ...

11 Exclusion of common law rules as to restraint of trade

(1) The purposes of a trade union are not, by reason only that they are in restraint of trade, unlawful so as –

(a) to make any member of the trade union liable to criminal proceedings for conspiracy or otherwise, or

(b) to make any agreement or trust void or voidable.

(2) No rule of a trade union is unlawful or unenforceable by reason only that it is in restraint of trade.

12 Property to be vested in trustees

(1) All property belonging to a trade union shall be vested in trustees in trust for it.

(2) A judgment, order or award made in proceedings of any description brought against a trade union is enforceable, by way of execution, diligence, punishment for contempt or otherwise, against any property held in trust for it to the same extent and in the same manner as if it were a body corporate ...

20 Liability of trade union in certain proceedings in tort

(1) Where proceedings in tort are brought against a trade union –

(a) on the ground that an act –

(i) induces another person to break a contract or interferes or induces another person to interfere with its performance, or

(ii) consists in threatening that a contract (whether one to which the union is a party or not) will be broken or its performance interfered with, or that the union will induce another person to break a contract or interfere with its performance, or

(b) in respect of an agreement or combination by two or more persons to do or to procure the doing of an act which, if it were done without any such agreement or combination, would be actionable in tort on such a ground,

then, for the purpose of determining in those proceedings whether the union is liable in respect of the act in question, that act shall be taken to have been done by the union if, but only if, it is to be taken to have been authorised or endorsed by the trade union in accordance with the following provisions.

(2) An act shall be taken to have been authorised or endorsed by a trade union if it was done, or was authorised or endorsed –

(a) by any person empowered by the rules to do, authorise or endorse acts of the kind in question, or

(b) by the principal executive committee or the president or general secretary, or

(c) by any other committee of the union or any other official of the union (whether employed by it or not).

(3) For the purposes of paragraph (c) of subsection (2) –

(a) any group of persons constituted in accordance with the rules of the union is a committee of the union; and

(b) an act shall be taken to have been done, authorised or endorsed by an official if it was done, authorised or endorsed by, or by any member of, any group of persons of which he was at the material time a member, the purposes of which included organising or co-ordinating industrial action.

(4) The provisions of paragraphs (b) and (c) of subsection (2) apply notwithstanding anything in the rules of the union, or in any contract or rule of law, but subject to the provisions of section 21 (repudiation by union of certain acts).

(5) Where for the purposes of any proceedings an act is by virtue of this section taken to have been done by a trade union, nothing in this section shall affect the liability of any other person, in those or any other proceedings, in respect of that act.

(6) In proceedings arising out of an act which is by virtue of this section taken to have been done by a trade union, the power of the court to grant an injunction or interdict includes power to require the union to take such steps as the court considers appropriate for ensuring –

(a) that there is no, or no further, inducement of persons to take part or to continue to take part in industrial action, and

(b) that no person engages in any conduct after the granting of the injunction or interdict by virtue of having been induced before it was granted to take part or to continue to take part in industrial action.

The provisions of subsection (2) to (4) above apply in relation to proceedings for failure to comply with any such injunction or interdict as they apply in relation to the original proceedings.

(7) In this section 'rules', in relation to a trade union, means the written rules of the union and any other written provision forming part of the contract between a member and the other members.

21 Repudiation by union of certain acts

(1) An act shall not be taken to have been authorised or endorsed by a trade union by virtue only of paragraph (c) of section 20(2) if it was repudiated by the executive, president or general secretary as soon as reasonably practicable after coming to the knowledge of any of them.

(2) Where an act is repudiated –

(a) written notice of the repudiation must be given to the committee or official in question, without delay, and

(b) the union must do its best to give individual written notice of the fact and date of repudiation, without delay –

(i) to every member of the union who the union has reason to believe is taking part, or might otherwise take part, in industrial action as a result of the act, and

(ii) to the employer of every such member.

(3) The notice given to members in accordance with paragraph (b)(i) of subsection

(2) must contain the following statement –

'Your union has repudiated the call (or calls) for industrial action to which this notice relates and will give no support to unofficial industrial action taken in response to it (or them). If you are dismissed while taking unofficial industrial action, you will have no right to complain of unfair dismissal.'

(4) If subsection (2) or (3) is not complied with, the repudiation shall be treated as ineffective.

(5) An act shall not be treated as repudiated if at any time after the union concerned purported to repudiate it the executive, president or general secretary has behaved in a manner which is inconsistent with the purported repudiation.

(6) The executive, president or general secretary shall be treated as so behaving if, on a request made to any of them within three months of the purported repudiation by a person who –

(a) is a party to a commercial contract whose performance has been or may be interfered with as a result of the act in question, and

(b) has not been given written notice by the union of the repudiation,

it is not forthwith confirmed in writing that the act has been repudiated.

(7) In this section 'commercial contract' means any contract other than –

(a) a contract of employment, or

(b) any other contract under which a person agrees personally to do work or perform services for another.

22   Limit on damages awarded against trade unions in actions in tort

(1) This section applies to any proceedings in tort brought against a trade union, except –

(a) proceedings for personal injury as a result of negligence, nuisance or breach of duty;

(b) proceedings for breach of duty in connection with the ownership, occupation, possession, control or use of property;

(c) proceedings brought by virtue of Part I of the Consumer Protection Act 1987 (product liability).

(2) In any proceedings in tort to which this section applies the amount which may be awarded against the union by way of damages shall not exceed the following limit –

Number of members of union	Maximum award of damages
Less than 5,000	£10,000
5,000 or more but less than 25,000	£50,000
25,000 or more but less than 100,000	£125,000
100,000 or more	£250,000

(3) The Secretary of State may by order amend subsection (2) so as to vary any of the sums specified; and the order may make such transitional provision as the Secretary of State considers appropriate.

(4) Any such order shall be made by statutory instrument which shall be subject to annulment in pursuance of a resolution of either House of Parliament.

(5) In this section –

'breach of duty' means breach of a duty imposed by any rule of law or by or under any enactment;

'personal injury' includes any disease and any impairment of a person's physical or mental condition; and

'property' means any property, whether real or personal (or in Scotland, heritable or moveable).

23   Restriction on enforcement of awards against certain property

(1) Where in any proceedings an amount is awarded by way of damages, costs or expenses –

    (a) against a trade union,

    (b) against trustees in whom property is vested in trust for a trade union, in their capacity as such (and otherwise than in respect of a breach of trust on their part), or

    (c) against members or officials of a trade union on behalf of themselves and all of the members of the union,

no part of that amount is recoverable by enforcement against any protected property.

(2) The following is protected property –

    (a) property belonging to the trustees otherwise than in their capacity as such;

    (b) property belonging to any member of the union otherwise than jointly or in common with the other members;

    (c) property belonging to an official of the union who is neither a member nor a trustee;

    (d) property comprised in the union's political fund where that fund –

        (i) is subject to rules of the union which prevent property which is or has been comprised in the fund from being used for financing strikes or other industrial action, and

        (ii) was so subject at the time when the act in respect of which the proceedings are brought was done;

    (e) property comprised in a separate fund maintained in accordance with the rules of the union for the purpose only of providing provident benefits.

(3) For this purpose 'provident benefits' includes –

(a) any payment expressly authorised by the rules of the union which is made –

(i) to a member during sickness or incapacity from personal injury or while out of work, or

(ii) to an aged member by way of superannuation, or

(iii) to a member who has met with an accident or has lost his tools by fire or theft;

(b) a payment in discharge or aid of funeral expenses on the death of a member or the wife of a member or as provision for the children of a deceased member.

119 Expressions relating to trade unions

In this Act, in relation to a trade union – ...

'branch or section', except where the context otherwise requires, includes a branch or section which is itself a trade union;

'executive' means the principal committee of the union exercising executive functions, by whatever name it is called; ...

'general secretary' means the official of the union who holds the office of general secretary or, where there is no such office, holds an office which is equivalent, or (except in section 14(4)) the nearest equivalent, to that of general secretary;

'officer' includes –

(a) any member of the governing body of the union, and

(b) any trustee of any fund applicable for the purposes of the union;

'official' means –

(a) an officer of the union or of a branch or section of the union, or

(b) a person elected or appointed in accordance with the rules of the union to be a representative of its members or of some of them,

and includes a person so elected or appointed who is an employee of the same employer as the members or one or more of the members whom he is to represent;

'president' means the official of the union who holds the office of president or, where there is no such office, who holds an office which is equivalent, or (except in section 14(4) or Chapter IV) the nearest equivalent, to that of president; and

'rules', except where the context otherwise requires, includes the rules of any branch or section of the union.

121 Meaning of 'the court'

In this Part 'the court' (except where the reference is expressed to be to the county court ...) means the High Court ...

122 Meaning of 'employers' association'

(1) In this Act an 'employers' association' means an organisation (whether temporary or permanent) –

(a) which consists wholly or mainly of employers or individual owners of undertakings of one or more descriptions and whose principal purposes include the regulation of relations between employers of that description or those descriptions and workers or trade unions; or

(b) which consists wholly or mainly of –

(i) constituent or affiliated organisations which fulfil the conditions in paragraph (a) (or themselves consist wholly or mainly of constituent or affiliated organisations which fulfil those conditions), or

(ii) representatives of such constituent or affiliated organisations,

and whose principal purposes include the regulation of relations between employers and workers or between employers and trade unions, or the regulation of relations between its constituent or affiliated organisations.

(2) References in this Act to employers' associations include combinations of employers and employers' associations.

127 Corporate or quasi-corporate status of employers' associations

(1) An employers' association may be either a body corporate or an unincorporated association.

(2) Where an employers' association is unincorporated –

(a) it is capable of making contracts;

(b) it is capable of suing and being sued in its own name, whether in proceedings relating to property or founded on contract or tort or any other cause of action; and

(c) proceedings for an offence alleged to have been committed by it or on its behalf may be brought against it in its own name.

130 Restriction on enforcement of awards against certain property

(1) Where in any proceedings an amount is awarded by way of damages, costs or expenses –

(a) against an employers' association,

(b) against trustees in whom property is vested in trust for an employers' association, in their capacity as such (and otherwise than in respect of a breach of trust on their part), or

(c) against members or officials of an employers' association on behalf of themselves and all of the members of the association,

no part of that amount is recoverable by enforcement against any protected property.

(2) The following is protected property –

(a) property belonging to the trustees otherwise than in their capacity as such;

(b) property belonging to any member of the association otherwise than jointly or in common with the other members;

(c) property belonging to an official of the association who is neither a member nor a trustee.

219 Protection from certain tort liabilities

(1) An act done by a person in contemplation or furtherance of a trade dispute is not actionable in tort on the ground only –

(a) that it induces another person to break a contract or interferes or induces another person to interfere with its performance, or

(b) that it consists in his threatening that a contract (whether one to which he is a party or not) will be broken or its performance interfered with, or that he will induce another person to break a contract or interfere with its performance.

(2) An agreement or combination by two or more persons to do or procure the doing of an act in contemplation or furtherance of a trade dispute is not actionable in tort if the act is one which if done without any such agreement or combination would not be actionable in tort.

(3) Nothing in subsection (1) and (2) prevents an act done in the course of picketing from being actionable in tort unless it is done in the course of attendance declared lawful by section 220 (peaceful picketing).

(4) Subsections (1) and (2) have effect subject to sections 222 to 225 (action excluded from protection) and to sections 226 (requirement of ballot before action by trade union) and 234A (requirement of notice to employer of industrial action); and in those sections 'not protected' means excluded from the protection afforded by this section or, where the expression is used with reference to a particular person, excluded from that protection as respects that person.

220 Peaceful picketing

(1) It is lawful for a person in contemplation or furtherance of a trade dispute to attend –

(a) at or near his own place of work, or

(b) if he is an official of a trade union, at or near the place of work of a member of the union whom he is accompanying and whom he represents,

for the purpose only of peacefully obtaining or communicating information, or peacefully persuading any person to work or abstain from working.

(2) If a person works or normally works –

(a) otherwise than at any one place, or

(b) at a place the location of which is such that attendance there for a purpose mentioned in subsection (1) is impracticable,

his place of work for the purposes of that subsection shall be any premises of his employer from which he works or from which his work is administered.

(3) In the case of a worker not in employment where –

(a) his last employment was terminated in connection with a trade dispute, or

(b) the termination of his employment was one of the circumstances giving rise to a trade dispute,

in relation to that dispute his former place of work shall be treated for the purposes of subsection (1) as being his place of work.

(4) A person who is an official of a trade union by virtue only of having been elected or appointed to be a representative of some of the members of the union shall be regarded for the purposes of subsection (1) as representing only those members; but otherwise an official of a union shall be regarded for those purposes as representing all its members.

221 Restrictions on grant of injunctions ...

(1) Where –

(a) an application for an injunction ... is made to a court in the absence of the party against whom it is sought or any representative of his, and

(b) he claims, or in the opinion of the court would be likely to claim, that he acted in contemplation or furtherance of a trade dispute,

the court shall not grant the injunction ... unless satisfied that all steps which in the circumstances were reasonable have been taken with a view to securing that notice of the application and an opportunity of being heard with respect to the application have been given to him.

(2) Where –

(a) an application for an interlocutory injunction is made to a court pending the trial of an action, and

(b) the party against whom it is sought claims that he acted in contemplation or furtherance of a trade dispute,

the court shall, in exercising its discretion whether or not to grant the injunction, have regard to the likelihood of that party's succeeding at the trial of the action in establishing any matter which would afford a defence to the action under section 219 (protection from certain tort liabilities) or section 220 (peaceful picketing) ...

222 Action to enforce trade union membership

(1) An act is not protected if the reason, or one of the reasons, for which it is done is the fact or belief that a particular employer –

(a) is employing, has employed or might employ a person who is not a member of a trade union, or

(b) is failing, has failed or might fail to discriminate against such a person.

(2) For the purposes of subsection (1)(b) an employer discriminates against a person if, but only if, he ensures that his conduct in relation to –

(a) persons, or persons of any description, employed by him, or who apply to be, or are, considered by him for employment, or

(b) the provision of employment for such persons,

is different, in some or all cases, according to whether or not they are members of a trade union, and is more favourable to those who are.

(3) An act is not protected if it constitutes, or is one of a number of acts which together constitute, an inducement or attempted inducement of a person –

(a) to incorporate in a contract to which that person is a party, or a proposed contract to which he intends to be a party, a term or condition which is or would be void by virtue of section 144 (union membership requirement in contract for goods or services), or

(b) to contravene section 145 (refusal to deal with person on grounds relating to union membership).

(4) References in this section to an employer employing a person are to a person acting in the capacity of the person for whom a worker works or normally works.

(5) References in this section to not being a member of a trade union are to not being a member of any trade union, of a particular trade union or of one of a number of particular trade unions. Any such reference includes a reference to not being a member of a particular branch or section of a trade union or of one of a number of particular branches or sections of a trade union.

223 Action taken because of dismissal for taking unofficial action

An act is not protected if the reason, or one of the reasons, for doing it is the fact or belief that an employer has dismissed one or more employees in circumstances such that by virtue of section 237 (dismissal in connection with unofficial action) they have no right to complain of unfair dismissal.

224 Secondary action

(1) An act is not protected if one of the facts relied on for the purpose of establishing liability is that there has been secondary action which is not lawful picketing.

(2) There is secondary action in relation to a trade dispute when, and only when, a person –

(a) induces another to break a contract of employment or interferes or induces another to interfere with its performance, or

(b) threatens that a contract of employment under which he or another is employed will be broken or its performance interfered with, or that he will induce another to break a contract of employment or to interfere with its performance,

and the employer under the contract of employment is not the employer party to the dispute.

(3) Lawful picketing means acts done in the course of such attendance as is declared lawful by section 220 (peaceful picketing) –

(a) by a worker employed (or, in the case of a worker not in employment, last employed) by the employer party to the dispute, or

(b) by a trade union official whose attendance is lawful by virtue of subsection (1)(b) of that section.

(4) For the purposes of this section an employer shall not be treated as party to a dispute between another employer and workers of that employer; and where more than one employer is in dispute with his workers, the dispute between each employer and his workers shall be treated as a separate dispute. In this subsection 'worker' has the same meaning as in section 244 (meaning of 'trade dispute').

(5) An act in contemplation or furtherance of a trade dispute which is primary action in relation to that dispute may not be relied on as secondary action in relation to another trade dispute.

Primary action means such action as is mentioned in paragraph (a) or (b) of subsection (2) where the employer under the contract of employment is the employer party to the dispute.

(6) In this section 'contract of employment' includes any contract under which one person personally does work or performs services for another, and related expressions shall be construed accordingly.

225 Pressure to impose union recognition requirement

(1) An act is not protected if it constitutes, or is one of a number of acts which together constitute, an inducement or attempted inducement of a person –

(a) to incorporate in a contract to which that person is a party, or a proposed contract to which he intends to be a party, a term or condition which is or would be void by virtue of section 186 (recognition requirement in contract for goods or services), or

(b) to contravene section 187 (refusal to deal with person on grounds of union exclusion).

(2) An act is not protected if –

(a) it interferes with the supply (whether or not under a contract) of goods or services, or can reasonably be expected to have that effect, and

(b) one of the facts relied upon for the purpose of establishing liability is that a person has –

(i) induced another to break a contract of employment or interfered or induced another to interfere with its performance, or

(ii) threatened that a contract of employment under which he or another is employed will be broken or its performance interfered with, or that he will induce another to break a contract of employment or to interfere with its performance, and

(c) the reason, or one of the reasons, for doing the act is the fact or belief that the supplier (not being the employer under the contract of employment mentioned in paragraph (b)) does not, or might not –

(i) recognise one or more trade unions for the purpose of negotiating on behalf of workers, or any class of worker, employed by him, or

(ii) negotiate or consult with, or with an official of, one or more trade unions.

226 Requirement of ballot before action by trade union

(1) An act done by a trade union to induce a person to take part, or continue to take part, in industrial action –

(a) is not protected unless the industrial action has the support of a ballot, and

(b) where section 226A falls to be complied with in relation to the person's employer, is not protected as respects the employer unless the trade union has complied with section 226A in relation to him.

In this section 'the relevant time', in relation to an act by a trade union to induce a person to take part, or continue to take part, in industrial action, means the time at which proceedings are commenced in respect of the act.

(2) Industrial action shall be regarded as having the support of a ballot only if –

(a) the union has held a ballot in respect of the action –

(i) in relation to which the requirements of section 226B [appointment of scrutineer] so far as applicable before and during the holding of the ballot were satisfied,

(ii) in relation to which the requirements of sections 227 to 231 were satisfied, and

(iii) in which the majority voting in the ballot answered 'Yes' to the question applicable in accordance with section 229(2) to industrial action of the kind to which the act of inducement relates;

(b) such of the requirements of the following sections as have fallen to be satisfied at the relevant time have been satisfied, namely –

(i) section 226B so far as applicable after the holding of the ballot, and

(ii) section 231B;

(bb) section 232A does not prevent the industrial action from being regarded as having the support of the ballot; and

(c) the requirements of section 233 (calling of industrial action with support of ballot) are satisfied.

Any reference in this subsection to a requirement of a provision which is disapplied or modified by section 232 has effect subject to that section.

(3) Where separate workplace ballots are held by virtue of section 228(1) –

(a) industrial action shall be regarded as having the support of a ballot if the conditions specified in subsection (2) are satisfied, and

(b) the trade union shall be taken to have complied with the requirements relating to a ballot imposed by section 226A [notice of ballot and sample voting paper for employers] if those requirements are complied with,

in relation to the ballot for the place of work of the person induced to take part, or continue to take part, in the industrial action.

(3A) If the requirements of section 231A fall to be satisfied in relation to an employer, as respects that employer industrial action shall not be regarded as having the support of a ballot unless those requirements are satisfied in relation to that employer.

(4) For the purposes of this section an inducement, in relation to a person, includes an inducement which is or would be ineffective, whether because of his unwillingness to be influenced by it or for any other reason.

236 No compulsion to work

No court shall, whether by way of –

(a) an order for specific performance ... of a contract of employment, or

(b) an injunction ... restraining a breach or threatened breach of such a contract,

compel an employee to do any work or attend at any place for the doing of any work.

244 Meaning of 'trade dispute' in Part V

(1) In this Part [ss219-246] a 'trade dispute' means a dispute between workers and their employer which relates wholly or mainly to one or more of the following –

(a) terms and conditions of employment, or the physical conditions in which any workers are required to work;

(b) engagement or non-engagement, or termination or suspension of employment or the duties of employment, of one or more workers;

(c) allocation of work or the duties of employment between workers or groups of workers;

(d) matters of discipline;

(e) a worker's membership or non-membership of a trade union;

(f) facilities for officials of trade unions; and

(g) machinery for negotiation or consultation, and other procedures, relating to any of the above matters, including the recognition by employers or employers' associations of the right of a trade union to represent workers in such negotiation or consultation or in the carrying out of such procedures.

(2) A dispute between a Minister of the Crown and any workers shall, notwithstanding that he is not the employer of those workers, be treated as a dispute between those workers and their employer if the dispute relates to matters which –

(a) have been referred for consideration by a joint body on which, by virtue of provision made by or under any enactment, he is represented, or

(b) cannot be settled without him exercising a power conferred on him by or under an enactment.

(3) There is a trade dispute even though it relates to matters occurring outside the United Kingdom, so long as the person or persons whose actions in the United Kingdom are said to be in contemplation or furtherance of a trade dispute relating to matters occurring outside the United Kingdom are likely to be affected in respect of one or more of the matters specified in subsection (1) by the outcome of the dispute.

(4) An act, threat or demand done or made by one person or organisation against another which, if resisted, would have led to a trade dispute with that other, shall be treated as being done or made in contemplation of a trade dispute with that other, notwithstanding that because that other submits to the act or threat or accedes to the demand no dispute arises.

(5) In this section –

'employment' includes any relationship whereby one person personally does work or performs services for another; and

'worker', in relation to a dispute with an employer, means –

(a) a worker employed by that employer; or

(b) a person who has ceased to be so employed if his employment was terminated in connection with the dispute or if the termination of his employment was one of the circumstances giving rise to the dispute.

298 Minor definitions: general

In this Act, unless the context otherwise requires –

'act' and 'action' each includes omission, and references to doing an act or taking action shall be construed accordingly;

'contravention' includes a failure to comply, and cognate expressions shall be construed accordingly; ...

As amended by the Trade Union Reform and Employment Rights Act 1993, ss18(1), 49(1), (2), Schedules 7, para 17, 8, paras 72, 73; Employment Relations Act 1999, s4, Schedule 3, paras 1, 2; Regulatory Reform (Removal of 20 Member Limit in Partnerships, etc) order 2002, art 4.

POLICE ACT 1996
(1996 c 16)

88   Liability for wrongful acts of constables

(1) The chief officer of police for a police area shall be liable in respect of any unlawful conduct of constables under his direction and control in the performance or purported performance of their functions in like manner as a master is liable in respect of any unlawful conduct of his servants in the course of their employment, and accordingly shall in the case of a tort be treated for all purposes as a joint tortfeasor.

(2) There shall be paid out of the police fund –

(a) any damages or costs awarded against the chief officer of police in any proceedings brought against him by virtue of this section and any costs incurred by him in any such proceedings so far as not recovered by him in the proceedings; and

(b) any sum required in connection with the settlement of any claim made against the chief officer of police by virtue of this section, if the settlement is approved by the police authority.

(3) Any proceedings in respect of a claim made by virtue of this section shall be brought against the chief officer of police for the time being or, in the case of a vacancy in that office, against the person for the time being performing the functions of the chief officer of police and references in subsections (1) and (2) to the chief officer of police shall be construed accordingly.

(4) A police authority may, in such cases and to such extent as appear to it to be appropriate, pay out of the police fund –

(a) any damages or costs awarded against a person to whom this subsection applies in proceedings for any unlawful conduct of that person,

(b) any costs incurred and not recovered by such a person in such proceedings, and

(c) any sum required in connection with the settlement of a claim that has or might have given rise to such proceedings.

(5) Subsection (4) applies to a person who is –

(a) a member of the police force maintained by the police authority,

(b) a constable for the time being required to serve with that force by virtue of section 24 or 98 of this Act or section 23 of the Police Act 1997, or

(c) a special constable appointed for the authority's police area.

(6) This section shall have effect where an international joint investigation team has been formed under the leadership of a constable who is a member of a police force as if –

(a) any unlawful conduct, in the performance or purported performance of his functions as such, of any member of that team who is neither a constable nor an employee of the police authority were unlawful conduct of a constable under the direction and control of the chief officer of police of that force; and

(b) subsection (4) applied, in the case of the police authority maintaining that forced, to every member of that team to whom it would not apply apart from this subsection.

(7) In this section 'international joint investigation team' means any investigation team formed in accordance with –

(a) any framework decision on joint investigation teams adopted under Article 34 of the Treaty on European Union;

(b) the Convention on Mutual Assistance in Criminal Matters between the Member States of the European Union, and the Protocol to that Convention, established in accordance with that Article of that Treaty; or

(c) any international agreement to which the United Kingdom is a party and which is specified for the purposes of this section in an order made by the Secretary of State.

(8) A statutory instrument containing an order under subsection (7) shall be subject to annulment in pursuance of a resolution of either House of Parliament.

As amended by the Police Act 1997, s134(1), Schedule 9, para 85; Police Reform Act 2002, ss102(1), (2)(a), (4), (5)(a), 103(1).

EMPLOYMENT RIGHTS ACT 1996
(1996 c 18)

203 Restrictions on contracting out

(1) Any provision in an agreement (whether a contract of employment or not) is void in so far as it purports –

(a) to exclude or limit the operation of any provision of this Act, or

(b) to preclude a person from bringing any proceedings under this Act before an employment tribunal.

(2) Subsection (1) –

(a) does not apply [in certain situations] ...

As amended by the Employment Rights (Dispute Resolution) Act 1998, s1(2)(a).

DEFAMATION ACT 1996
(1996 c 31)

1   Responsibility for publication

(1) In defamation proceedings a person has a defence if he shows that –

(a) he was not the author, editor or publisher of the statement complained of,

(b) he took reasonable care in relation to its publication, and

(c) he did not know, and had no reason to believe, that what he did caused or contributed to the publication of a defamatory statement.

(2) For this purpose 'author', 'editor' and 'publisher' have the following meanings, which are further explained in subsection (3) –

'author' means the originator of the statement, but does not include a person who did not intend that his statement be published at all;

'editor' means a person having editorial or equivalent responsibility for the content of the statement or the decision to publish it; and

'publisher' means a commercial publisher, that is, a person whose business is issuing material to the public, or a section of the public, who issues material containing the statement in the course of that business.

(3) A person shall not be considered the author, editor or publisher of a statement if he is only involved –

(a) in printing, producing, distributing or selling printed material containing the statement;

(b) in processing, making copies of, distributing, exhibiting or selling a film or sound recording (as defined in Part I of the Copyright, Designs and Patents Act 1988) containing the statement;

(c) in processing, making copies of, distributing or selling any electronic medium in or on which the statement is recorded, or in operating or providing any equipment, system or service by means of which the statement is retrieved, copied, distributed or made available in electronic form;

(d) as the broadcaster of a live programme containing the statement in circumstances in which he has no effective control over the maker of the statement;

(e) as the operator of or provider of access to a communications system by means of which the statement is transmitted, or made available, by a person over whom he has no effective control.

In a case not within paragraphs (a) to (e) the court may have regard to those provisions by way of analogy in deciding whether a person is to be considered the author, editor or publisher of a statement.

(4) Employees or agents of an author, editor or publisher are in the same position as their employer or principal to the extent that they are responsible for the content of the statement or the decision to publish it.

(5) In determining for the purposes of this section whether a person took reasonable care, or had reason to believe that what he did caused or contributed to the publication of a defamatory statement, regard shall be had to –

(a) the extent of his responsibility for the content of the statement or the decision to publish it,

(b) the nature or circumstances of the publication, and

(c) the previous conduct or character of the author, editor or publisher.

(6) This section does not apply to any cause of action which arose before the section came into force.

2   Offer to make amends

(1) A person who has published a statement alleged to be defamatory of another may offer to make amends under this section.

(2) The offer may be in relation to the statement generally or in relation to a specific defamatory meaning which the person making the offer accepts that the statement conveys ('a qualified offer').

(3) An offer to make amends –

(a) must be in writing,

(b) must be expressed to be an offer to make amends under section 2 of the Defamation Act 1996, and

(c) must state whether it is a qualified offer and, if so, set out the defamatory meaning in relation to which it is made.

(4) An offer to make amends under this section is an offer –

(a) to make a suitable correction of the statement complained of and a sufficient apology to the aggrieved party,

(b) to publish the correction and apology in a manner that is reasonable and practicable in the circumstances, and

(c) to pay to the aggrieved party such compensation (if any), and such costs, as may be agreed or determined to be payable.

The fact that the offer is accompanied by an offer to take specific steps does not affect the fact that an offer to make amends under this section is an offer to do all the things mentioned in paragraphs (a) to (c).

(5) An offer to make amends under this section may not be made by a person after

serving a defence in defamation proceedings brought against him by the aggrieved party in respect of the publication in question.

(6) An offer to make amends under this section may be withdrawn before it is accepted; and a renewal of an offer which has been withdrawn shall be treated as a new offer.

3   Accepting an offer to make amends

(1) If an offer to make amends under section 2 is accepted by the aggrieved party, the following provisions apply.

(2) The party accepting the offer may not bring or continue defamation proceedings in respect of the publication concerned against the person making the offer, but he is entitled to enforce the offer to make amends, as follows.

(3) If the parties agree on the steps to be taken in fulfilment of the offer, the aggrieved party may apply to the court for an order that the other party fulfil his offer by taking the steps agreed.

(4) If the parties do not agree on the steps to be taken by way of correction, apology and publication, the party who made the offer may take such steps as he thinks appropriate, and may in particular –

   (a) make the correction and apology by a statement in open court in terms approved by the court, and
   (b) give an undertaking to the court as to the manner of their publication.

(5) If the parties do not agree on the amount to be paid by way of compensation, it shall be determined by the court on the same principles as damages in defamation proceedings. The court shall take account of any steps taken in fulfilment of the offer and (so far as not agreed between the parties) of the suitability of the correction, the sufficiency of the apology and whether the manner of their publication was reasonable in the circumstances, and may reduce or increase the amount of compensation accordingly.

(6) If the parties do not agree on the amount to be paid by way of costs, it shall be determined by the court on the same principles as costs awarded in court proceedings.

(7) The acceptance of an offer by one person to make amends does not affect any cause of action against another person in respect of the same publication, subject as follows.

(8) In England and Wales or Northern Ireland, for the purposes of the Civil Liability (Contribution) Act 1978 –

   (a) the amount of compensation paid under the offer shall be treated as paid in bona fide settlement or compromise of the claim; and
   (b) where another person is liable in respect of the same damage (whether jointly or otherwise), the person whose offer to make amends was accepted is not required to pay by virtue of any contribution under section 1 of that Act a

greater amount than the amount of the compensation payable in pursuance of the offer. ...

(10) Proceedings under this section shall be heard and determined without a jury.

4 Failure to accept offer to make amends

(1) If an offer to make amends under section 2, duly made and not withdrawn, is not accepted by the aggrieved party, the following provisions apply.

(2) The fact that the offer was made is a defence (subject to subsection (3)) to defamation proceedings in respect of the publication in question by that party against the person making the offer. A qualified offer is only a defence in respect of the meaning to which the offer related.

(3) There is no such defence if the person by whom the offer was made knew or had reason to believe that the statement complained of –

(a) referred to the aggrieved party or was likely to be understood as referring to him, and

(b) was both false and defamatory of that party;

but it shall be presumed until the contrary is shown that he did not know and had no reason to believe that was the case.

(4) The person who made the offer need not rely on it by way of defence, but if he does he may not rely on any other defence. If the offer was a qualified offer, this applies only in respect of the meaning to which the offer related.

(5) The offer may be relied on in mitigation of damages whether or not it was relied on as a defence.

7 Ruling on the meaning of a statement

In defamation proceedings the court shall not be asked to rule whether a statement is arguably capable, as opposed to capable, of bearing a particular meaning or meanings attributed to it.

8 Summary disposal of claim

(1) In defamation proceedings the court may dispose summarily of the plaintiff's claim in accordance with the following provisions.

(2) The court may dismiss the plaintiff's claim if it appears to the court that it has no realistic prospect of success and there is no reason why it should be tried.

(3) The court may give judgment for the plaintiff and grant him summary relief (see section 9) if it appears to the court that there is no defence to the claim which has a realistic prospect of success, and that there is no other reason why the claim should be tried. Unless the plaintiff asks for summary relief, the court shall not act under this subsection unless it is satisfied that summary relief will adequately compensate him for the wrong he has suffered.

(4) In considering whether a claim should be tried the court shall have regard to –

(a) whether all the persons who are or might be defendants in respect of the publication complained of are before the court;

(b) whether summary disposal of the claim against another defendant would be inappropriate;

(c) the extent to which there is a conflict of evidence;

(d) the seriousness of the alleged wrong (as regards the content of the statement and the extent of publication); and

(e) whether it is justifiable in the circumstances to proceed to a full trial.

(5) Proceedings under this section shall be heard and determined without a jury.

9 Meaning of summary relief

(1) For the purposes of section 8 (summary disposal of claim) 'summary relief' means such of the following as may be appropriate –

(a) a declaration that the statement was false and defamatory of the plaintiff;

(b) an order that the defendant publish or cause to be published a suitable correction and apology;

(c) damages not exceeding £10,000 or such other amount as may be prescribed by order of the Lord Chancellor;

(d) an order restraining the defendant from publishing or further publishing the matter complained of.

(2) The content of any correction and apology, and the time, manner, form and place of publication, shall be for the parties to agree. If they cannot agree on the content, the court may direct the defendant to publish or cause to be published a summary of the court's judgment agreed by the parties or settled by the court in accordance with rules of court. If they cannot agree on the time, manner, form or place of publication, the court may direct the defendant to take such reasonable and practicable steps as the court considers appropriate.

(3) Any order under subsection (1)(c) shall be made by statutory instrument which shall be subject to annulment in pursuance of a resolution of either House of Parliament.

10 Summary disposal: rules of court

(1) Provision may be made by rules of court as to the summary disposal of the plaintiff's claim in defamation proceedings.

(2) Without prejudice to the generality of that power, provision may be made –

(a) authorising a party to apply for summary disposal at any stage of the proceedings;

(b) authorising the court at any stage of the proceedings –

(i) to treat any application, pleading or other step in the proceedings as an application for summary disposal, or

(ii) to make an order for summary disposal without any such application;

(c) as to the time for serving pleadings or taking any other step in the proceedings in a case where there are proceedings for summary disposal;

(d) requiring the parties to identify any question of law or construction which the court is to be asked to determine in the proceedings;

(e) as to the nature of any hearing on the question of summary disposal, and in particular –

(i) authorising the court to order affidavits or witness statements to be prepared for use as evidence at the hearing, and

(ii) requiring the leave of the court for the calling of oral evidence, or the introduction of new evidence, at the hearing;

(f) authorising the court to require a defendant to elect, at or before the hearing, whether or not to make an offer to make amends under section 2.

13   Evidence concerning proceedings in Parliament

(1) Where the conduct of a person in or in relation to proceedings in Parliament is in issue in defamation proceedings, he may waive for the purposes of those proceedings, so far as concerns him, the protection of any enactment or rule of law which prevents proceedings in Parliament being impeached or questioned in any court or place out of Parliament.

(2) Where a person waives that protection –

(a) any such enactment or rule of law shall not apply to prevent evidence being given, questions being asked or statements, submissions, comments or findings being made about his conduct, and

(b) none of those things shall be regarded as infringing the privilege of either House of Parliament.

(3) The waiver by one person of that protection does not affect its operation in relation to another person who has not waived it.

(4) Nothing in this section affects any enactment or rule of law so far as it protects a person (including a person who has waived the protection referred to above) from legal liability for words spoken or things done in the course of, or for the purposes of or incidental to, any proceedings in Parliament.

(5) Without prejudice to the generality of subsection (4), that subsection applies to –

(a) the giving of evidence before either House or a committee;

(b) the presentation or submission of a document to either House or a committee;

(c) the preparation of a document for the purposes of or incidental to the transacting of any such business;

(d) the formulation, making or publication of a document, including a report, by or pursuant to an order of either House or a committee; and

(e) any communication with the Parliamentary Commissioner for Standards or any person having functions in connection with the registration of members' interests.

In this subsection 'a committee' means a committee of either House or a joint committee of both Houses of Parliament.

14 Reports of court proceedings absolutely privileged

(1) A fair and accurate report of proceedings in public before a court to which this section applies, if published contemporaneously with proceedings, is absolutely privileged.

(2) A report of proceedings which by an order of the court, or as a consequence of any statutory provision, is required to be postponed shall be treated as published contemporaneously if it is published as soon as practicable after publication is permitted.

(3) This section applies to –

(a) any court in the United Kingdom,

(b) the European Court of Justice or any court attached to that court,

(c) the European Court of Human Rights, and

(d) any international criminal tribunal established by the Security Council of the United Nations or by an international agreement to which the United Kingdom is a party.

In paragraph (a) 'court' includes any tribunal or body exercising the judicial power of the State. ...

15 Reports, etc protected by qualified privilege

(1) The publication of any report or other statement mentioned in Schedule 1 to this Act is privileged unless the publication is shown to be made with malice, subject as follows.

(2) In defamation proceedings in respect of the publication of a report or other statement mentioned in Part II of that Schedule, there is no defence under this section if the plaintiff shows that the defendant –

(a) was requested by him to publish in a suitable manner a reasonable letter or statement by way of explanation or contradiction, and

(b) refused or neglected to do so.

For this purpose 'in a suitable manner' means in the same manner as the publication complained of or in a manner that is adequate and reasonable in the circumstances.

(3) This section does not apply to the publication to the public, or a section of the

public, of matter which is not of public concern and the publication of which is not for the public benefit.

(4) Nothing in this section shall be construed –

(a) as protecting the publication of matter the publication of which is prohibited by law, or

(b) as limiting or abridging any privilege subsisting apart from this section.

17   Interpretation

(1) In this Act –

'publication' and 'publish', in relation to a statement, have the meaning they have for the purposes of the law of defamation generally, but 'publisher' is specially defined for the purposes of section l;

'statement' means words, pictures, visual images, gestures or any other method of signifying meaning; and

'statutory provision' means –

(a) a provision contained in an Act or in subordinate legislation within the meaning of the Interpretation Act 1978,

(aa) a provision contained in an Act of the Scottish Parliament or in an instrument made under such an Act, or

(b) a statutory provision within the meaning given by section 1(f) of the Interpretation Act (Northern Ireland) 1954.

20   Short title and saving ...

(2) Nothing in this Act affects the law relating to criminal libel.

SCHEDULE 1

QUALIFIED PRIVILEGE

PART I

STATEMENTS HAVING QUALIFIED PRIVILEGE WITHOUT
EXPLANATION OR CONTRADICTION

1. A fair and accurate report of proceedings in public of a legislature anywhere in the world.

2. A fair and accurate report of proceedings in public before a court anywhere in the world.

3. A fair and accurate report of proceedings in public of a person appointed to hold a public inquiry by a government or legislature anywhere in the world.

4. A fair and accurate report of proceedings in public anywhere in the world of an international organisation or an international conference.

5. A fair and accurate copy of or extract from any register or other document required by law to be open to public inspection.

6. A notice or advertisement published by or on the authority of a court, or of a judge or officer of a court, anywhere in the world.

7. A fair and accurate copy of or extract from matter published by or on the authority of a government or legislature anywhere in the world.

8. A fair and accurate copy of or extract from matter published anywhere in the world by an international organisation or an international conference.

PART II

STATEMENTS PRIVILEGED SUBJECT TO EXPLANATION OR CONTRADICTION

9. (1) A fair and accurate copy of or extract from a notice or other matter issued for the information of the public by or on behalf of –

(a) a legislature in any member State or the European Parliament;

(b) the government of any member State, or any authority performing governmental functions in any member State or part of a member State, or the European Commission;

(c) an international organisation or international conference.

(2) In this paragraph 'governmental functions' includes police functions.

10. A fair and accurate copy of or extract from a document made available by a court in any member State or the European Court of Justice (or any court attached to that court), or by a judge or officer of any such court.

11. (1) A fair and accurate report of proceedings at any public meeting or sitting in the United Kingdom of –

(a) a local authority or local authority committee;

(aa) in the case of a local authority which are operating executive arrangements, the executive of that authority or a committee of that executive;

(b) a justice or justices of the peace acting otherwise than as a court exercising judicial authority;

(c) a commission, tribunal, committee or person appointed for the purposes of any inquiry by any statutory provision, by Her Majesty or by a Minister of the Crown, a member of the Scottish Executive or a Northern Ireland Department;

(d) a person appointed by a local authority to hold a local inquiry in pursuance of any statutory provision;

(e) any other tribunal, board, committee or body constituted by or under, and exercising functions under, any statutory provision.

(1A) In the case of a local authority which are operating executive arrangements, a fair and accurate record of any decision made by any member of the executive where that record is required to be made and available for public inspection by virtue of section 22 of the Local Government Act 2000 or of any provision in regulations made under that section.

(2) In sub-paragraph (1)(a), (1)(aa) and (1A) –

'local authority' means –

(a) in relation to England and Wales, a principal council within the meaning of the Local Government Act 1972, any body falling within any paragraph of section 100J(1) of that Act or an authority or body to which the Public Bodies (Admission to Meetings) Act 1960 applies, ... and

'local authority committee' means any committee of a local authority or of local authorities, and includes –

(a) any committee or sub-committee in relation to which sections 100A to 100D of the Local Government Act 1972 apply by virtue of section 100E of that Act (whether or not also by virtue of section 100J of that Act), ...

(2A) In sub-paragraphs (1) and (1A) –

'executive' and 'executive arrangements' have the same meaning as in Part II of the Local Government Act 2000.

(3) A fair and accurate report of any corresponding proceedings in any of the Channel Islands or the Isle of Man or in another member State.

12. (1) A fair and accurate report of proceedings at any public meeting held in a member State.

(2) In this paragraph a 'public meeting' means a meeting bona fide and lawfully held for a lawful purpose and for the furtherance or discussion of a matter of public concern, whether admission to the meeting is general or restricted.

13. (1) A fair and accurate report of proceedings at a general meeting of a UK public company.

(2) A fair and accurate copy of or extract from any document circulated to members of a UK public company –

(a) by or with the authority of the board of directors of the company,

(b) by the auditors of the company, or

(c) by any member of the company in pursuance of a right conferred by any statutory provision.

(3) A fair and accurate copy of or extract from any document circulated to members of a UK public company which relates to the appointment, resignation, retirement or dismissal of directors of the company.

(4) In this paragraph 'UK public company' means –

(a) a public company within the meaning of section 1(3) of the Companies Act 1985 or Article 12(3) of the Companies (Northern Ireland) Order 1986, or

(b) a body corporate incorporated by or registered under any other statutory provision, or by Royal Charter, or formed in pursuance of letters patent.

(5) A fair and accurate report of proceedings at any corresponding meeting of, or copy of or extract from any corresponding document circulated to members of, a public company formed under the law of any of the Channel Islands or the Isle of Man or of another member State.

14. A fair and accurate report of any finding or decision of any of the following descriptions of association, formed in the United Kingdom or another member State, or of any committee or governing body of such an association –

(a) an association formed for the purpose of promoting or encouraging the exercise of or interest in any art, science, religion or learning, and empowered by its constitution to exercise control over or adjudicate on matters of interest or concern to the association, or the actions or conduct of any person subject to such control or adjudication;

(b) an association formed for the purpose of promoting or safeguarding the interests of any trade, business, industry or profession, or of the persons carrying on or engaged in any trade, business, industry or profession, and empowered by its constitution to exercise control over or adjudicate upon matters connected with that trade, business, industry or profession, or the actions or conduct of those persons;

(c) an association formed for the purpose of promoting or safeguarding the interests of a game, sport or pastime to the playing or exercise of which members of the public are invited or admitted, and empowered by its constitution to exercise control over or adjudicate upon persons connected with or taking part in the game, sport or pastime;

(d) an association formed for the purpose of promoting charitable objects or other objects beneficial to the community and empowered by its constitution to exercise control over or to adjudicate on matters of interest or concern to the association, or the actions or conduct of any person subject to such control or adjudication.

15. (1) A fair and accurate report of, or copy of or extract from, any adjudication, report, statement or notice issued by a body, officer or other person designated for the purposes of this paragraph –

(a) for England and Wales or Northern Ireland, by order of the Lord Chancellor,
...

(2) An order under this paragraph shall be made by statutory instrument which shall be subject to annulment in pursuance of a resolution of either House of Parliament.

PART III

SUPPLEMENTARY PROVISIONS

16. (1) In this Schedule –

'court' includes any tribunal or body exercising the judicial power of the State;

'international conference' means a conference attended by representatives of two or more governments;

'international organisation' means an organisation of which two or more governments are members, and includes any committee or other subordinate body of such an organisation; and

'legislature' includes a local legislature.

(2) References in this Schedule to a member State include any European dependent territory of a member State.

(3) In paragraphs 2 and 6 'court' includes –

(a) the European Court of Justice (or any court attached to that court) and the Court of Auditors of the European Communities,

(b) the European Court of Human Rights,

(c) any international criminal tribunal established by the Security Council of the United Nations or by an international agreement to which the United Kingdom is a party, and

(d) the International Court of Justice and any other judicial or arbitral tribunal deciding matters in dispute between States.

(4) In paragraphs 1, 3 and 7 'legislature' includes the European Parliament.

17. (1) Provision may be made by order identifying –

(a) for the purposes of paragraph 11, the corresponding proceedings referred to in sub-paragraph (3);

(b) for the purposes of paragraph 13, the corresponding meetings and documents referred to in sub-paragraph (5).

(2) An order under this paragraph may be made –

(a) for England and Wales or Northern Ireland, by the Lord Chancellor, …

(3) An order under this paragraph shall be made by statutory instrument which shall be subject to annulment in pursuance of a resolution of either House of Parliament.

NB As to Wales, for amendments to Schedule 1, Pt II, para 11 see the Local Authorities (Executive and Alternative Arrangements) (Modification of Enactments and Other Provisions) (Wales) Order 2002, arts 2(p), 30.

As amended by the Scotland Act 1998, s125(1), Schedule 8, para 33; Local Authorities (Executive and Alternative Arrangements) (Modification of Enactments and Other Provisions) (England) Order 2001, art 31(b); Local Authorities (Executive Arrangements) (Modification of Enactments) (England) Order 2002, art 12.

DAMAGES ACT 1996
(1996 c 48)

1   Assumed rate of return on investment of damages

(1) In determining the return to be expected from the investment of a sum awarded as damages for future pecuniary loss in an action for personal injury the court shall, subject to and in accordance with rules of court made for the purposes of this section, take into account such rate of return (if any) as may from time to time be prescribed by an order made by the Lord Chancellor.

(2) Subsection (1) above shall not however prevent the court taking a different rate of return into account if any party to the proceedings shows that it is more appropriate in the case in question.

(3) An order under subsection (1) above may prescribe different rates of return for different classes of case.

(4) Before making an order under subsection (1) above the Lord Chancellor shall consult the Government Actuary and the Treasury; and any order under that subsection shall be made by statutory instrument subject to annulment in pursuance of a resolution of either House of Parliament. ...

2   Consent orders for periodical payments

(1) A court awarding damages in an action for personal injury may, with the consent of the parties, make an order under which the damages are wholly or partly to take the form of periodical payments.

(2) In this section 'damages' includes an interim payment which the court, by virtue of rules of court in that behalf, orders the defendant to make to the plaintiff ...

(3) This section is without prejudice to any powers exercisable apart from this section.

See Appendix, Courts Act 2003, s100(1).

3   Provisional damages and fatal accident claims

(1) This section applies where a person –

    (a) is awarded provisional damages; and
    (b) subsequently dies as a result of the act or omission which gave rise to the cause of action for which the damages were awarded.

(2) The award of the provisional damages shall not operate as a bar to an action in respect of that person's death under the Fatal Accidents Act 1976.

(3) Such part (if any) of –

(a) the provisional damages; and

(b) any further damages awarded to the person in question before his death,

as was intended to compensate him for pecuniary loss in a period which in the event falls after his death shall be taken into account in assessing the amount of any loss of support suffered by the person or persons for whose benefit the action under the Fatal Accidents Act 1976 is brought.

(4) No award of further damages made in respect of that person after his death shall include any amount for loss of income in respect of any period after his death.

(5) In this section 'provisional damages' means damages awarded by virtue of subsection (2)(a) of section 32A of the Supreme Court Act 1981 or section 51 of the County Courts Act 1984 and 'further damages' means damages awarded by virtue of subsection (2)(b) of either of those sections.

(6) Subsection (2) above applies whether the award of provisional damages was before or after the coming into force of that subsection; and subsections (3) and (4) apply to any award of damages under the 1976 Act or, as the case may be, further damages after the coming into force of those subsections. ...

4   Enhanced protection for structured settlement annuitants

(1) In relation to an annuity purchased for a person pursuant to a structured settlement from an authorised insurance company within the meaning of the Policyholders Protection Act 1975 (and in respect of which that person as annuitant is accordingly the policyholder for the purposes of that Act) sections 10 and 11 of that Act (protection in the event of liquidation of the insurer) as applied by any transitional provisions made by order under section 426 of the 2000 Act shall have effect as if any reference to ninety per cent of the amount of the liability, of any future benefit or of the value attributed to the policy were a reference to the full amount of the liability, benefit or value.

(2) Those sections as applied by any transitional provisions made by order under section 426 of the 2000 Act shall also have effect as mentioned in subsection (1) above in relation to an annuity purchased from an authorised insurance company within the meaning of the 1975 Act pursuant to any order incorporating terms corresponding to those of a structured settlement which a court makes when awarding damages for personal injury.

(3) Those sections as applied by any transitional provisions made by order under section 426 of the 2000 Act shall also have effect as mentioned in subsection (1) above in relation to an annuity purchased from or otherwise provided by an authorised insurance company within the meaning of the 1975 Act pursuant to terms corresponding to those of a structured settlement contained in an agreement made by –

(a) the Motor Insurers' Bureau; or

(b) a Domestic Regulations Insurer,

in respect of damages for personal injury which the Bureau or Insurer undertakes to pay in satisfaction of a claim or action against an uninsured driver.

(3A) In relation to an annuity –

(a) purchased for a person pursuant to a structured settlement from an authorised insurer;

(b) purchased from such an insurer pursuant to any order of the kind referred to in subsection (2); or

(c) purchased from or otherwise provided by such an insurer pursuant to terms corresponding to those of a structured settlement contained in an agreement of the kind referred to in subsection (3),

any long term insurance provision in the Financial Services Compensation Scheme has effect in accordance with subsection (3B).

(3B) To the extent that any long term insurance provision limits the obligation of the scheme manager to make payments or secure continuity of insurance by reference to any amount less than the full amount of any liability, benefit or value due under a contract of long term insurance, the provision has effect as if the reference to that amount were a reference to the full amount of the liability, benefit or value.

(3C) In this section –

'the 2000 Act' means the Financial Services and Markets Act 2000;

'authorised insurer' means an authorised person within the meaning of the 2000 Act with permission under that Act to effect or carry out contracts of insurance as principal;

'Financial Services Compensation Scheme' means the Financial Services Compensation Scheme referred to in section 213(2) of the Financial Services and Markets Act 2000;

'long term insurance provision' means any provision in the Financial Services Compensation Scheme requiring the scheme manager to –

(a) pay compensation in respect of a liability of an authorised insurer in liquidation under a contract of long term insurance;

(b) secure continuity of insurance for parties to contracts of long term insurance in the event that an authorised insurer goes into liquidation; or

(c) secure that payments are made in respect of benefits falling due under contracts of long term insurance during any period while the scheme manager is seeking to make arrangements to secure continuity of insurance as mentioned in (b) above;

'scheme manager' means a body corporate established in accordance with section 212(1) of the 2000 Act.

(3D) In subsections (3B) and (3C) above –

(a) a reference to a contract of long term insurance must be read with –

(i) section 22 of the 2000 Act;

(ii) any relevant order under that section; and

(iii) Schedule 2 to that Act;

(b) an authorised insurer is in liquidation when –

(i) a resolution has been passed in accordance with the provisions of the Insolvency Act 1986 ... for the voluntary winding up of the insurer, otherwise than merely for the purpose of reconstruction of the insurer or of amalgamation with another insurer; or

(ii) without any such resolution having been passed beforehand, an order has been made for the winding up of the insurer by the court under that Act or that Order.

(4) In subsection (3) above 'the Motor Insurers' Bureau' means the company of that name incorporated on 14th June 1946 under the Companies Act 1929 and 'a Domestic Regulations Insurer' has the meaning given in the Bureau's Domestic Regulations.

(5) Subsections (1) to (3) of this section apply if the liquidation of the authorised insurance company begins (within the meaning of the 1975 Act) after the coming into force of this section irrespective of when the annuity was purchased or provided.

(6) Subsections (3A) to (3D) of this section apply if the liquidation of the authorised insurer begins (within the meaning of subsection (3D)) after the coming into force of section 19 of the 2000 Act, irrespective of when the annuity was purchased or provided.

See Appendix, Courts Act 2003, s101(1).

5   Meaning of structured settlement

(1) In section 4 above a 'structured settlement' means an agreement settling a claim or action for damages for personal injury on terms whereby –

(a) the damages are to consist wholly or partly of periodical payments; and

(b) the person to whom the payments are to be made is to receive them as the annuitant under one or more annuities purchased for him by the person against whom the claim or action is brought or, if he is insured against the claim, by his insurer.

(2) The periodical payments may be for the life of the claimant, for a specified period or of a specified number or minimum number or include payments of more than one of those descriptions.

(3) The amounts of the periodical payments (which need not be at a uniform rate or payable at uniform intervals) may be –

(a) specified in the agreement, with or without provision for increases of specified amounts or percentages; or

(b) subject to adjustment in a specified manner so as to preserve their real value; or

(c) partly specified as mentioned in paragraph (a) above and partly subject to adjustment as mentioned in paragraph (b) above.

(4) The annuity or annuities must be such as to provide the annuitant with sums which as to amount and time of payment correspond to the periodical payments described in the agreement.

(5) Payments in respect of the annuity or annuities may be received on behalf of the annuitant by another person or received and held on trust for his benefit under a trust of which he is, during his lifetime, the sole beneficiary.

(6) The Lord Chancellor may by an order made by statutory instrument provide that there shall for the purposes of this section be treated as an insurer any body specified in the order, being a body which, though not an insurer, appears to him to fulfil corresponding functions in relation to damages for personal injury claimed or awarded against persons of any class or description, and the reference in subsection (1)(b) above to a person being insured against the claim and his insurer shall be construed accordingly. ...

(8) Where –

(a) an agreement is made settling a claim or action for damages for personal injury on terms whereby the damages are to consist wholly or partly of periodical payments;

(b) the person against whom the claim or action is brought (or, if he is insured against the claim, his insurer) purchases one or more annuities; and

(c) a subsequent agreement is made under which the annuity is, or the annuities are, assigned in favour of the person entitled to the payments (so as to secure that from a future date he receives the payments as the annuitant under the annuity or annuities),

then, for the purposes of section 4 above, the agreement settling the claim or action shall be treated as a structured settlement and any such annuity assigned in favour of that person shall be treated as an annuity purchased for him pursuant to the settlement.

(9) Subsections (2) to (7) [Scotland] above shall apply to an agreement to which subsection (8) above applies as they apply to a structured settlement as defined in subsection (1) above (the reference in subsection (6) to subsection (1)(b) being read as a reference to subsection (8)(b)).

See Appendix, Courts Act 2003, s101(1).

6   Guarantees for public sector settlements

(1) This section applies where –

(a) a claim or action for damages for personal injury is settled on terms corresponding to those of a structured settlement as defined in section 5 above except that the person to whom the payments are to be made is not to receive them as mentioned in subsection (1)(b) of that section; or

(b) a court awarding damages for personal injury makes an order incorporating such terms.

(2) If it appears to a Minister of the Crown that the payments are to be made by a body in relation to which he has, by virtue of this section, power to do so, he may guarantee the payments to be made under the agreement or order.

(3) The bodies in relation to which a Minister may give such a guarantee shall, subject to subsection (4) below, be such bodies as are designated in relation to the relevant government department by guidelines agreed upon between that department and the Treasury.

(4) A guarantee purporting to be given by a Minister under this section shall not be invalidated by any failure on his part to act in accordance with such guidelines as are mentioned in subsection (3) above.

(5) A guarantee under this section shall be given on such terms as the Minister concerned may determine but those terms shall in every case require the body in question to reimburse the Minister, with interest, for any sums paid by him in fulfilment of the guarantee.

(6) Any sums required by a Minister for fulfilling a guarantee under this section shall be defrayed out of money provided by Parliament and any sums received by him by way of reimbursement or interest shall be paid into the Consolidated Fund.

(7) A Minister who has given one or more guarantees under this section shall, as soon as possible after the end of each financial year, lay before each House of Parliament a statement showing what liabilities are outstanding in respect of the guarantees in that year, what sums have been paid in that year in fulfilment of the guarantees and what sums (including interest) have been recovered in that year in respect of the guarantees or are still owing.

(8) In this section 'government department' means any department of Her Majesty's government in the United Kingdom and for the purposes of this section a government department is a relevant department in relation to a Minister if he has responsibilities in respect of that department. ...

See Appendix, Courts Act 2003, s101(2).

7   Interpretation

(1) Subject to subsection (2) below, in this Act 'personal injury' includes any disease and any impairment of a person's physical or mental condition and references to a claim or action for personal injury include references to such a claim or action brought by virtue of the Law Reform (Miscellaneous Provisions) Act 1934 and to a claim or action brought by virtue of the Fatal Accidents Act 1976. ...

As amended by the Financial Services and Markets Act 2000 (Consequential Amendments and Repeals) Order 2001, art 350.

HOUSING GRANTS, CONSTRUCTION AND REGENERATION ACT 1996

(1996 c 53)

PART II

CONSTRUCTION CONTRACTS

104 Construction contracts

(1) In this Part a 'construction contract' means an agreement with a person for any of the following –

(a) the carrying out of construction operations;

(b) arranging for the carrying out of construction operations by others, whether under sub-contract to him or otherwise;

(c) providing his own labour, or the labour of others, for the carrying out of construction operations.

(2) References in this Part to a construction contract include an agreement –

(a) to do architectural, design, or surveying work, or

(b) to provide advice on building, engineering, interior or exterior decoration or on the laying-out of landscape, in relation to construction operations.

(3) References in this Part to a construction contract do not include a contract of employment (within the meaning of the Employment Rights Act 1996).

(5) Where an agreement relates to construction operations and other matters, this Part applies to it only so far as it relates to construction operations. An agreement relates to construction operations so far as it makes provision of any kind within subsection (1) or (2).

(6) This Part applies only to construction contracts which –

(a) are entered into after the commencement of this Part, and

(b) relate to the carrying out of construction operations in England, Wales or Scotland.

(7) This Part applies whether or not the law of England and Wales or Scotland is otherwise the applicable law in relation to the contract.

105 Meaning of 'construction operations'

(1) In this Part 'construction operations' means, subject as follows, operations of any of the following descriptions –

(a) construction, alteration, repair, maintenance, extension, demolition or dismantling of buildings, or structures forming, or to form, part of the land (whether permanent or not);

(b) construction, alteration, repair, maintenance, extension, demolition or dismantling of any works forming, or to form, part of the land, including (without prejudice to the foregoing) walls, roadworks, power-lines, electronic communications apparatus, aircraft runways, docks and harbours, railways, inland waterways, pipe-lines, reservoirs, water-mains, wells, sewers, industrial plant and installations for purposes of land drainage, coast protection or defence;

(c) installation in any building or structure of fittings forming part of the land, including (without prejudice to the foregoing) systems of heating, lighting, air-conditioning, ventilation, power supply, drainage, sanitation, water supply or fire protection, or security or communications systems;

(d) external or internal cleaning of buildings and structures, so far as carried out in the course of their construction, alteration, repair, extension or restoration;

(e) operations which form an integral part of, or are preparatory to, or are for rendering complete, such operations as are previously described in this subsection, including site clearance, earth-moving, excavation, tunnelling and boring, laying of foundations, erection, maintenance or dismantling of scaffolding, site restoration, landscaping and the provision of roadways and other access works;

(f) painting or decorating the internal or external surfaces of any building or structure.

(2) The following operations are not construction operations within the meaning of this Part –

(a) drilling for, or extraction of, oil or natural gas;

(b) extraction (whether by underground or surface working) of minerals; tunnelling or boring, or construction of underground works, for this purpose;

(c) assembly, installation or demolition of plant or machinery, or erection or demolition of steelwork for the purposes of supporting or providing access to plant or machinery, on a site where the primary activity is –

(i) nuclear processing, power generation, or water or effluent treatment, or

(ii) the production, transmission, processing or bulk storage (other than warehousing) of chemicals, pharmaceuticals, oil, gas, steel or food and drink; Housing Grants, Construction and Regeneration Act 1996, s 105

(d) manufacture or delivery to site of –

(i) building or engineering components or equipment,

(ii) materials, plant or machinery, or

(iii) components for systems of heating, lighting, air-conditioning, ventilation, power supply, drainage, sanitation, water supply or fire protection, or for security or communications systems,

except under a contract which also provides for their installation;

(e) the making, installation and repair of artistic works, being sculptures, murals and other works which are wholly artistic in nature. ...

106 Provisions not applicable to contract with residential occupier

(1) This Part does not apply –

(a) to a construction contract with a residential occupier (see below), or

(b) to any other description of construction contract excluded from the operation of this Part by order of the Secretary of State.

(2) A construction contract with a residential occupier means a construction contract which principally relates to operations on a dwelling which one of the parties to the contract occupies, or intends to occupy, as his residence. In this subsection 'dwelling' means a dwelling-house or a flat; and for this purpose –

'dwelling-house' does not include a building containing a flat; and

'flat' means separate and self-contained premises constructed or adapted for use for residential purposes and forming part of a building from some other part of which the premises are divided horizontally. ...

107 Provisions applicable only to agreements in writing

(1) The provisions of this Part apply only where the construction contract is in writing, and any other agreement between the parties as to any matter is effective for the purposes of this Part only if in writing. The expressions 'agreement', 'agree' and 'agreed' shall be construed accordingly.

(2) There is an agreement in writing –

(a) if the agreement is made in writing (whether or not it is signed by the parties),

(b) if the agreement is made by exchange of communications in writing, or

(c) if the agreement is evidenced in writing.

(3) Where parties agree otherwise than in writing by reference to terms which are in writing, they make an agreement in writing.

(4) An agreement is evidenced in writing if an agreement made otherwise than in writing is recorded by one of the parties, or by a third party, with the authority of the parties to the agreement.

(5) An exchange of written submissions in adjudication proceedings, or in arbitral or legal proceedings in which the existence of an agreement otherwise than in writing is alleged by one party against another party and not denied by the other

party in his response constitutes as between those parties an agreement in writing to the effect alleged.

(6) References in this Part to anything being written or in writing include its being recorded by any means.

108 Right to refer disputes to adjudication

(1) A party to a construction contract has the right to refer a dispute arising under the contract for adjudication under a procedure complying with this section. For this purpose 'dispute' includes any difference. ...

(3) The contract shall provide that the decision of the adjudicator is binding until the dispute is finally determined by legal proceedings, by arbitration (if the contract provides for arbitration or the parties otherwise agree to arbitration) or by agreement. The parties may agree to accept the decision of the adjudicator as finally determining the dispute. ...

109 Entitlement to stage payments

(1) A party to a construction contract is entitled to payment by instalments, stage payments or other periodic payments for any work under the contract unless –

(a) it is specified in the contract that the duration of the work is to be less than 45 days, or

(b) it is agreed between the parties that the duration of the work is estimated to be less than 45 days.

(2) The parties are free to agree the amounts of the payments and the intervals at which, or circumstances in which, they become due.

(3) In the absence of such agreement, the relevant provisions of the Scheme for Construction Contracts apply.

(4) References in the following sections to a payment under the contract include a payment by virtue of this section.

110 Dates for payment

(1) Every construction contract shall –

(a) provide an adequate mechanism for determining what payments become due under the contract, and when, and

(b) provide for a final date for payment in relation to any sum which becomes due.

The parties are free to agree how long the period is to be between the date on which a sum becomes due and the final date for payment.

(2) Every construction contract shall provide for the giving of notice by a party not later than five days after the date on which a payment becomes due from him under the contract, or would have become due if –

(a) the other party had carried out his obligations under the contract, and

(b) no set-off or abatement was permitted by reference to any sum claimed to be due under one or more other contracts,

specifying the amount (if any) of the payment made or proposed to be made, and the basis on which that amount was calculated.

(3) If or to the extent that a contract does not contain such provision as is mentioned in subsection (1) or (2), the relevant provisions of the Scheme for Construction Contracts apply.

111 Notice of intention to withhold payment

(1) A party to a construction contract may not withhold payment after the final date for payment of a sum due under the contract unless he has given an effective notice of intention to withhold payment. The notice mentioned in section 110(2) may suffice as a notice of intention to withhold payment if it complies with the requirements of this section.

(2) To be effective such a notice must specify –

(a) the amount proposed to be withheld and the ground for withholding payment, or

(b) if there is more than one ground, each ground and the amount attributable to it,

and must be given not later than the prescribed period before the final date for payment.

(3) The parties are free to agree what that prescribed period is to be. In the absence of such agreement, the period shall be that provided by the Scheme for Construction Contracts.

(4) Where an effective notice of intention to withhold payment is given, but on the matter being referred to adjudication it is decided that the whole or part of the amount should be paid, the decision shall be construed as requiring payment not later than –

(a) seven days from the date of the decision, or

(b) the date which apart from the notice would have been the final date for payment,

whichever is the later.

112 Right to suspend performance for non-payment

(1) Where a sum due under a construction contract is not paid in full by the final date for payment and no effective notice to withhold payment has been given, the person to whom the sum is due has the right (without prejudice to any other right or remedy) to suspend performance of his obligations under the contract to the party by whom payment ought to have been made ('the party in default').

(2) The right may not be exercised without first giving to the party in default at least seven days' notice of intention to suspend performance, stating the ground or grounds on which it is intended to suspend performance.

(3) The right to suspend performance ceases when the party in default makes payment in full of the amount due.

(4) Any period during which performance is suspended in pursuance of the right conferred by this section shall be disregarded in computing for the purposes of any contractual time limit the time taken, by the party exercising the right or by a third party, to complete any work directly or indirectly affected by the exercise of the right. Where the contractual time limit is set by reference to a date rather than a period, the date shall be adjusted accordingly.

113   Prohibition of conditional payment provisions

(1) A provision making payment under a construction contract conditional on the payer receiving payment from a third person is ineffective, unless that third person, or any other person payment by whom is under the contract (directly or indirectly) a condition of payment by that third person, is insolvent. ...

(6) Where a provision is rendered ineffective by subsection (1), the parties are free to agree other terms for payment. In the absence of such agreement, the relevant provisions of the Scheme for

114   The Scheme for Construction Contracts

(1) The Minister shall by regulations make a scheme ('the Scheme for Construction Contracts') containing provision about the matters referred to in the preceding provisions of this Part. ...

(4) Where any provisions of the Scheme for Construction Contracts apply by virtue of this Part in default of contractual provision agreed by the parties, they have effect as implied terms of the contract concerned. ...

116   Reckoning periods of time

(1) For the purposes of this Part periods of time shall be reckoned as follows.

(2) Where an act is required to be done within a specified period after or from a specified date, the period begins immediately after that date.

(3) Where the period would include Christmas Day, Good Friday or a day which under the Banking and Financial Dealings Act 1971 is a bank holiday in England and Wales or, as the case may be, in Scotland, that day shall be excluded.

117   Crown application

(1) This Part applies to a construction contract entered into by or on behalf of the Crown otherwise than by or on behalf of Her Majesty in her private capacity. ...

As amended by the Communications Act 2003, s406(1), Schedule 17, para 137.

SOCIAL SECURITY (RECOVERY OF BENEFITS) ACT 1997

(1997 c 27)

1   Cases in which this Act applies

(1) This Act applies in cases where –

(a) a person makes a payment (whether on his own behalf or not) to or in respect of any other person in consequence of any accident, injury or disease suffered by the other, and

(b) any listed benefits have been, or are likely to be, paid to or for the other during the relevant period in respect of the accident, injury or disease.

(2) The reference above to a payment in consequence of any accident, injury or disease is to a payment made –

(a) by or on behalf of a person who is, or is alleged to be, liable to any extent in respect of the accident, injury or disease, or

(b) in pursuance of a compensation scheme for motor accidents;

but does not include a payment mentioned in Part I of Schedule 1.

(3) Subsection (1)(a) applies to a payment made –

(a) voluntarily, or in pursuance of a court order or an agreement, or otherwise, and

(b) in the United Kingdom or elsewhere.

(4) In a case where this Act applies –

(a) the 'injured person' is the person who suffered the accident, injury or disease,

(b) the 'compensation payment' is the payment within subsection (1)(a), and

(c) 'recoverable benefit' is any listed benefit which has been or is likely to be paid as mentioned in subsection (1)(b).

2   Compensation payments to which this Act applies

This Act applies in relation to compensation payments made on or after the day on which this section comes into force, unless they are made in pursuance of a court order or agreement made before that day.

3 'The relevant period'

(1) In relation to a person ('the claimant') who has suffered any accident, injury or disease, 'the relevant period' has the meaning given by the following subsections.

(2) Subject to subsection (4), if it is a case of accident or injury, the relevant period is the period of five years immediately following the day on which the accident or injury in question occurred.

(3) Subject to subsection (4), if it is a case of disease, the relevant period is the period of five years beginning with the date on which the claimant first claims a listed benefit in consequence of the disease.

(4) If at any time before the end of the period referred to in subsection (2) or (3) –

(a) a person makes a compensation payment in final discharge of any claim made by or in respect of the claimant and arising out of the accident, injury or disease, or

(b) an agreement is made under which an earlier compensation payment is treated as having been made in final discharge of any such claim,

the relevant period ends at that time.

4 Applications for certificates of recoverable benefits

(1) Before a person ('the compensator') makes a compensation payment he must apply to the Secretary of State for a certificate of recoverable benefits.

(2) Where the compensator applies for a certificate of recoverable benefits, the Secretary of State must –

(a) send to him a written acknowledgement of receipt of his application, and

(b) subject to subsection (7), issue the certificate before the end of the following period.

(3) The period is –

(a) the prescribed period, or

(b) if there is no prescribed period, the period of four weeks,

which begins with the day following the day on which the application is received.

(4) The certificate is to remain in force until the date specified in it for that purpose.

(5) The compensator may apply for fresh certificates from time to time.

(6) Where a certificate of recoverable benefits ceases to be in force, the Secretary of State may issue a fresh certificate without an application for one being made.

(7) Where the compensator applies for a fresh certificate while a certificate ('the existing certificate') remains in force, the Secretary of State must issue the fresh certificate before the end of the following period.

(8) The period is –

(a) the prescribed period, or

(b) if there is no prescribed period, the period of four weeks,

which begins with the day following the day on which the existing certificate ceases to be in force.

(9) For the purposes of this Act, regulations may provide for the day on which an application for a certificate of recoverable benefits is to be treated as received.

5   Information contained in certificates

(1) A certificate of recoverable benefits must specify, for each recoverable benefit –

(a) the amount which has been or is likely to have been paid on or before a specified date, and

(b) if the benefit is paid or likely to be paid after the specified date, the rate and period for which, and the intervals at which, it is or is likely to be so paid.

(2) In a case where the relevant period has ended before the day on which the Secretary of State receives the application for the certificate, the date specified in the certificate for the purposes of subsection (1) must be the day on which the relevant period ended.

(3) In any other case, the date specified for those purposes must not be earlier than the day on which the Secretary of State received the application.

(4) The Secretary of State may estimate, in such manner as he thinks fit, any of the amounts, rates or periods specified in the certificate.

(5) Where the Secretary of State issues a certificate of recoverable benefits, he must provide the information contained in the certificate to –

(a) the person who appears to him to be the injured person, or

(b) any person who he thinks will receive a compensation payment in respect of the injured person.

(6) A person to whom a certificate of recoverable benefits is issued or who is provided with information under subsection (5) is entitled to particulars of the manner in which any amount, rate or period specified in the certificate has been determined, if he applies to the Secretary of State for those particulars.

6   Liability to pay Secretary of State amount of benefits

(1) A person who makes a compensation payment in any case is liable to pay to the Secretary of State an amount equal to the total amount of the recoverable benefits.

(2) The liability referred to in subsection (1) arises immediately before the compensation payment or, if there is more than one, the first of them is made.

(3) No amount becomes payable under this section before the end of the period of 14 days following the day on which the liability arises.

(4) Subject to subsection (3), an amount becomes payable under this section at the end of the period of 14 days beginning with the day on which a certificate of

recoverable benefits is first issued showing that the amount of recoverable benefit to which it relates has been or is likely to have been paid before a specified date.

7 Recovery of payments due under section 6

(1) This section applies where a person has made a compensation payment but –

(a) has not applied for a certificate of recoverable benefits, or

(b) has not made a payment to the Secretary of State under section 6 before the end of the period allowed under that section.

(2) The Secretary of State may –

(a) issue the person who made the compensation payment with a certificate of recoverable benefits, if none has been issued, or

(b) issue him with a copy of the certificate of recoverable benefits or (if more than one has been issued) the most recent one,

and (in either case) issue him with a demand that payment of any amount due under section 6 be made immediately.

(3) The Secretary of State may, in accordance with subsections (4) and (5), recover the amount for which a demand for payment is made under subsection (2) from the person who made the compensation payment.

(4) If the person who made the compensation payment resides or carries on business in England and Wales and a county court so orders, any amount recoverable under subsection (3) is recoverable by execution issued from the county court or otherwise as if it were payable under an order of that court.

(5) If the person who made the payment resides or carries on business in Scotland, any amount recoverable under subsection (3) may be enforced in like manner as an extract registered decree arbitral bearing a warrant for execution issued by the sheriff court of any sheriffdom in Scotland.

(6) A document bearing a certificate which –

(a) is signed by a person authorised to do so by the Secretary of State, and

(b) states that the document, apart from the certificate, is a record of the amount recoverable under subsection (3),

is conclusive evidence that that amount is so recoverable.

(7) A certificate under subsection (6) purporting to be signed by a person authorised to do so by the Secretary of State is to be treated as so signed unless the contrary is proved.

8 Reduction of compensation payment

(1) This section applies in a case where, in relation to any head of compensation listed in column 1 of Schedule 2 –

(a) any of the compensation payment is attributable to that head, and

(b) any recoverable benefit is shown against that head in column 2 of the Schedule.

(2) In such a case, any claim of a person to receive the compensation payment is to be treated for all purposes as discharged if –

(a) he is paid the amount (if any) of the compensation payment calculated in accordance with this section, and

(b) if the amount of the compensation payment so calculated is nil, he is given a statement saying so by the person who (apart from this section) would have paid the gross amount of the compensation payment.

(3) For each head of compensation listed in column 1 of the Schedule for which paragraphs (a) and (b) of subsection (1) are met, so much of the gross amount of the compensation payment as is attributable to that head is to be reduced (to nil, if necessary) by deducting the amount of the recoverable benefit or, as the case may be, the aggregate amount of the recoverable benefits shown against it.

(4) Subsection (3) is to have effect as if a requirement to reduce a payment by deducting an amount which exceeds that payment were a requirement to reduce that payment to nil.

(5) The amount of the compensation payment calculated in accordance with this section is –

(a) the gross amount of the compensation payment, less

(b) the sum of the reductions made under subsection (3),

(and, accordingly, the amount may be nil).

9   Section 8: supplementary

(1) A person who makes a compensation payment calculated in accordance with section 8 must inform the person to whom the payment is made –

(a) that the payment has been so calculated, and

(b) of the date for payment by reference to which the calculation has been made.

(2) If the amount of a compensation payment calculated in accordance with section 8 is nil, a person giving a statement saying so is to be treated for the purposes of this Act as making a payment within section 1(1)(a) on the day on which he gives the statement.

(3) Where a person –

(a) makes a compensation payment calculated in accordance with section 8, and

(b) if the amount of the compensation payment so calculated is nil, gives a statement saying so,

he is to be treated, for the purpose of determining any rights and liabilities in respect of contribution or indemnity, as having paid the gross amount of the compensation payment.

(4) For the purposes of this Act –

(a) the gross amount of the compensation payment is the amount of the compensation payment apart from section 8, and

(b) the amount of any recoverable benefit is the amount determined in accordance with the certificate of recoverable benefits.

10   Review of certificates of recoverable benefits

(1) Any certificate of recoverable benefits may be reviewed by the Secretary of State –

(a) either within the prescribed period or in prescribed cases or circumstances; and

(b) either on an application made for the purpose or on his own initiative.

(2) On a review under this section the Secretary of State may either –

(a) confirm the certificate, or

(b) (subject to subsection (3)) issue a fresh certificate containing such variations as he considers appropriate, or

(c) revoke the certificate.

(3) The Secretary of State may not vary the certificate so as to increase the total amount of the recoverable benefits unless it appears to him that the variation is required as a result of the person who applied for the certificate supplying him with incorrect or insufficient information.

11   Appeals against certificates of recoverable benefits

(1) An appeal against a certificate of recoverable benefits may be made on the ground –

(a) that any amount, rate or period specified in the certificate is incorrect, or

(b) that listed benefits which have been, or are likely to be, paid otherwise than in respect of the accident, injury or disease in question have been brought into account, or

(c) that listed benefits which have not been, and are not likely to be, paid to the injured person during the relevant period have been brought into account, or

(d) that the payment on the basis of which the certificate was issued is not a payment within section 1(1)((a).

(2) An appeal under this section may be made by –

(a) the person who applied for the certificate of recoverable benefits, or

(aa) (in a case where that certificate was issued under section 7(2)(a)) the person to whom it was so issued, or

(b) (in a case where the amount of the compensation payment has been calculated under section 8) the injured person or other person to whom the payment is made.

(3) No appeal may be made under this section until –

(a) the claim giving rise to the compensation payment has been finally disposed of, and

(b) the liability under section 6 has been discharged.

(4) For the purposes of subsection (3)(a), if an award of damages in respect of a claim has been made under or by virtue of –

(a) section 32A(2)(a) of the Supreme Court Act 1981,

(b) section 12(2)(a) of the Administration of Justice Act 1982, or

(c) section 51(2)(a) of the County Courts Act 1984,

(orders for provisional damages in personal injury cases), the claim is to be treated as having been finally disposed of. ...

12   Reference of questions to medical appeal tribunal

(1) The Secretary of State must refer an appeal under section 11 to an appeal tribunal.

(3) In determining any appeal under section 11, the tribunal must take into account any decision of a court relating to the same, or any similar, issue arising in connection with the accident, injury or disease in question. ...

13   Appeal to Social Security Commissioner

(1) An appeal may be made to a Commissioner against any decision of an appeal tribunal under section 12 on the ground that the decision was erroneous in point of law.

(2) An appeal under this section may be made by –

(a) the Secretary of State,

(b) the person who applied for the certificate of recoverable benefits,

(bb) (in a case where that certificate was issued under section 7(2)(a)) the person to whom it was so issued, or

(c) (in a case where the amount of the compensation payment has been calculated in accordance with section 8) the injured person or other person to whom the payment is made. ...

15   Court orders

(1) This section applies where a court makes an order for a compensation payment to be made in any case, unless the order is made with the consent of the injured person and the person by whom the payment is to be made.

(2) The court must, in the case of each head of compensation listed in column 1 of

Schedule 2 to which any of the compensation payment is attributable, specify in the order the amount of the compensation payment which is attributable to that head.

17 Benefits irrelevant to assessment of damages

In assessing damages in respect of any accident, injury or disease, the amount of any listed benefits paid or likely to be paid is to be disregarded.

21 Compensation payments to be disregarded

(1) If, when a compensation payment is made, the first and second conditions are met, the payment is to be disregarded for the purposes of sections 6 and 8.

(2) The first condition is that the person making the payment –

(a) has made an application for a certificate of recoverable benefits which complies with subsection (3), and

(b) has in his possession a written acknowledgment of the receipt of his application.

(3) An application complies with this subsection if it –

(a) accurately states the prescribed particulars relating to the injured person and the accident, injury or disease in question, and

(b) specifies the name and address of the person to whom the certificate is to be sent.

(4) The second condition is that the Secretary of State has not sent the certificate to the person, at the address, specified in the application, before the end of the period allowed under section 4.

(5) In any case where –

(a) by virtue of subsection (1), a compensation payment is disregarded for the purposes of sections 6 and 8, but

(b) the person who made the compensation payment nevertheless makes a payment to the Secretary of State for which (but for subsection (1)) he would be liable under section 6,

subsection (1) is to cease to apply in relation to the compensation payment.

(6) If, in the opinion of the Secretary of State, circumstances have arisen which adversely affect normal methods of communication –

(a) he may by order provide that subsection (1) is not to apply during a specified period not exceeding three months, and

(b) he may continue any such order in force for further periods not exceeding three months at a time.

22 Liability of insurers

(1) If a compensation payment is made in a case where –

(a) a person is liable to any extent in respect of the accident, injury or disease, and

(b) the liability is covered to any extent by a policy of insurance,

the policy is also to be treated as covering any liability of that person under section 6.

(2) Liability imposed on the insurer by subsection (1) cannot be excluded or restricted.

(3) For that purpose excluding or restricting liability includes –

(a) making the liability or its enforcement subject to restrictive or onerous conditions,

(b) excluding or restricting any right or remedy in respect of the liability, or subjecting a person to any prejudice in consequence of his pursuing any such right or remedy, or

(c) excluding or restricting rules of evidence or procedure. ...

28   The Crown

This Act applies to the Crown.

29   General interpretation

In this Act –

'appeal tribunal' means an appeal tribunal constituted under Chapter I of Part I of the Social Security Act 1998;

'benefit' means any benefit under the Social Security Contributions and Benefits Act 1992, a jobseeker's allowance or mobility allowance,

'Commissioner' has the same meaning as in Chapter II of Part I of the Social Security Act 1998 (see section 39);

'compensation scheme for motor accidents' means any scheme or arrangement under which funds are available for the payment of compensation in respect of motor accidents caused, or alleged to have been caused, by uninsured or unidentified persons;

'listed benefit' means a benefit listed in column 2 of Schedule 2;

'payment' means payment in money or money's worth, and related expressions are to be interpreted accordingly;

'prescribed' means prescribed by regulations; and

'regulations' means regulations made by the Secretary of State.

SCHEDULE 1

COMPENSATION PAYMENTS

PART I

EXEMPTED PAYMENTS

1. Any small payment (defined in Part II of this Schedule).

2. Any payment made to or for the injured person under section 130 of the Powers of Criminal Courts (Sentencing) Act 2000 … (compensation orders against convicted persons). …

5. – (1) Any payment made to the injured person by an insurer under the terms of any contract of insurance entered into between the injured person and the insurer before –

    (a) the date on which the injured person first claims a listed benefit in consequence of the disease in question, or

    (b) the occurrence of the accident or injury in question.

(2) 'Insurer' means –

    (a) a person who has permission under Part 4 of the Financial Services and Markets Act 2000 to effect or carry out contracts of insurance; or

    (b) an EEA firm of the kind mentioned in paragraph 5(d) of Schedule 3 to that Act which has permission under paragraph 15 of that Schedule (as a result of qualifying for authorisation under paragraph 12 of that Schedule) to effect or carry out contracts of insurance.

(3) Sub-paragraph (2) must be read with –

    (a) section 22 of the Financial Services and Markets Act 2000;

    (b) any relevant order under that section; and

    (c) Schedule 2 to that Act.

6. Any redundancy payment falling to be taken into account in the assessment of damages in respect of an accident, injury or disease.

7. So much of any payment as is referable to costs.

8. Any prescribed payment.

PART II

POWER TO DISREGARD SMALL PAYMENTS

9. – (1) Regulations may make provision for compensation payments to be disregarded for the purposes of sections 6 and 8 in prescribed cases where the amount of the compensation payment, or the aggregate amount of two or more connected compensation payments, does not exceed the prescribed sum.

(2) A compensation payment disregarded by virtue of this paragraph is referred to in paragraph 1 as a 'small payment'.

(3) For the purposes of this paragraph –

(a) two or more compensation payments are 'connected' if each is made to or in respect of the same injured person and in respect of the same accident, injury or disease, and

(b) any reference to a compensation payment is a reference to a payment which would be such a payment apart from paragraph 1.

SCHEDULE 2

CALCULATION OF COMPENSATION PAYMENT

(1) Head of compensation	(2) Benefit
1. Compensation for earnings lost during the relevant period	Disablement pension payable under section 103 of the 1992 Act Incapacity benefit Income support Invalidity pension and allowance Jobseeker's allowance Reduced earnings allowance Severe disablement allowance Sickness benefit Statutory sick pay Unemployability supplement Unemployment benefit
2. Compensation for cost of care incurred during the relevant period	Attendance allowance Care component of disability living allowance Disablement pension increase payable under section 104 or 105 of the 1992 Act
3. Compensation for loss of mobility during the relevant period	Mobility allowance Mobility component of disability living allowance

NOTES

1. – (1) References to incapacity benefit, invalidity pension and allowance, severe disablement allowance, sickness benefit and unemployment benefit also include any income support paid with each of those benefits on the same instrument of payment or paid concurrently with each of those benefits by means of an instrument for benefit payment.

(2) For the purpose of this Note, income support includes personal expenses addition, special transitional additions and transitional addition as defined in the Income Support (Transitional) Regulations 1987.

2. Any reference to statutory sick pay –

(a) includes only 80 per cent. of payments made between 6th April 1991 and 5th April 1994, and

(b) does not include payments made on or after 6th April 1994.

3. In this Schedule 'the 1992 Act' means the Social Security Contributions and Benefits Act 1992.

As amended by the Social Security Act 1998, s86(1), Schedule 7, paras 149–153; Tax Credits Act 1999, ss2(3), 19(4), Schedule 2, Pt IV, para 18(1)(a), (2), Schedule 6; Powers of Criminal Courts (Sentencing) Act 2000, s165(1), Schedule 9, para 181; Financial Services and Markets Act 2000 (Consequential Amendments and Repeals) Order 2001, art 358.

PROTECTION FROM HARASSMENT ACT 1997
(1997 c 40)

1 Prohibition of harassment

(1) A person must not pursue a course of conduct –

(a) which amounts to harassment of another, and

(b) which he knows or ought to know amounts to harassment of the other.

(2) For the purposes of this section, the person whose course of conduct is in question ought to know that it amounts to harassment of another if a reasonable person in possession of the same information would think the course of conduct amounted to harassment of the other.

(3) Subsection (1) does not apply to a course of conduct if the person who pursued it shows –

(a) that it was pursued for the purpose of preventing or detecting crime,

(b) that it was pursued under any enactment or rule of law or to comply with any condition or requirement imposed by any person under any enactment, or

(c) that in the particular circumstances the pursuit of the course of conduct was reasonable.

3 Civil remedy

(1) An actual or apprehended breach of section 1 may be the subject of a claim in civil proceedings by the person who is or may be the victim of the course of conduct in question.

(2) On such a claim, damages may be awarded for (among other things) any anxiety caused by the harassment and any financial loss resulting from the harassment.

(3) Where –

(a) in such proceedings the High Court or a county court grants an injunction for the purpose of restraining the defendant from pursuing any conduct which amounts to harassment, and

(b) the plaintiff considers that the defendant has done anything which he is prohibited from doing by the injunction,

the plaintiff may apply for the issue of a warrant for the arrest of the defendant. ...

7   Interpretation of this group of sections

(1) This section applies for the interpretation of sections 1 to 5.

(2) References to harassing a person include alarming the person or causing the person distress.

(3) A 'course of conduct' must involve conduct on at least two occasions.

(3A) A person's conduct on any occasion shall be taken, if aided, abetted, counselled or procured by another –

(a) to be conduct on that occasion of the other (as well as conduct of the person whose conduct it is); and

(b) to be conduct in relation to which the other's knowledge and purpose, and what he ought to have known, are the same as they were in relation to what was contemplated or reasonably foreseeable at the time of the aiding, abetting, counselling or procuring.

(4) 'Conduct' includes speech.

As amended by the Criminal Justice and Police Act 2001, s44.

LATE PAYMENT OF COMMERCIAL DEBTS (INTEREST) ACT 1998

(1998 c 20)

PART I

STATUTORY INTEREST ON QUALIFYING DEBTS

1 Statutory interest

(1) It is an implied term in a contract to which this Act applies that any qualifying debt created by the contract carries simple interest subject to and in accordance with this Part.

(2) Interest carried under that implied term (in this Act referred to as 'statutory interest') shall be treated, for the purposes of any rule of law or enactment (other than this Act) relating to interest on debts, in the same way as interest carried under an express contract term.

(3) This Part has effect subject to Part II (which in certain circumstances permits contract terms to oust or vary the right to statutory interest that would otherwise be conferred by virtue of the term implied by subsection (1)).

2 Contracts to which Act applies

(1) This Act applies to a contract for the supply of goods or services where the purchaser and the supplier are each acting in the course of a business, other than an excepted contract.

(2) In this Act 'contract for the supply of goods or services' means –

(a) a contract of sale of goods; or

(b) a contract (other than a contract of sale of goods) by which a person does any, or any combination, of the things mentioned in subsection (3) for a consideration that is (or includes) a money consideration.

(3) Those things are –

(a) transferring or agreeing to transfer to another the property in goods;

(b) bailing or agreeing to bail goods to another by way of hire or, in Scotland, hiring or agreeing to hire goods to another; and

(c) agreeing to carry out a service.

(4) For the avoidance of doubt a contract of service or apprenticeship is not a contract for the supply of goods or services.

(5) The following are excepted contracts –

(a) a consumer credit agreement;

(b) a contract intended to operate by way of mortgage, pledge, charge or other security.

(7) In this section –

'business' includes a profession and the activities of any government department or local or public authority;

'consumer credit agreement' has the same meaning as in the Consumer Credit Act 1974;

'contract of sale of goods' and 'goods' have the same meaning as in the Sale of Goods Act 1979;

'government department' includes any part of the Scottish Administration;

'property in goods' means the general property in them and not merely a special property.

3   Qualifying debts

(1) A debt created by virtue of an obligation under a contract to which this Act applies to pay the whole or any part of the contract price is a 'qualifying debt' for the purposes of this Act, unless (when created) the whole of the debt is prevented from carrying statutory interest by this section.

(2) A debt does not carry statutory interest if or to the extent that it consists of a sum to which a right to interest or to charge interest applies by virtue of any enactment (other than section 1 of this Act). This subsection does not prevent a sum from carrying statutory interest by reason of the fact that a court, arbitrator or arbiter would, apart from this Act, have power to award interest on it.

(3) A debt does not carry (and shall be treated as never having carried) statutory interest if or to the extent that a right to demand interest on it, which exists by virtue of any rule of law, is exercised.

4   Period for which statutory interest runs

(1) Statutory interest runs in relation to a qualifying debt in accordance with this section (unless section 5 applies).

(2) Statutory interest starts to run on the day after the relevant day for the debt, at the rate prevailing under section 6 at the end of the relevant day.

(3) Where the supplier and the purchaser agree a date for payment of the debt (that is, the day on which the debt is to be created by the contract), that is the relevant day unless the debt relates to an obligation to make an advance payment. A date so agreed may be a fixed one or may depend on the happening of an event or the failure of an event to happen.

(4) Where the debt relates to an obligation to make an advance payment, the relevant day is the day on which the debt is treated by section 11 as having been created.

(5) In any other case, the relevant day is the last day of the period of 30 days beginning with –

(a) the day on which the obligation of the supplier to which the debt relates is performed; or

(b) the day on which the purchaser has notice of the amount of the debt or (where that amount is unascertained) the sum which the supplier claims is the amount of the debt,

whichever is the later.

(6) Where the debt is created by virtue of an obligation to pay a sum due in respect of a period of hire of goods, subsection (5)(a) has effect as if it referred to the last day of that period.

(7) Statutory interest ceases to run when the interest would cease to run if it were carried under an express contract term.

(8) In this section 'advance payment' has the same meaning as in section 11.

5   Remission of statutory interest

(1) This section applies where, by reason of any conduct of the supplier, the interests of justice require that statutory interest should be remitted in whole or part in respect of a period for which it would otherwise run in relation to a qualifying debt.

(2) If the interests of justice require that the supplier should receive no statutory interest for a period, statutory interest shall not run for that period.

(3) If the interests of justice require that the supplier should receive statutory interest at a reduced rate for a period, statutory interest shall run at such rate as meets the justice of the case for that period.

(4) Remission of statutory interest under this section may be required –

(a) by reason of conduct at any time (whether before or after the time at which the debt is created); and

(b) for the whole period for which statutory interest would otherwise run or for one or more parts of that period.

(5) In this section 'conduct' includes any act or omission.

5A   Compensation arising out of late payment

(1) Once statutory interest begins to run in relation to a qualifying debt, the supplier shall be entitled to a fixed sum (in addition to the statutory interest on the debt).

(2) That sum shall be –

(a) for a debt less than £1,000, the sum of £40;

(b) for a debt of £1,000 or more, but less than £10,000, the sum of £70;

(c) for a debt of £10,000 or more, the sum of £100.

(3) The obligation to pay an additional fixed sum under this section in respect of a qualifying debt shall be treated as part of the term implied by section 1(1) in the contract creating the debt.

6 Rate of statutory interest

(1) The Secretary of State shall by order made with the consent of the Treasury set the rate of statutory interest by prescribing –

(a) a formula for calculating the rate of statutory interest; or

(b) the rate of statutory interest.

(2) Before making such an order the Secretary of State shall, among other things, consider the extent to which it may be desirable to set the rate so as to –

(a) protect suppliers whose financial position makes them particularly vulnerable if their qualifying debts are paid late; and

(b) deter generally the late payment of qualifying debts.

PART II

CONTRACT TERMS RELATING TO LATE PAYMENT OF QUALIFYING DEBTS

7 Purpose of Part II

(1) This Part deals with the extent to which the parties to a contract to which this Act applies may by reference to contract terms oust or vary the right to statutory interest that would otherwise apply when a qualifying debt created by the contract (in this Part referred to as 'the debt') is not paid.

(2) This Part applies to contract terms agreed before the debt is created; after that time the parties are free to agree terms dealing with the debt.

(3) This Part has effect without prejudice to any other ground which may affect the validity of a contract term.

8 Circumstances where statutory interest may be ousted or varied

(1) Any contract terms are void to the extent that they purport to exclude the right to statutory interest in relation to the debt, unless there is a substantial contractual remedy for late payment of the debt.

(2) Where the parties agree a contractual remedy for late payment of the debt that is a substantial remedy, statutory interest is not carried by the debt (unless they agree otherwise).

(3) The parties may not agree to vary the right to statutory interest in relation to the debt unless either the right to statutory interest as varied or the overall remedy for late payment of the debt is a substantial remedy.

(4) Any contract terms are void to the extent that they purport to –

(a) confer a contractual right to interest that is not a substantial remedy for late payment of the debt, or

(b) vary the right to statutory interest so as to provide for a right to statutory interest that is not a substantial remedy for late payment of the debt,

unless the overall remedy for late payment of the debt is a substantial remedy.

(5) Subject to this section, the parties are free to agree contract terms which deal with the consequences of late payment of the debt.

9 Meaning of 'substantial remedy'

(1) A remedy for the late payment of the debt shall be regarded as a substantial remedy unless –

(a) the remedy is insufficient either for the purpose of compensating the supplier for late payment or for deterring late payment; and

(b) it would not be fair or reasonable to allow the remedy to be relied on to oust or (as the case may be) to vary the right to statutory interest that would otherwise apply in relation to the debt.

(2) In determining whether a remedy is not a substantial remedy, regard shall be had to all the relevant circumstances at the time the terms in question are agreed.

(3) In determining whether subsection (1)(b) applies, regard shall be had (without prejudice to the generality of subsection (2)) to the following matters –

(a) the benefits of commercial certainty;

(b) the strength of the bargaining positions of the parties relative to each other;

(c) whether the term was imposed by one party to the detriment of the other (whether by the use of standard terms or otherwise); and

(d) whether the supplier received an inducement to agree to the term.

10 Interpretation of Part II

(1) In this Part –

'contract term' means a term of the contract creating the debt or any other contract term binding the parties (or either of them);

'contractual remedy' means a contractual right to interest or any contractual remedy other than interest;

'contractual right to interest' includes a reference to a contractual right to charge interest;

'overall remedy', in relation to the late payment of the debt, means any combination of a contractual right to interest, a varied right to statutory interest or a contractual remedy other than interest;

'substantial remedy' shall be construed in accordance with section 9.

(2) In this Part a reference (however worded) to contract terms which vary the right to statutory interest is a reference to terms altering in any way the effect of Part I in relation to the debt (for example by postponing the time at which interest starts to run or by imposing conditions on the right to interest).

(3) In this Part a reference to late payment of the debt is a reference to late payment of the sum due when the debt is created (excluding any part of that sum which is prevented from carrying statutory interest by section 3).

PART III

GENERAL AND SUPPLEMENTARY

11   Treatment of advance payments of the contract price

(1) A qualifying debt created by virtue of an obligation to make an advance payment shall be treated for the purposes of this Act as if it was created on the day mentioned in subsection (3), (4) or (5) (as the case may be).

(2) In this section 'advance payment' means a payment falling due before the obligation of the supplier to which the whole contract price relates ('the supplier's obligation') is performed, other than a payment of a part of the contract price that is due in respect of any part performance of that obligation and payable on or after the day on which that part performance is completed.

(3) Where the advance payment is the whole contract price, the debt shall be treated as created on the day on which the supplier's obligation is performed.

(4) Where the advance payment is a part of the contract price, but the sum is not due in respect of any part performance of the supplier's obligation, the debt shall be treated as created on the day on which the supplier's obligation is performed.

(5) Where the advance payment is a part of the contract price due in respect of any part performance of the supplier's obligation, but is payable before that part performance is completed, the debt shall be treated as created on the day on which the relevant part performance is completed.

(6) Where the debt is created by virtue of an obligation to pay a sum due in respect of a period of hire of goods, this section has effect as if –

(a) references to the day on which the supplier's obligation is performed were references to the last day of that period; and

(b) references to part performance of that obligation were references to part of that period.

(7) For the purposes of this section an obligation to pay the whole outstanding balance of the contract price shall be regarded as an obligation to pay the whole contract price and not as an obligation to pay a part of the contract price.

12   Conflict of laws

(1) This Act does not have effect in relation to a contract governed by the law of a part of the United Kingdom by choice of the parties if –

(a) there is no significant connection between the contract and that part of the United Kingdom; and

(b) but for that choice, the applicable law would be a foreign law.

(2) This Act has effect in relation to a contract governed by a foreign law by choice of the parties if –

(a) but for that choice, the applicable law would be the law of a part of the United Kingdom; and

(b) there is no significant connection between the contract and any country other than that part of the United Kingdom.

(3) In this section –

'contract' means a contract falling within section 2(1); and

'foreign law' means the law of a country outside the United Kingdom.

13   Assignments, etc

(1) The operation of this Act in relation to a qualifying debt is not affected by –

(a) any change in the identity of the parties to the contract creating the debt; or

(b) the passing of the right to be paid the debt, or the duty to pay it (in whole or in part) to a person other than the person who is the original creditor or the original debtor when the debt is created.

(2) Any reference in this Act to the supplier or the purchaser is a reference to the person who is for the time being the supplier or the purchaser or, in relation to a time after the debt in question has been created, the person who is for the time being the creditor or the debtor, as the case may be.

(3) Where the right to be paid part of a debt passes to a person other than the person who is the original creditor when the debt is created, any reference in this Act to a debt shall be construed as (or, if the context so requires, as including) a reference to part of a debt.

(4) A reference in this section to the identity of the parties to a contract changing, or to a right or duty passing, is a reference to it changing or passing by assignment or assignation, by operation of law or otherwise.

14   Contract terms relating to the date for payment of the contract price

(1) This section applies to any contract term which purports to have the effect of postponing the time at which a qualifying debt would otherwise be created by a contract to which this Act applies.

(2) Sections 3(2)(b) and 17(1)(b) of the Unfair Contract Terms Act 1977 (no reliance to be placed on certain contract terms) shall apply in cases where such a contract term is not contained in written standard terms of the purchaser as well as in cases where the term is contained in such standard terms.

(3) In this section 'contract term' has the same meaning as in section 10(1).

16   Interpretation

(1) In this Act –

'contract for the supply of goods or services' has the meaning given in section 2(2);

'contract price' means the price in a contract of sale of goods or the money consideration referred to in section 2(2)(b) in any other contract for the supply of goods or services;

'purchaser' means (subject to section 13(2)) the buyer in a contract of sale or the person who contracts with the supplier in any other contract for the supply of goods or services;

'qualifying debt' means a debt falling within section 3(1);

'statutory interest' means interest carried by virtue of the term implied by section 1(1); and

'supplier' means (subject to section 13(2)) the seller in a contract of sale of goods or the person who does one or more of the things mentioned in section 2(3) in any other contract for the supply of goods or services.

(2) In this Act any reference (however worded) to an agreement or to contract terms includes a reference to both express and implied terms (including terms established by a course of dealing or by such usage as binds the parties).

17   Short title, commencement and extent ...

(2) This Act (apart from this section) shall come into force on such day as the Secretary of State may by order appoint; and different days may be appointed for different descriptions of contract or for other different purposes. An order under this subsection may specify a description of contract by reference to any feature of the contract (including the parties). ...

(4) This Act does not affect contracts of any description made before this Act comes into force for contracts of that description. ...

NB The Late Payment of Commercial Debts (Interest) Act 1998 (Commencement No 1) Order 1998 brought this Act into force on 1 November 1998 in relation to commercial contracts for the supply of goods or services where the supplier is a small business (50 or fewer full-time employees) and the purchaser is a large business (more than 50 full-time employees) or a United Kingdom public authority, eg a government department or a local authority.

The Late Payment of Commercial Debts (Interest) Act 1998 (Commencement No

2) Order 1999 extended the Act's provisions, with effect from 1 July 1999, to contracts between a small business supplier and, inter alia, the National Assembly for Wales and the Auditor General for Wales.

The Late Payment of Commercial Debts (Interest) Act 1998 (Commencement No 3) Order 2000 extended the Act's provisions, with effect from 1 September 2000, to contracts between a small business supplier and, inter alia, the Metropolitan Police Authority or the London Fire and Emergency Planning Authority.

The Late Payment of Commercial Debts (Interest) Act 1998 (Commencement No 4) Order 2000 extended the Act's provisions, with effect from 1 November 2000, to contracts between a small business supplier and a small business purchaser.

The Late Payment of Commercial Debts (Interest) Act 1998 (Commencement No 5) Order 2002 brought into force on 7 August 2002 the provisions of the Act which were not then in force.

As amended by the Scotland Act 1998 (Consequential Modifications) Order 1999, art 4, Schedule 2, Pt I, para 132; Late Payment of Commercial Debts Regulations 2002, reg 2(2)–(4).

GOVERNMENT OF WALES ACT 1998
(1998 c 38)

77   Defamation

(1) For the purposes of the law of defamation –

(a) any statement made in, for the purposes of or for purposes incidental to proceedings of the Assembly (including proceedings of a committee of the Assembly or of a sub-committee of such a committee), and

(b) the publication by or under the authority of the Assembly of a report of such proceedings,

is absolutely privileged.

(2) Subsection (1)(a) applies, in particular, to any statement made in –

(a) evidence given before the Assembly, a committee of the Assembly or a sub-committee of such a committee,

(b) a document laid before the Assembly or such a committee or sub-committee,

(c) a document prepared for the purposes of, or for the purposes incidental to, the transaction of business by the Assembly or such a committee or sub-committee,

(d) a document (other than a report to which subsection (1)(b) applies) formulated, made or published by or under the authority of the Assembly or such a committee or sub-committee,

(e) any communication –

(i) between any person and a person having functions in connection with the registration of interests of Assembly members, or

(ii) between any person and an Assembly member,

in connection with such registration, or

(f) any communication –

(i) between any person and a person having functions in connection with the investigation of complaints about actions or failures on the part of the Assembly, or

(ii) between any person and an Assembly member,

in connection with any such complaint.

(3) In subsections (1) and (2) 'statement' has the same meaning as in the Defamation Act 1996.

(4) The Assembly –

(a) is a legislature for the purposes of Schedule 1 to that Act (qualified privilege for fair and accurate report of public proceedings of legislatures etc), and

(b) shall be treated as if it were a Minister of the Crown for the purposes of paragraph 11(1)(c) of that Schedule (report of proceedings of person appointed by a Minister etc for the purposes of an inquiry).

(5) Section 10 of the Defamation Act 1952 ... (limitation on privilege at elections) [has] effect in relation to elections of Assembly members as to elections to Parliament.

NATIONAL MINIMUM WAGE ACT 1998
(1998 c 39)

1   Workers to be paid at least the national minimum wage

(1) A person who qualifies for the national minimum wage shall be remunerated by his employer in respect of his work in any pay reference period at a rate which is not less than the national minimum wage.

(2) A person qualifies for the national minimum wage if he is an individual who –

(a) is a worker;

(b) is working, or ordinarily works, in the United Kingdom under his contract; and

(c) has ceased to be of compulsory school age.

(3) The national minimum wage shall be such single hourly rate as the Secretary of State may from time to time prescribe.

(4) For the purposes of this Act a 'pay reference period' is such period as the Secretary of State may prescribe for the purpose.

(5) Subsections (1) to (4) above are subject to the following provisions of this Act.

49   Restrictions on contracting out

(1) Any provision in any agreement (whether a worker's contract or not) is void in so far as it purports –

(a) to exclude or limit the operation of any provision of this Act; or

(b) to preclude a person from bringing proceedings under this Act before an employment tribunal.

(2) Subsection (1) above does not apply [in certain situations] ...

HUMAN RIGHTS ACT 1998
(1998 c 42)

1   The Convention Rights

(1) In this Act 'the Convention rights' means the rights and fundamental freedoms set out in –

  (a) Articles 2 to 12 and 14 of the Convention,
  (b) Articles 1 to 3 of the First Protocol, and
  (c) Article 1 of the Thirteenth Protocol,

as read with Articles 16 to 18 of the Convention. ...

6   Acts of public authorities

(1) It is unlawful for a public authority to act in a way which is incompatible with a Convention right.

(2) Subsection (1) does not apply to an act if –

  (a) as the result of one or more provisions of primary legislation, the authority could not have acted differently; or
  (b) in the case of one or more provisions of, or made under, primary legislation which cannot be read or given effect in a way which is compatible with the Convention rights, the authority was acting so as to give effect to or enforce those provisions.

(3) In this section 'public authority' includes –

  (a) a court or tribunal, and
  (b) any person certain of whose functions are functions of a public nature,

but does not include either House of Parliament or a person exercising functions in connection with proceedings in Parliament.

(4) In subsection (3) 'Parliament' does not include the House of Lords in its judicial capacity.

(5) In relation to a particular act, a person is not a public authority by virtue only of subsection (3)(b) if the nature of the act is private.

(6) 'An act' includes a failure to act but does not include a failure to –

  (a) introduce in, or lay before, Parliament a proposal for legislation; or
  (b) make any primary legislation or remedial order.

8   Judicial remedies

(1) In relation to any act (or proposed act) of a public authority which the court finds is (or would be) unlawful, it may grant such relief or remedy, or make such order, within its powers as it considers just and appropriate.

(2) But damages may be awarded only by a court which has power to award damages, or to order the payment of compensation, in civil proceedings.

(3) No award of damages is to be made unless, taking account of all the circumstances of the case, including –

(a) any other relief or remedy granted, or order made, in relation to the act in question (by that or any other court), and

(b) the consequences of any decision (of that or any other court) in respect of that act,

the court is satisfied that the award is necessary to afford just satisfaction to the person in whose favour it is made.

(4) In determining –

(a) whether to award damages, or

(b) the amount of an award,

the court must take into account the principles applied by the European Court of Human Rights in relation to the award of compensation under Article 41 of the Convention.

(5) A public authority against which damages are awarded is to be treated – ...

(b) for the purposes of the Civil Liability (Contribution) Act 1978 as liable in respect of damage suffered by the person to whom the award is made.

(6) In this section –

'court' includes a tribunal;
'damages' means damages for an unlawful act of a public authority; and
'unlawful' means unlawful under section 6(1).

21   Interpretation, etc

(1) In this Act – ...

'the Convention' means the Convention for the Protection of Human Rights and Fundamental Freedoms, agreed by the Council of Europe at Rome on 4th November 1950 as it has effect for the time being in relation to the United Kingdom; ...

'primary legislation' means any –

(a) public general Act;

(b) local and personal Act;

(c) private Act;

(d) Measure of the Church Assembly;

(e) Measure of the General Synod of the Church of England;

(f) Order in Council –

(i) made in exercise of Her Majesty's Royal Prerogative;

(ii) made under section 38(1)(a) of the Northern Ireland Constitution Act 1973 or the corresponding provision of the Northern Ireland Act 1998; or

(iii) amending an Act of a kind mentioned in paragraph (a), (b) or (c);

and includes an order or other instrument made under primary legislation (otherwise than by the National Assembly for Wales, a member of the Scottish Executive, a Northern Ireland Minister or a Northern Ireland department) to the extent to which it operates to bring one or more provisions of that legislation into force or amends any primary legislation;

'the First Protocol' means the protocol to the Convention agreed at Paris on 20th March 1952; ...

'the Thirteenth Protocol' means the protocol to the Convention (concerning the abolition of the death penalty in all circumstances) agreed at Vilnius on 3rd May 2002;

'remedial order' means an order under section 10; ...

'tribunal' means any tribunal in which legal proceedings may be brought. ...

As amended by the Human Rights Act 1998 (Amendment) Order 2004, art 2(1), (2).

CONTRACTS (RIGHTS OF THIRD PARTIES) ACT 1999

(1999 c 31)

1 Right of third party to enforce contractual term

(1) Subject to the provisions of this Act, a person who is not a party to a contract (a 'third party') may in his own right enforce a term of the contract if –

    (a) the contract expressly provides that he may, or

    (b) subject to subsection (2), the term purports to confer a benefit on him.

(2) Subsection (1)(b) does not apply if on a proper construction of the contract it appears that the parties did not intend the term to be enforceable by the third party.

(3) The third party must be expressly identified in the contract by name, as a member of a class or as answering a particular description but need not be in existence when the contract is entered into.

(4) This section does not confer a right on a third party to enforce a term of a contract otherwise than subject to and in accordance with any other relevant terms of the contract.

(5) For the purpose of exercising his right to enforce a term of the contract, there shall be available to the third party any remedy that would have been available to him in an action for breach of contract if he had been a party to the contract (and the rules relating to damages, injunctions, specific performance and other relief shall apply accordingly).

(6) Where a term of a contract excludes or limits liability in relation to any matter references in this Act to the third party enforcing the term shall be construed as references to his availing himself of the exclusion or limitation.

(7) In this Act, in relation to a term of a contract which is enforceable by a third party –

    'the promisor' means the party to the contract against whom the term is enforceable by the third party, and

    'the promisee' means the party to the contract by whom the term is enforceable against the promisor.

2   Variation and rescission of contract

(1) Subject to the provisions of this section, where a third party has a right under section 1 to enforce a term of the contract, the parties to the contract may not, by agreement, rescind the contract, or vary it in such a way as to extinguish or alter his entitlement under that right, without his consent if –

    (a) the third party has communicated his assent to the term to the promisor,

    (b) the promisor is aware that the third party has relied on the term, or

    (c) the promisor can reasonably be expected to have foreseen that the third party would rely on the term and the third party has in fact relied on it.

(2) The assent referred to in subsection (1)(a) –

    (a) may be by words or conduct, and

    (b) if sent to the promisor by post or other means, shall not be regarded as communicated to the promisor until received by him.

(3) Subsection (1) is subject to any express term of the contract under which –

    (a) the parties to the contract may by agreement rescind or vary the contract without the consent of the third party, or

    (b) the consent of the third party is required in circumstances specified in the contract instead of those set out in subsection (1)(a) to (c).

(4) Where the consent of a third party is required under subsection (1) or (3), the court or arbitral tribunal may, on the application of the parties to the contract, dispense with his consent if satisfied –

    (a) that his consent cannot be obtained because his whereabouts cannot reasonably be ascertained, or

    (b) that he is mentally incapable of giving his consent.

(5) The court or arbitral tribunal may, on the application of the parties to a contract, dispense with any consent that may be required under subsection (1)(c) if satisfied that it cannot reasonably be ascertained whether or not the third party has in fact relied on the term.

(6) If the court or arbitral tribunal dispenses with a third party's consent, it may impose such conditions as it thinks fit, including a condition requiring the payment of compensation to the third party.

(7) The jurisdiction conferred on the court by subsections (4) to (6) is exercisable by both the High Court and a county court.

3   Defences, etc available to promisor

(1) Subsections (2) to (5) apply where, in reliance on section 1, proceedings for the enforcement of a term of a contract are brought by a third party.

(2) The promisor shall have available to him by way of defence or set-off any matter that –

(a) arises from or in connection with the contract and is relevant to the term, and

(b) would have been available to him by way of defence or set-off if the proceedings had been brought by the promisee.

(3) The promisor shall also have available to him by way of defence or set-off any matter if –

(a) an express term of the contract provides for it to be available to him in proceedings brought by the third party, and

(b) it would have been available to him by way of defence or set-off if the proceedings had been brought by the promisee.

(4) The promisor shall also have available to him –

(a) by way of defence or set-off any matter, and

(b) by way of counterclaim any matter not arising from the contract, that would have been available to him by way of defence or set-off or, as the case may be, by way of counterclaim against the third party if the third party had been a party to the contract.

(5) Subsections (2) and (4) are subject to any express term of the contract as to the matters that are not to be available to the promisor by way of defence, set-off or counterclaim.

(6) Where in any proceedings brought against him a third party seeks in reliance on section 1 to enforce a term of a contract (including, in particular, a term purporting to exclude or limit liability), he may not do so if he could not have done so (whether by reason of any particular circumstances relating to him or otherwise) had he been a party to the contract.

4   Enforcement of contract by promisee

Section 1 does not affect any right of the promisee to enforce any term of the contract.

5   Protection of promisor from double liability

Where under section 1 a term of a contract is enforceable by a third party, and the promisee has recovered from the promisor a sum in respect of –

(a) the third party's loss in respect of the term, or

(b) the expense to the promisee of making good to the third party the default of the promisor, then, in any proceedings brought in reliance on that section by the third party, the court or arbitral tribunal shall reduce any award to the third party to such extent as it thinks appropriate to take account of the sum recovered by the promisee.

6   Exceptions

(1) Section 1 confers no rights on a third party in the case of a contract on a bill of exchange, promissory note or other negotiable instrument.

(2) Section 1 confers no rights on a third party in the case of any contract binding on a company and its members under section 14 of the Companies Act 1985 [effect of memorandum and articles].

(2A) Section 1 confers no rights on a third party in the case of any incorporation document of a limited liability partnership or any limited liability partnership agreement as defined in the Limited Liability Partnerships Regulations 2001 (SI No 2001/1090).

(3) Section 1 confers no right on a third party to enforce –

(a) any term of a contract of employment against an employee,

(b) any term of a worker's contract against a worker (including a home worker), or

(c) any term of a relevant contract against an agency worker.

(4) In subsection (3) –

(a) 'contract of employment', 'employee', 'worker's contract', and 'worker' have the meaning given by section 54 of the National Minimum Wage Act 1998,

(b) 'home worker' has the meaning given by section 35(2) of that Act,

(c) 'agency worker' has the same meaning as in section 34(1) of that Act, and

(d) 'relevant contract' means a contract entered into, in a case where section 34 of that Act applies, by the agency worker as respects work falling within subsection (1)(a) of that section.

(5) Section 1 confers no rights on a third party in the case of –

(a) a contract for the carriage of goods by sea, or

(b) a contract for the carriage of goods by rail or road, or for the carriage of cargo by air, which is subject to the rules of the appropriate international transport convention, except that a third party may in reliance on that section avail himself of an exclusion or limitation of liability in such a contract.

'sea' means a contract of carriage –

(a) contained in or evidenced by a bill of lading, sea waybill or a corresponding electronic transaction, or

(b) under or for the purposes of which there is given an undertaking which is contained in a ship's delivery order or a corresponding electronic transaction.

(7) For the purposes of subsection (6) –

(a) 'bill of lading', 'sea waybill' and 'ship's delivery order' have the same meaning as in the Carriage of Goods by Sea Act 1992, and

(b) a corresponding electronic transaction is a transaction within section 1(5) of that Act which corresponds to the issue, indorsement, delivery or transfer of a bill of lading, sea waybill or ship's delivery order.

(8) In subsection (5) 'the appropriate international transport convention' means –

(a) in relation to a contract for the carriage of goods by rail, the Convention which has the force of law in the United Kingdom under section 1 of the International Transport Conventions Act 1983,

(b) in relation to a contract for the carriage of goods by road, the Convention which has the force of law in the United Kingdom under section 1 of the Carriage of Goods by Road Act 1965, and

(c) in relation to a contract for the carriage of cargo by air –

(i) the Convention which has the force of law in the United Kingdom under section 1 of the Carriage by Air Act 1961, or

(ii) the Convention which has the force of law under section 1 of the Carriage by Air (Supplementary Provisions) Act 1962, or

(iii) either of the amended Conventions set out in Part B of Schedule 2 or 3 to the Carriage by Air Acts (Application of Provisions) Order 1967.

7   Supplementary provisions relating to third party

(1) Section 1 does not affect any right or remedy of a third party that exists or is available apart from this Act.

(2) Section 2(2) of the Unfair Contract Terms Act 1977 (restriction on exclusion etc. of liability for negligence) shall not apply where the negligence consists of the breach of an obligation arising from a term of a contract and the person seeking to enforce it is a third party acting in reliance on section 1.

(3) In sections 5 and 8 of the Limitation Act 1980 the references to an action founded on a simple contract and an action upon a specialty shall respectively include references to an action brought in reliance on section 1 relating to a simple contract and an action brought in reliance on that section relating to a specialty.

(4) A third party shall not, by virtue of section 1(5) or 3(4) or (6), be treated as a party to the contract for the purposes of any other Act (or any instrument made under any other Act).

8   Arbitration provisions

(1) Where –

(a) a right under section 1 to enforce a term ('the substantive term') is subject to a term providing for the submission of disputes to arbitration ('the arbitration agreement'), and

(b) the arbitration agreement is an agreement in writing for the purposes of Part I of the Arbitration Act 1996, the third party shall be treated for the purposes of that Act as a party to the arbitration agreement as regards disputes between himself and the promisor relating to the enforcement of the substantive term by the third party.

(2) Where –

(a) a third party has a right under section 1 to enforce a term providing for one or more descriptions of dispute between the third party and the promisor to be submitted to arbitration ('the arbitration agreement'),

(b) the arbitration agreement is an agreement in writing for the purposes of Part I of the Arbitration Act 1996, and

(c) the third party does not fall to be treated under subsection (1) as a party to the arbitration agreement, the third party shall, if he exercises the right, be treated for the purposes of that Act as a party to the arbitration agreement in relation to the matter with respect to which the right is exercised, and be treated as having been so immediately before the exercise of the right.

10   Short title, commencement and extent ...

(2) This Act comes into force on the day on which it is passed but, subject to subsection (3), does not apply in relation to a contract entered into before the end of the period of six months beginning with that day.

(3) The restriction in subsection (2) does not apply in relation to a contract which –

(a) is entered into on or after the day on which this Act is passed, and

(b) expressly provides for the application of this Act. ...

NB This Act received the Royal Assent on 11 November 1999.

As amended by the Limited Liability Partnerships Regulations 2001, reg 9, Schedule 5, para 20.

FINANCIAL SERVICES AND MARKETS ACT 2000
(2000 c 8)

412 Gaming contracts

(1) No contract to which this section applies is void or unenforceable because of –

(a) section 18 of the Gaming Act 1845, section 1 of the Gaming Act 1892 ...

(2) This section applies to a contract if –

(a) it is entered into by either or each party by way of business;

(b) the entering into or performance of it by either party constitutes an activity of a specified kind or one which falls within a specified class of activity; and

(c) it relates to an investment of a specified kind or one which falls within a specified class of investment.

(3) Part II of Schedule 2 applies for the purposes of subsection (2)(c), with the references to section 22 being read as references to that subsection.

(4) Nothing in Part II of Schedule 2, as applied by subsection (3), limits the power conferred by subsection (2)(c).

(5) 'Investment' includes any asset, right or interest.

(6) 'Specified' means specified in an order made by the Treasury.

SCHEDULE 2

PART II

INVESTMENTS

10. The matters with respect to which provision may be made under section 22(1) in respect of investments include, in particular, those described in general terms in this Part of this Schedule.

11. – (1) Shares or stock in the share capital of a company.

(2) 'Company' includes –

(a) any body corporate (wherever incorporated), and

(b) any unincorporated body constituted under the law of a country or territory outside the United Kingdom,

other than an open-ended investment company.

12. Any of the following –

(a) debentures;

(b) debenture stock;

(c) loan stock;

(d) bonds;

(e) certificates of deposit;

(f) any other instruments creating or acknowledging a present or future indebtedness. ...

17. Options to acquire or dispose of property.

18. Rights under a contract for the sale of a commodity or property of any other description under which delivery is to be made at a future date.

19. Rights under –

(a) a contract for differences; or

(b) any other contract the purpose or pretended purpose of which is to secure a profit or avoid a loss by reference to fluctuations in –

(i) the value or price of property of any description; or

(ii) an index or other factor designated for that purpose in the contract.

20. Rights under a contract of insurance ...

LIMITED LIABILITY PARTNERSHIPS ACT 2000
(2000 c 12)

1 Limited liability partnerships

(1) There shall be a new form of legal entity to be known as a limited liability partnership.

(2) A limited liability partnership is a body corporate (with legal personality separate from that of its members) which is formed by being incorporated under this Act; and –

(a) in the following provisions of this Act (except in the phrase 'oversea limited liability partnership'), and

(b) in any other enactment (except where provision is made to the contrary or the context otherwise requires),

references to a limited liability partnership are to such a body corporate.

(3) A limited liability partnership has unlimited capacity.

(4) The members of a limited liability partnership have such liability to contribute to its assets in the event of its being wound up as is provided for by virtue of this Act.

(5) Accordingly, except as far as otherwise provided by this Act or any other enactment, the law relating to partnerships does not apply to a limited liability partnership.

(6) The Schedule (which makes provision about the names and registered offices of limited liability partnerships) has effect.

2 Incorporation document, etc

(1) For a limited liability partnership to be incorporated –

(a) two or more persons associated for carrying on a lawful business with a view to profit must have subscribed their names to an incorporation document,

(b) there must have been delivered to the registrar either the incorporation document or a copy authenticated in a manner approved by him, and

(c) there must have been so delivered a statement in a form approved by the registrar, made by either a solicitor engaged in the formation of the limited liability partnership or anyone who subscribed his name to the incorporation document, that the requirement imposed by paragraph (a) has been complied with. ...

4 Members

(1) On the incorporation of a limited liability partnership its members are the persons who subscribed their names to the incorporation document (other than any who have died or been dissolved).

(2) Any other person may become a member of a limited liability partnership by and in accordance with an agreement with the existing members.

(3) A person may cease to be a member of a limited liability partnership (as well as by death or dissolution) in accordance with an agreement with the other members or, in the absence of agreement with the other members as to cessation of membership, by giving reasonable notice to the other members.

(4) A member of a limited liability partnership shall not be regarded for any purpose as employed by the limited liability partnership unless, if he and the other members were partners in a partnership, he would be regarded for that purpose as employed by the partnership.

5 Relationship of members, etc

(1) Except as far as otherwise provided by this Act or any other enactment, the mutual rights and duties of the members of a limited liability partnership, and the mutual rights and duties of a limited liability partnership and its members, shall be governed –

(a) by agreement between the members, or between the limited liability partnership and its members, or

(b) in the absence of agreement as to any matter, by any provision made in relation to that matter by regulations under section 15(c).

(2) An agreement made before the incorporation of a limited liability partnership between the persons who subscribe their names to the incorporation document may impose obligations on the limited liability partnership (to take effect at any time after its incorporation).

6 Members as agents

(1) Every member of a limited liability partnership is the agent of the limited liability partnership.

(2) But a limited liability partnership is not bound by anything done by a member in dealing with a person if –

(a) the member in fact has no authority to act for the limited liability partnership by doing that thing, and

(b) the person knows that he has no authority or does not know or believe him to be a member of the limited liability partnership.

(3) Where a person has ceased to be a member of a limited liability partnership, the former member is to be regarded (in relation to any person dealing with the limited liability partnership) as still being a member of the limited liability partnership unless –

(a) the person has notice that the former member has ceased to be a member of the limited liability partnership, or

(b) notice that the former member has ceased to be a member of the limited liability partnership has been delivered to the registrar.

(4) Where a member of a limited liability partnership is liable to any person (other than another member of the limited liability partnership) as a result of a wrongful act or omission of his in the course of the business of the limited liability partnership or with its authority, the limited liability partnership is liable to the same extent as the member.

COUNTRYSIDE AND RIGHTS OF WAY ACT 2000

(2000 c 37)

PART I

ACCESS TO THE COUNTRYSIDE

CHAPTER I

RIGHT OF ACCESS

1   Principal definitions for Part I

(1) In this Part 'access land' means any land which –

(a) is shown as open country on a map in conclusive form issued by the appropriate countryside body for the purposes of this Part,

(b) is shown on such a map as registered common land,

(c) is registered common land in any area outside Inner London for which no such map relating to registered common land has been issued,

(d) is situated more than 600 metres above sea level in any area for which no such map relating to open country has been issued, or

(e) is dedicated for the purposes of this Part under section 16,

but does not (in any of those cases) include excepted land or land which is treated by section 15(1) as being accessible to the public apart from this Act.

(2) In this Part –

'access authority' –

(a) in relation to land in a National Park, means the National Park authority, and

(b) in relation to any other land, means the local highway authority in whose area the land is situated;

'the appropriate countryside body' means –

(a) in relation to England, the Countryside Agency, and

(b) in relation to Wales, the Countryside Council for Wales;

'excepted land' means land which is for the time being of any of the descriptions specified in Part I of Schedule 1, those descriptions having effect subject to Part II of that Schedule;

'mountain' includes, subject to the following definition, any land situated more than 600 metres above sea level;

'mountain, moor, heath or down' does not include land which appears to the appropriate countryside body to consist of improved or semi-improved grassland;

'open country' means land which –

(a) appears to the appropriate countryside body to consist wholly or predominantly of mountain, moor, heath or down, and

(b) is not registered common land.

(3) In this Part 'registered common land' means –

(a) land which is registered as common land under the Commons Registration Act 1965 (in this section referred to as 'the 1965 Act') and whose registration under that Act has become final, or

(b) subject to subsection (4), land which fell within paragraph (a) on the day on which this Act is passed or at any time after that day but has subsequently ceased to be registered as common land under the 1965 Act on the register of common land in which it was included being amended by reason of the land having ceased to be common land within the meaning of that Act.

(4) Subsection (3)(b) does not apply where –

(a) the amendment of the register of common land was made in pursuance of an application made before the day on which this Act is passed, or

(b) the land ceased to be common land by reason of the exercise of –

(i) any power of compulsory purchase, of appropriation or of sale which is conferred by an enactment,

(ii) any power so conferred under which land may be made common land within the meaning of the 1965 Act in substitution for other land.

2   Rights of public in relation to access land

(1) Any person is entitled by virtue of this subsection to enter and remain on any access land for the purposes of open-air recreation, if and so long as –

(a) he does so without breaking or damaging any wall, fence, hedge, stile or gate, and

(b) he observes the general restrictions in Schedule 2 and any other restrictions imposed in relation to the land under Chapter II.

(2) Subsection (1) has effect subject to subsections (3) and (4) and to the provisions of Chapter II [Exclusion or restriction of access].

(3) Subsection (1) does not entitle a person to enter or be on any land, or do anything

on any land, in contravention of any prohibition contained in or having effect under any enactment, other than an enactment contained in a local or private Act.

(4) If a person becomes a trespasser on any access land by failing to comply with –

(a) subsection (1)(a),

(b) the general restrictions in Schedule 2, or

(c) any other restrictions imposed in relation to the land under Chapter II,

he may not, within 72 hours after leaving that land, exercise his right under subsection (1) to enter that land again or to enter other land in the same ownership.

(5) In this section 'owner', in relation to any land which is subject to a farm business tenancy within the meaning of the Agricultural Tenancies Act 1995 or a tenancy to which the Agricultural Holdings Act 1986 applies, means the tenant under that tenancy, and 'ownership' shall be construed accordingly.

12 Effect of right of access on rights and liabilities of owners

(1) The operation of section 2(1) in relation to any access land does not increase the liability, under any enactment not contained in this Act or under any rule of law, of a person interested in the access land or any adjoining land in respect of the state of the land or of things done or omitted to be done on the land.

(2) Any restriction arising under a covenant or otherwise as to the use of any access land shall have effect subject to the provisions of this Part, and any liability of a person interested in any access land in respect of such a restriction is limited accordingly.

(3) For the purposes of any enactment or rule of law as to the circumstances in which the dedication of a highway or the grant of an easement may be presumed, or may be established by prescription, the use by the public or by any person of a way across land in the exercise of the right conferred by section 2(1) is to be disregarded.

(4) The use of any land by the inhabitants of any locality for the purposes of open-air recreation in the exercise of the right conferred by section 2(1) is to be disregarded in determining whether the land has become a town or village green.

45 Interpretation of Part I

(1) In this Act, unless a contrary intention appears – ...

'interest', in relation to land, includes any estate in land and any right over land, whether the right is exercisable by virtue of the ownership of an estate or interest in land or by virtue of a licence or agreement, and in particular includes rights of common and sporting rights, and references to a person interested in land shall be construed accordingly; ...

SCHEDULE 2

RESTRICTIONS TO BE OBSERVED BY PERSONS
EXERCISING RIGHT OF ACCESS

1. Section 2(1) does not entitle a person to be on any land if, in or on that land, he –

(a) drives or rides any vehicle other than an invalid carriage as defined by section 20(2) of the Chronically Sick and Disabled Persons Act 1970,

(b) uses a vessel or sailboard on any non-tidal water,

(c) has with him any animal other than a dog,

(d) commits any criminal offence,

(e) lights or tends a fire or does any act which is likely to cause a fire,

(f) intentionally or recklessly takes, kills, injures or disturbs any animal, bird or fish,

(g) intentionally or recklessly takes, damages or destroys any eggs or nests,

(h) feeds any livestock,

(i) bathes in any non-tidal water,

(j) engages in any operations of or connected with hunting, shooting, fishing, trapping, snaring, taking or destroying of animals, birds or fish or has with him any engine, instrument or apparatus used for hunting, shooting, fishing, trapping, snaring, taking or destroying animals, birds or fish,

(k) uses or has with him any metal detector,

(l) intentionally removes, damages or destroys any plant, shrub, tree or root or any part of a plant, shrub, tree or root,

(m) obstructs the flow of any drain or watercourse, or opens, shuts or otherwise interferes with any sluice-gate or other apparatus,

(n) without reasonable excuse, interferes with any fence, barrier or other device designed to prevent accidents to people or to enclose livestock,

(o) neglects to shut any gate or to fasten it where any means of doing so is provided, except where it is reasonable to assume that a gate is intended to be left open,

(p) affixes or writes any advertisement, bill, placard or notice,

(q) in relation to any lawful activity which persons are engaging in or are about to engage in on that or adjoining land, does anything which is intended by him to have the effect –

(i) of intimidating those persons so as to deter them or any of them from engaging in that activity,

(ii) of obstructing that activity, or

(iii) of disrupting that activity,

(r) without reasonable excuse, does anything which (whether or not intended by him to have the effect mentioned in paragraph (q)) disturbs, annoys or obstructs any persons engaged in a lawful activity on the land,

(s) engages in any organised games, or in camping, hang-gliding or para-gliding, or

(t) engages in any activity which is organised or undertaken (whether by him or another) for any commercial purpose.

2. – (1) In paragraph 1(k), 'metal detector' means any device designed or adapted for detecting or locating any metal or mineral in the ground.

(2) For the purposes of paragraph 1(q) and (r), activity on any occasion on the part of a person or persons on land is 'lawful' if he or they may engage in the activity on the land on that occasion without committing an offence or trespassing on the land.

3. Regulations may amend paragraphs 1 and 2.

4. During the period beginning with 1st March and ending with 31st July in each year, section 2(1) does not entitle a person to be on any land if he takes, or allows to enter or remain, any dog which is not on a short lead.

5. Whatever the time of year, section 2(1) does not entitle a person to be on any land if he takes, or allows to enter or remain, any dog which is not on a short lead and which is in the vicinity of livestock.

6. In paragraphs 4 and 5, 'short lead' means a lead of fixed length and of not more than two metres. ...

UNFAIR TERMS IN CONSUMER CONTRACTS REGULATIONS 1999

(SI 1999 No 2083)

1   Citation and commencement

These Regulations may be cited as the Unfair Terms in Consumer Contracts Regulations 1999 and shall come into force on 1st October 1999.

2   Revocation

The Unfair Terms in Consumer Contracts Regulations 1994 are hereby revoked.

3   Interpretation

(1) In these Regulations –

'the Community' means the European Community;

'consumer' means any natural person who, in contracts covered by these Regulations, is acting for purposes which are outside his trade, business or profession;

'court' in relation to England and Wales and Northern Ireland means a county court or the High Court, and in relation to Scotland, the Sheriff or the Court of Session;

'EEA Agreement' means the Agreement on the European Economic Area signed at Oporto on 2nd May 1992 as adjusted by the protocol signed at Brussels on 17th March 1993;

'Member State' means a State which is a contracting party to the EEA Agreement;

'notified' means notified in writing;

'the OFT' means the Office of Fair Trading;

'qualifying body' means a person specified in Schedule 1;

'seller or supplier' means any natural or legal person who, in contracts covered by these Regulations, is acting for purposes relating to his trade, business or profession, whether publicly owned or privately owned;

'unfair terms' means the contractual terms referred to in regulation 5.

(1A) The references –

(a) in regulation 4(1) to a seller or a supplier, and

(b) in regulation 8(1) to a seller or supplier,

include references to a distance supplier and to an intermediary.

(1B) In paragraph (1A) and regulation 5(6) –

'distance supplier' means –

(a) a supplier under a distance contract within the meaning of the Financial Services (Distance Marketing) Regulations 2004, or

(b) a supplier of unsolicited financial services within regulation 15 of those Regulations; and

'intermediary' has the same meaning as in those Regulations. ...

4 Terms to which these Regulations apply

(1) These Regulations apply in relation to unfair terms in contracts concluded between a seller or a supplier and a consumer.

(2) These Regulations do not apply to contractual terms which reflect –

(a) mandatory statutory or regulatory provisions (including such provisions under the law of any Member State or in Community legislation having effect in the United Kingdom without further enactment);

(b) the provisions or principles of international conventions to which the Member States or the Community are party.

5 Unfair terms

(1) A contractual term which has not been individually negotiated shall be regarded as unfair if, contrary to the requirement of good faith, it causes a significant imbalance in the parties' rights and obligations arising under the contract, to the detriment of the consumer.

(2) A term shall always be regarded as not having been individually negotiated where it has been drafted in advance and the consumer has therefore not been able to influence the substance of the term.

(3) Notwithstanding that a specific term or certain aspects of it in a contract has been individually negotiated, these Regulations shall apply to the rest of a contract if an overall assessment of it indicates that it is a pre-formulated standard contract.

(4) It shall be for any seller or supplier who claims that a term was individually negotiated to show that it was.

(5) Schedule 2 to these Regulations contains an indicative and non-exhaustive list of the terms which may be regarded as unfair.

(6) Any contractual term providing that a customer bears the burden of proof in respect of showing whether a distance supplier or an intermediary complied with

any or all of the obligations placed upon him resulting from the Directive and any rule or enactment implementing it shall always be regarded as unfair.

(7) In paragraph (6) –

'the Directive' means Directive 2002/65/EC of the European Parliament and of the Council of 23 September 2002 concerning the distance marketing of consumer financial services and amending Council Directive 90/619/EEC and Directives 97/7/EC and 98/27EC; and

'rule' means a rule made by the Financial Services Authority under the Financial Services and Markets Act 2000 or by a designated professional body within the meaning of section 326(2) of that Act.

6   Assessment of unfair terms

(1) Without prejudice to regulation 12, the unfairness of a contractual term shall be assessed, taking into account the nature of the goods or services for which the contract was concluded and by referring, at the time of conclusion of the contract, to all the circumstances attending the conclusion of the contract and to all the other terms of the contract or of another contract on which it is dependent.

(2) In so far as it is in plain intelligible language, the assessment of fairness of a term shall not relate –

(a) to the definition of the main subject matter of the contract, or

(b) to the adequacy of the price or remuneration, as against the goods or services supplied in exchange.

7   Written contracts

(1) A seller or supplier shall ensure that any written term of a contract is expressed in plain, intelligible language.

(2) If there is doubt about the meaning of a written term, the interpretation which is most favourable to the consumer shall prevail but this rule shall not apply in proceedings brought under regulation 12.

8   Effect of unfair term

(1) An unfair term in a contract concluded with a consumer by a seller or supplier shall not be binding on the consumer.

(2) The contract shall continue to bind the parties if it is capable of continuing in existence without the unfair term.

9   Choice of law clauses

These Regulations shall apply notwithstanding any contract term which applies or purports to apply the law of a non-Member State, if the contract has a close connection with the territory of the Member States.

10 Complaints – consideration by the OFT

(1) It shall be the duty of the OFT to consider any complaint made to it that any contract term drawn up for general use is unfair, unless –

(a) the complaint appears to the OFT to be frivolous or vexatious; or

(b) a qualifying body has notified the OFT that it agrees to consider the complaint.

(2) The OFT shall give reasons for its decision to apply or not to apply, as the case may be, for an injunction under regulation 12 in relation to any complaint which these Regulations require him to consider.

(3) In deciding whether or not to apply for an injunction in respect of a term which the OFT considers to be unfair, it may, if it considers it appropriate to do so, have regard to any undertakings given to it by or on behalf of any person as to the continued use of such a term in contracts concluded with consumers.

11 Complaints – consideration by qualifying bodies

(1) If a qualifying body specified in Part One of Schedule 1 notifies the OFT that it agrees to consider a complaint that any contract term drawn up for general use is unfair, it shall be under a duty to consider that complaint.

(2) Regulation 10(2) and (3) shall apply to a qualifying body which is under a duty to consider a complaint as they apply to the OFT.

12 Injunctions to prevent continued use of unfair terms

(1) The OFT or, subject to paragraph (2), any qualifying body may apply for an injunction (including an interim injunction) against any person appearing to the OFT or that body to be using, or recommending use of, an unfair term drawn up for general use in contracts concluded with consumers.

(2) A qualifying body may apply for an injunction only where –

(a) it has notified the OFT of its intention to apply at least fourteen days before the date on which the application is made, beginning with the date on which the notification was given; or

(b) the OFT consents to the application being made within a shorter period.

(3) The court on an application under this regulation may grant an injunction on such terms as it thinks fit.

(4) An injunction may relate not only to use of a particular contract term drawn up for general use but to any similar term, or a term having like effect, used or recommended for use by any person.

13 Powers of the OFT and qualifying bodies to obtain documents and information

(1) The OFT may exercise the power conferred by this regulation for the purpose of –

(a) facilitating its consideration of a complaint that a contract term drawn up for general use is unfair; or

(b) ascertaining whether a person has complied with an undertaking or court order as to the continued use, or recommendation for use, of a term in contracts concluded with consumers.

(2) A qualifying body specified in Part One of Schedule 1 may exercise the power conferred by this regulation for the purpose of –

(a) facilitating its consideration of a complaint that a contract term drawn up for general use is unfair; or

(b) ascertaining whether a person has complied with –

(i) an undertaking given to it or to the court following an application by that body, or

(ii) a court order made on an application by that body,

as to the continued use, or recommendation for use, of a term in contracts concluded with consumers.

(3) The OFT may require any person to supply to it, and a qualifying body specified in Part One of Schedule 1 may require any person to supply to it –

(a) a copy of any document which that person has used or recommended for use, at the time the notice referred to in paragraph (4) below is given, as a pre-formulated standard contract in dealings with consumers;

(b) information about the use, or recommendation for use, by that person of that document or any other such document in dealings with consumers.

(4) The power conferred by this regulation is to be exercised by a notice in writing which may –

(a) specify the way in which and the time within which it is to be complied with; and

(b) be varied or revoked by a subsequent notice.

(5) Nothing in this regulation compels a person to supply any document or information which he would be entitled to refuse to produce or give in civil proceedings before the court.

(6) If a person makes default in complying with a notice under this regulation, the court may, on the application of the OFT or of the qualifying body, make such order as the court thinks fit for requiring the default to be made good, and any such order may provide that all the costs or expenses of and incidental to the application shall be borne by the person in default or by any officers of a company or other association who are responsible for its default.

14   Notification of undertakings and orders to the OFT

A qualifying body shall notify the OFT –

(a) of any undertaking given to it by or on behalf of any person as to the continued use of a term which that body considers to be unfair in contracts concluded with consumers;

(b) of the outcome of any application made by it under regulation 12, and of the terms of any undertaking given to, or order made by, the court;

(c) of the outcome of any application made by it to enforce a previous order of the court.

15 Publication, information and advice

(1) The OFT shall arrange for the publication in such form and manner as it considers appropriate, of –

(a) details of any undertaking or order notified to it under regulation 14;

(b) details of any undertaking given to it by or on behalf of any person as to the continued use of a term which the OFT considers to be unfair in contracts concluded with consumers;

(c) details of any application made by it under regulation 12, and of the terms of any undertaking given to, or order made by, the court;

(d) details of any application made by the OFT to enforce a previous order of the court.

(2) The OFT shall inform any person on request whether a particular term to which these Regulations apply has been –

(a) the subject of an undertaking given to the OFT or notified to it by a qualifying body; or

(b) the subject of an order of the court made upon application by it or notified to it by a qualifying body;

and shall give that person details of the undertaking or a copy of the order, as the case may be, together with a copy of any amendments which the person giving the undertaking has agreed to make to the term in question.

(3) The OFT may arrange for the dissemination in such form and manner as it considers appropriate of such information and advice concerning the operation of these Regulations as may appear to it to be expedient to give to the public and to all persons likely to be affected by these Regulations.

16 The functions of the Financial Services Authority

The functions of the Financial Services Authority under these Regulations shall be treated as functions of the Financial Services Authority under the Financial Services and Markets Act 2000.

SCHEDULE 1

REGULATION 3

QUALIFYING BODIES

PART ONE

1. The Information Commissioner.

2. The Gas and Electricity Markets Authority.

3. The Director General of Electricity Supply for Northern Ireland.

4. The Director General of Gas for Northern Ireland.

5. The Office of Communications.

6. The Director General of Water Services.

7. The Office of Rail Regulation.

8. Every weights and measures authority in Great Britain.

9. The Department of Enterprise, Trade and Investment in Northern Ireland.

10. The Financial Services Authority.

PART TWO

11. Consumers' Association.

SCHEDULE 2

REGULATION 5(5)

INDICATIVE AND NON-EXHAUSTIVE LIST OF TERMS WHICH
MAY BE REGARDED AS UNFAIR

1. Terms which have the object or effect of –

(a) excluding or limiting the legal liability of a seller or supplier in the event of the death of a consumer or personal injury to the latter resulting from an act or omission of that seller or supplier;

(b) inappropriately excluding or limiting the legal rights of the consumer vis-à-vis the seller or supplier or another party in the event of total or partial non-performance or inadequate performance by the seller or supplier of any of the contractual obligations, including the option of offsetting a debt owed to the seller or supplier against any claim which the consumer may have against him;

(c) making an agreement binding on the consumer whereas provision of services by the seller or supplier is subject to a condition whose realisation depends on his own will alone;

(d) permitting the seller or supplier to retain sums paid by the consumer where the latter decides not to conclude or perform the contract, without providing for the consumer to receive compensation of an equivalent amount from the seller or supplier where the latter is the party cancelling the contract;

(e) requiring any consumer who fails to fulfil his obligation to pay a disproportionately high sum in compensation;

(f) authorising the seller or supplier to dissolve the contract on a discretionary basis where the same facility is not granted to the consumer, or permitting the seller or supplier to retain the sums paid for services not yet supplied by him where it is the seller or supplier himself who dissolves the contract;

(g) enabling the seller or supplier to terminate a contract of indeterminate duration without reasonable notice except where there are serious grounds for doing so;

(h) automatically extending a contract of fixed duration where the consumer does not indicate otherwise, when the deadline fixed for the consumer to express his desire not to extend the contract is unreasonably early;

(i) irrevocably binding the consumer to terms with which he had no real opportunity of becoming acquainted before the conclusion of the contract;

(j) enabling the seller or supplier to alter the terms of the contract unilaterally without a valid reason which is specified in the contract;

(k) enabling the seller or supplier to alter unilaterally without a valid reason any characteristics of the product or service to be provided;

(l) providing for the price of goods to be determined at the time of delivery or allowing a seller of goods or supplier of services to increase their price without in both cases giving the consumer the corresponding right to cancel the contract if the final price is too high in relation to the price agreed when the contract was concluded;

(m) giving the seller or supplier the right to determine whether the goods or services supplied are in conformity with the contract, or giving him the exclusive right to interpret any term of the contract;

(n) limiting the seller's or supplier's obligation to respect commitments undertaken by his agents or making his commitments subject to compliance with a particular formality;

(o) obliging the consumer to fulfil all his obligations where the seller or supplier does not perform his;

(p) giving the seller or supplier the possibility of transferring his rights and obligations under the contract, where this may serve to reduce the guarantees for the consumer, without the latter's agreement;

(q) excluding or hindering the consumer's right to take legal action or exercise any other legal remedy, particularly by requiring the consumer to take disputes exclusively to arbitration not covered by legal provisions, unduly restricting the evidence available to him or imposing on him a burden of proof which, according to the applicable law, should lie with another party to the contract.

2. Scope of paragraphs 1(g), (j) and (l)

(a) Paragraph 1(g) is without hindrance to terms by which a supplier of financial services reserves the right to terminate unilaterally a contract of indeterminate duration without notice where there is a valid reason, provided that the supplier is required to inform the other contracting party or parties thereof immediately.

(b) Paragraph 1(j) is without hindrance to terms under which a supplier of financial services reserves the right to alter the rate of interest payable by the consumer or due to the latter, or the amount of other charges for financial services without notice where there is a valid reason, provided that the supplier is required to inform the other contracting party or parties thereof at the earliest opportunity and that the latter are free to dissolve the contract immediately.

Paragraph 1(j) is also without hindrance to terms under which a seller or supplier reserves the right to alter unilaterally the conditions of a contract of indeterminate duration, provided that he is required to inform the consumer with reasonable notice and that the consumer is free to dissolve the contract.

(c) Paragraphs 1(g), (j) and (l) do not apply to:

– transactions in transferable securities, financial instruments and other products or services where the price is linked to fluctuations in a stock exchange quotation or index or a financial market rate that the seller or supplier does not control;

– contracts for the purchase or sale of foreign currency, traveller's cheques or international money orders denominated in foreign currency;

(d) Paragraph 1(l) is without hindrance to price indexation clauses, where lawful, provided that the method by which prices vary is explicitly described.

As amended by the Unfair Terms in Consumer Contracts (Amendment) Regulations 2001, art 2; Financial Services and Markets Act 2000 (Consequential Amendments and Repeals) Order 2001, art 583; Enterprise Act 2002, s2; Railways and Transport Safety Act 2003, s16; Communications Act 2003 (Consequential Amendments No 2) Order 2003, art 2; Financial Services (Distance Marketing) Regulations 2004, reg 24.

ELECTRONIC COMMERCE (EC DIRECTIVE) REGULATIONS 2002
(SI 2002 No 2013)

2 Interpretation

(1) In these Regulations and in the Schedule – ...

'consumer' means any natural person who is acting for purposes other than those of his trade, business or profession; ...

'the Directive' means Directive 2000/31/EC of the European Parliament and of the Council of 8 June 2000 on certain legal aspects of information society services, in particular electronic commerce, in the Internal Market (Directive on electronic commerce); ...

'service provider' means any person providing an information society service; ...

(3) Terms used in the Directive other than those in paragraph (1) above shall have the same meaning as in the Directive.

9 Information to be provided where contracts are concluded by electronic means

(1) Unless parties who are not consumers have agreed otherwise, where a contract is to be concluded by electronic means a service provider shall, prior to an order being placed by the recipient of a service, provide to that recipient in a clear, comprehensible and unambiguous manner the information set out in (a) to (d) below –

(a) the different technical steps to follow to conclude the contract;

(b) whether or not the concluded contract will be filed by the service provider and whether it will be accessible;

(c) the technical means for identifying and correcting input errors prior to the placing of the order; and

(d) the languages offered for the conclusion of the contract.

(2) Unless parties who are not consumers have agreed otherwise, a service provider shall indicate which relevant codes of conduct he subscribes to and give information on how those codes can be consulted electronically.

(3) Where the service provider provides terms and conditions applicable to the

contract to the recipient, the service provider shall make them available to him in a way that allows him to store and reproduce them.

(4) The requirements of paragraphs (1) and (2) above shall not apply to contracts concluded exclusively by exchange of electronic mail or by equivalent individual communications.

11   Placing of the order

(1) Unless parties who are not consumers have agreed otherwise, where the recipient of the service places his order through technological means, a service provider shall –

  (a) acknowledge receipt of the order to the recipient of the service without undue delay and by electronic means; and

  (b) make available to the recipient of the service appropriate, effective and accessible technical means allowing him to identify and correct input errors prior to the placing of the order.

(2) For the purposes of paragraph (1)(a) above –

  (a) the order and the acknowledgement of receipt will be deemed to be received when the parties to whom they are addressed are able to access them; and

  (b) the acknowledgement of receipt may take the form of the provision of the service paid for where that service is an information society service.

(3) The requirements of paragraph (1) above shall not apply to contracts concluded exclusively by exchange of electronic mail or by equivalent individual communications.

12   Meaning of the term 'order'

Except in relation to regulation 9(1)(c) and regulation 11(1)(b) where 'order' shall be the contractual offer, 'order' may be but need not be the contractual offer for the purposes of regulations 9 and 11.

13   Liability of the service provider

The duties imposed by regulations … 9(1) and 11(1)(a) shall be enforceable, at the suit of any recipient of a service, by an action against the service provider for damages for breach of statutory duty.

14   Compliance with Regulation 9(3)

Where on request a service provider has failed to comply with the requirement in regulation 9(3), the recipient may seek an order from any court having jurisdiction in relation to the contract requiring that service provider to comply with that requirement.

15 Right to rescind contract

Where a person –

(a) has entered into a contract to which these Regulations apply, and

(b) the service provider has not made available means of allowing him to identify and correct input errors in compliance with regulation 11(1)(b),

he shall be entitled to rescind the contract unless any court having jurisdiction in relation to the contract in question orders otherwise on the application of the service provider.

SALE AND SUPPLY OF GOODS TO CONSUMERS REGULATIONS 2002
(SI 2002 No 3045)

2   Interpretation

In these Regulations –

'consumer' means any natural person who, in the contracts covered by these Regulations, is acting for purposes which are outside his trade, business or profession;

'consumer guarantee' means any undertaking to a consumer by a person acting in the course of his business, given without extra charge, to reimburse the price paid or to replace, repair or handle consumer goods in any way if they do not meet the specifications set out in the guarantee statement or in the relevant advertising;

'court' in relation to England and Wales ... means a county court or the High Court ...;

'enforcement authority' means the Office of Fair Trading, every local weights and measures authority in Great Britain ...;

'goods' has the same meaning as in section 61 of the Sale of Goods Act 1979;

'guarantor' means a person who offers a consumer guarantee to a consumer; and

'supply' includes supply by way of sale, lease, hire or hire-purchase.

15   Consumer guarantees

(1) Where goods are sold or otherwise supplied to a consumer which are offered with a consumer guarantee, the consumer guarantee takes effect at the time the goods are delivered as a contractual obligation owed by the guarantor under the conditions set out in the guarantee statement and the associated advertising.

(2) The guarantor shall ensure that the guarantee sets out in plain intelligible language the contents of the guarantee and the essential particulars necessary for making claims under the guarantee, notably the duration and territorial scope of the guarantee as well as the name and address of the guarantor.

(3) On request by the consumer to a person to whom paragraph (4) applies, the guarantee shall within a reasonable time be made available in writing or in another durable medium available and accessible to him.

(4) This paragraph applies to the guarantor and any other person who offers to consumers the goods which are the subject of the guarantee for sale or supply.

(5) Where consumer goods are offered with a consumer guarantee, and where those goods are offered within the territory of the United Kingdom, then the guarantor shall ensure that the consumer guarantee is written in English.

(6) If the guarantor fails to comply with the provisions of paragraphs (2) or (5) above, or a person to whom paragraph (4) applies fails to comply with paragraph (3) then the enforcement authority may apply for an injunction ... against that person requiring him to comply.

(7) The court on application under this Regulation may grant an injunction ... on such terms as it thinks fit.

As amended by the Enterprise Act 2002, s2.

APPENDIX

COURTS ACT 2003
(2003 c 39)

100 Periodical payments

(1) For section 2 of the Damages Act 1996 (c 48) (periodical payments by consent) substitute –

'2 Periodical payments

(1) A court awarding damages for future pecuniary loss in respect of personal injury –

    (a) may order that the damages are wholly or partly to take the form of periodical payments, and

    (b) shall consider whether to make that order.

(2) A court awarding other damages in respect of personal injury may, if the parties consent, order that the damages are wholly or partly to take the form of periodical payments.

(3) A court may not make an order for periodical payments unless satisfied that the continuity of payment under the order is reasonably secure.

(4) For the purpose of subsection (3) the continuity of payment under an order is reasonably secure if –

    (a) it is protected by a guarantee given under section 6 of or the Schedule to this Act,

    (b) it is protected by a scheme under section 213 of the Financial Services and Markets Act 2000 (compensation) (whether or not as modified by section 4 of this Act), or

    (c) the source of payment is a government or health service body.

(5) An order for periodical payments may include provision –

    (a) requiring the party responsible for the payments to use a method (selected or to be selected by him) under which the continuity of payment is reasonably secure by virtue of subsection (4);

    (b) about how the payments are to be made, if not by a method under which the continuity of payment is reasonably secure by virtue of subsection (4);

    (c) requiring the party responsible for the payments to take specified action to secure continuity of payment, where continuity is not reasonably secure by virtue of subsection (4);

(d) enabling a party to apply for a variation of provision included under paragraph (a), (b) or (c).

(6) Where a person has a right to receive payments under an order for periodical payments, or where an arrangement is entered into in satisfaction of an order which gives a person a right to receive periodical payments, that person's right under the order or arrangement may not be assigned or charged without the approval of the court which made the order; and –

(a) a court shall not approve an assignment or charge unless satisfied that special circumstances make it necessary, and

(b) a purported assignment or charge, or agreement to assign or charge, is void unless approved by the court.

(7) Where an order is made for periodical payments, an alteration of the method by which the payments are made shall be treated as a breach of the order (whether or not the method was specified under subsection (5)(b)) unless –

(a) the court which made the order declares its satisfaction that the continuity of payment under the new method is reasonably secure,

(b) the new method is protected by a guarantee given under section 6 of or the Schedule to this Act,

(c) the new method is protected by a scheme under section 213 of the Financial Services and Markets Act 2000 (compensation) (whether or not as modified by section 4 of this Act), or

(d) the source of payment under the new method is a government or health service body.

(8) An order for periodical payments shall be treated as providing for the amount of payments to vary by reference to the retail prices index (within the meaning of section 833(2) of the Income and Corporation Taxes Act 1988) at such times, and in such a manner, as may be determined by or in accordance with Civil Procedure Rules.

(9) But an order for periodical payments may include provision –

(a) disapplying subsection (8), or

(b) modifying the effect of subsection (8).

2A Periodical payments: supplementary

(1) Civil Procedure Rules may require a court to take specified matters into account in considering –

(a) whether to order periodical payments;

(b) the security of the continuity of payment;

(c) whether to approve an assignment or charge.

(2) For the purposes of section 2(4)(c) and (7)(d) "government or health service body" means a body designated as a government body or a health service body by order made by the Lord Chancellor.

(3) An order under subsection (2) –

(a) shall be made by statutory instrument, and

(b) shall be subject to annulment in pursuance of a resolution of either House of Parliament.

(4) Section 2(6) is without prejudice to a person's power to assign a right to the scheme manager established under section 212 of the Financial Services and Markets Act 2000.

(5) In section 2 "damages" includes an interim payment which a court orders a defendant to make to a claimant. ...

(7) Section 2 is without prejudice to any power exercisable apart from that section.

2B Variation of orders and settlements

(1) The Lord Chancellor may by order enable a court which has made an order for periodical payments to vary the order in specified circumstances (otherwise than in accordance with section 2(5)(d)).

(2) The Lord Chancellor may by order enable a court in specified circumstances to vary the terms on which a claim or action for damages for personal injury is settled by agreement between the parties if the agreement –

(a) provides for periodical payments, and

(b) expressly permits a party to apply to a court for variation in those circumstances.

(3) An order under this section may make provision –

(a) which operates wholly or partly by reference to a condition or other term of the court's order or of the agreement;

(b) about the nature of an order which may be made by a court on a variation;

(c) about the matters to be taken into account on considering variation;

(d) of a kind that could be made by Civil Procedure Rules ... (and which may be expressed to be with or without prejudice to the power to make those rules).

(4) An order under this section may apply (with or without modification) or amend an enactment about provisional or further damages.

(5) An order under this section shall be subject to any order under section 1 of the Courts and Legal Services Act 1990 (allocation between High Court and county courts).

(6) An order under this section –

(a) shall be made by statutory instrument,

(b) may not be made unless the Lord Chancellor has consulted such persons as he thinks appropriate,

(c) may not be made unless a draft has been laid before and approved by resolution of each House of Parliament, and

(d) may include transitional, consequential or incidental provision.

(7) In subsection (4) –

"provisional damages" means damages awarded by virtue of subsection (2)(a) of section 32A of the Supreme Court Act 1981 or section 51 of the County Courts Act 1984 ..., and

"further damages" means damages awarded by virtue of subsection (2)(b) of either of those sections ...'

101   Periodical payments: security

(1) For sections 4 and 5 of the Damages Act 1996 (c 48) (enhanced protection for structured settlement annuitant) substitute –

'4   Enhanced protection for periodical payments

(1) Subsection (2) applies where –

(a) a person has a right to receive periodical payments, and

(b) his right is protected by a scheme under section 213 of the Financial Services and Markets Act 2000 (compensation), but only as to part of the payments.

(2) The protection provided by the scheme shall extend by virtue of this section to the whole of the payments.

(3) Subsection (4) applies where –

(a) one person ("the claimant") has a right to receive periodical payments from another person ("the defendant"),

(b) a third person ("the insurer") is required by or in pursuance of an arrangement entered into with the defendant (whether or not together with other persons and whether before or after the creation of the claimant's right) to make payments in satisfaction of the claimant's right or for the purpose of enabling it to be satisfied, and

(c) the claimant's right to receive the payments would be wholly or partly protected by a scheme under section 213 of the Financial Services and Markets Act 2000 if it arose from an arrangement of the same kind as that mentioned in paragraph (b) but made between the claimant and the insurer.

(4) For the purposes of the scheme under section 213 of that Act –

(a) the claimant shall be treated as having a right to receive the payments from the insurer under an arrangement of the same kind as that mentioned in subsection (3)(b),

(b) the protection under the scheme in respect of those payments shall extend by virtue of this section to the whole of the payments, and

(c) no person other than the claimant shall be entitled to protection under the scheme in respect of the payments.

(5) In this section "periodical payments" means periodical payments made pursuant to –

(a) an order of a court in so far as it is made in reliance on section 2 above (including an order as varied), or

(b) an agreement in so far as it settles a claim or action for damages in respect of personal injury (including an agreement as varied).

(6) In subsection (5)(b) the reference to an agreement in so far as it settles a claim or action for damages in respect of personal injury includes a reference to an undertaking given by the Motor Insurers' Bureau (being the company of that name incorporated on 14th June 1946 under the Companies Act 1929), or an Article 75 insurer under the Bureau's Articles of Association, in relation to a claim or action in respect of personal injury.'

(2) In section 6(1) of the Damages Act 1996 (c 48) (guarantee for public sector settlement) for the words 'on terms corresponding to those of a structured settlement as defined in section 5 above except that the person to whom the payments are to be made is not to receive them as mentioned in subsection (1)(b) of that section' substitute 'on terms whereby the damages are to consist wholly or partly of periodical payments'.

HEALTH AND SOCIAL CARE (COMMUNITY HEALTH AND STANDARDS) ACT 2003

(2003 c 43)

PART 3

RECOVERY OF NHS CHARGES

150 Liability to pay NHS charges

(1) This section applies if –

(a) a person makes a compensation payment to or in respect of any other person (the 'injured person') in consequence of any injury, whether physical or psychological, suffered by the injured person, and

(b) the injured person has –

(i) received NHS treatment at a health service hospital as a result of the injury,

(ii) been provided with NHS ambulance services as a result of the injury for the purpose of taking him to a health service hospital for NHS treatment (unless he was dead on arrival at that hospital), or

(iii) received treatment as mentioned in sub-paragraph (i) and been provided with ambulance services as mentioned in sub-paragraph (ii).

(2) The person making the compensation payment is liable to pay the relevant NHS charges –

(a) in respect of –

(i) the treatment, in so far as received at a hospital in England or Wales,

(ii) the ambulance services, in so far as provided to take the injured person to such a hospital,

to the Secretary of State ...

(3) 'Compensation payment' means a payment, including a payment in money's worth, made –

(a) by or on behalf of a person who is, or is alleged to be, liable to any extent in respect of the injury, or

(b) in pursuance of a compensation scheme for motor accidents,

but does not include a payment mentioned in Schedule 10.

(4) Subsection (1)(a) applies –

    (a) to a payment made –

        (i) voluntarily, or in pursuance of a court order or an agreement, or otherwise, and

        (ii) in the United Kingdom or elsewhere, and

    (b) if more than one payment is made, to each payment.

(5) 'Injury' does not include any disease.

(6) Nothing in subsection (5) prevents this Part from applying to –

    (a) treatment received as a result of any disease suffered by the injured person, or

    (b) ambulance services provided as a result of any disease suffered by him,

if the disease in question is attributable to the injury suffered by the injured person (and accordingly that treatment is received or those services are provided as a result of the injury). …

(10) 'Relevant NHS charges' means the amount (or amounts) specified in a certificate of NHS charges –

    (a) issued under this Part, in respect of the injured person, to the person making the compensation payment, and

    (b) in force.

(11) 'Compensation scheme for motor accidents' means any scheme or arrangement under which funds are available for the payment of compensation in respect of motor accidents caused, or alleged to have been caused, by uninsured or unidentified persons.

(12) Regulations may amend Schedule 10 by omitting or modifying any payment for the time being specified in that Schedule.

(13) This section applies in relation to any injury which occurs after the date on which this section comes into force.

(14) For the purposes of this Part, it is irrelevant whether a compensation payment is made with or without an admission of liability.

163 Regulations governing lump sums, periodical payments, etc

(1) Regulations may make provision (including provision modifying this Part) –

    (a) for cases to which section 150(2) applies in which two or more compensation payments in the form of lump sums are made by the same person in respect of the same injury,

(b) for cases to which section 150(2) applies in which an agreement is entered into for the making of –

(i) periodical compensation payments (whether of an income or capital nature), or

(ii) periodical compensation payments and lump sum compensation payments,

(c) for cases in which the compensation payment to which section 150(2) applies is an interim payment of damages which a court orders to be repaid.

(2) Regulations made by virtue of subsection (1)(a) may (among other things) provide –

(a) for giving credit for amounts already paid, and

(b) for the payment by any person of any balance or the recovery from any person of any excess.

(3) Regulations may make provision modifying the application of this Part in relation to cases in which a payment into court is made and, in particular, may provide –

(a) for the making of a payment into court to be treated in prescribed circumstances as the making of a compensation payment,

(b) for application for, and issue of, certificates.

164 Liability of insurers

(1) If a compensation payment is made in a case where –

(a) a person is liable to any extent in respect of the injury, and

(b) the liability is covered to any extent by a policy of insurance,

the policy is also to be treated as covering any liability of that person under section 150(2).

(2) Liability imposed on the insurer by subsection (1) cannot be excluded or restricted.

(3) For that purpose excluding or restricting liability includes –

(a) making the liability or its enforcement subject to restrictive or onerous conditions,

(b) excluding or restricting any right or remedy in respect of the liability, or subjecting a person to any prejudice in consequence of his pursuing any such right or remedy, or

(c) excluding or restricting rules of evidence or procedure.

(4) Regulations may in prescribed cases limit the amount of the liability imposed on the insurer by subsection (1).

(5) This section applies in relation to policies of insurance issued before (as well as those issued after) the date on which it comes into force.

(6) References in this section to policies of insurance and their issue include references to contracts of insurance and their making

166 The Crown

This Part binds the Crown.

SCHEDULE 10

RECOVERY OF NHS CHARGES: EXEMPTED PAYMENTS

1. Any payment made to or for the injured person under –

(a) section 130 of the Powers of Criminal Courts (Sentencing) Act 2000 (c 6) (compensation orders against convicted persons) ...

2. Any payment made in the exercise of a discretion out of property held subject to a trust in a case where no more than 50 per cent by value of the capital contributed to the trust was directly or indirectly provided by persons who are, or are alleged to be, liable in respect of –

(a) the injury suffered by the injured person, or

(b) any connected injury suffered by another.

3. Any payment made out of property held for the purposes of a prescribed trust.

4. – (1) Any payment made to the injured person by an insurer under the terms of any contract of insurance entered into between the injured person and the insurer before the occurrence of the injury in question.

(2) In sub-paragraph (1), 'insurer' means –

(a) a person who has permission under Part 4 of the Financial Services and Markets Act 2000 (c 8) to effect or carry out contracts of insurance, or

(b) an EEA firm of the kind mentioned in paragraph 5(d) of Schedule 3 to that Act which has permission under paragraph 15 of that Schedule (as a result of qualifying for authorisation under paragraph 12 of that Schedule) to effect or carry out contracts of insurance.

(3) Sub-paragraph (2) must be read with –

(a) section 22 of the Financial Services and Markets Act 2000,

(b) any relevant order under that section, and

(c) Schedule 2 to that Act.

5. Any payment which apart from this paragraph would be made by –

(a) the responsible body of the health service hospital to whom the payment would subsequently be passed under section 162,

(b) the relevant ambulance trust to whom the payment would subsequently be passed under that section.

6. Any payment to the extent that it is made –

(a) in consequence of an action under the Fatal Accidents Act 1976 (c 30) ...

(c) in circumstances where, had an action been brought, it would have been brought under that Act ...

8. Any payment of a prescribed description, either generally or in such circumstances as may be prescribed.

INDEX

Law Update 2005–
due March 2005

An annual review of the most recent developments in specific legal subject areas, useful for law students at degree and professional levels, others with law elements in their courses and also practitioners seeking a quick update.

Published around March every year, the Law Update summarises the major legal developments during the course of the previous year. In conjunction with Old Bailey Press textbooks it gives the student a significant advantage when revising for examinations.

Contents
Administrative Law • Commercial Law • Company Law • Conflict of Laws • Constitutional Law • Contract Law • Conveyancing • Criminal Law • Criminology • Employment Law • English and European Legal Systems • Equity and Trusts • European Union Law • Evidence • Family Law • Jurisprudence • Land Law • Law of International Trade • Public International Law • Revenue Law • Tort

For further information on contents or to place an order, please contact:

Mail Order
Old Bailey Press
at Holborn College
Woolwich Road
Charlton
London
SE7 8LN

Telephone: 020 8317 6039
Fax: 020 8317 6004
Website: www.oldbaileypress.co.uk
E-Mail: mailorder@oldbaileypress.co.uk

ISBN 1 85836 571 6
Soft cover 246 x 175 mm
400 pages approx
£10.95
Due March 2005

Revision Aids

Designed for the undergraduate, the 101 Questions & Answers series and the Suggested Solutions series are for all those who have a positive commitment to passing their law examinations. Each series covers a different examinable topic and comprises a selection of answers to examination questions and, in the case of the 101 Questions and Answers, interrograms. The majority of questions represent examination 'bankers' and are supported by full-length essay solutions. These titles will undoubtedly assist you with your research and further your understanding of the subject in question.

101 Questions & Answers Series

Only £7.95 Published December 2003

Constitutional Law
ISBN: 1 85836 522 8

Criminal Law
ISBN: 1 85836 432 9

Land Law
ISBN: 1 85836 515 5

Law of Contract
ISBN: 1 85836 517 1

Law of Tort
ISBN: 1 85836 516 3

Suggested Solutions to Past Examination Questions 2001–2002 Series

Only £6.95 Published December 2003

Company Law
ISBN: 1 85836 519 8

Employment Law
ISBN: 1 85836 520 1

European Union Law
ISBN: 1 85836 524 4

Evidence
ISBN: 1 85836 521 X

Family Law
ISBN: 1 85836 525 2

For further information or to place an order, please contact:

Mail Order
Old Bailey Press at Holborn College
Woolwich Road
Charlton
London
SE7 8LN

Telephone: 020 8317 6039
Fax: 020 8317 6004
Website: www.oldbaileypress.co.uk
E-Mail: mailorder@oldbaileypress.co.uk

Unannotated Cracknell's Statutes for Use in Examinations

New Editions of Cracknell's Statutes

Only £11.95   Due 2005

Cracknell's Statutes provide a comprehensive series of essential statutory provisions for each subject. Amendments are consolidated, avoiding the need to cross-refer to amending legislation. Unannotated, they are suitable for use in examinations, and provide the precise wording of vital Acts of Parliament for the diligent student.

Company Law
ISBN: 1 85836 563 5

Equity and Trusts
ISBN: 1 85836 589 9

Constitutional & Administrative Law
ISBN: 1 85836 584 8

European Union Legislation
ISBN: 1 85836 590 2

Contract, Tort and Remedies
ISBN: 1 85836 583 X

Family Law
ISBN: 1 85836 566 X

Criminal Law
ISBN: 1 85836 586 4

Land: The Law of Real Property
ISBN: 1 85836 585 6

Employment Law
ISBN: 1 85836 587 2

Law of International Trade
ISBN: 1 85836 582 1

English Legal System
ISBN: 1 85836 588 0

Medical Law
ISBN: 1 85836 567 8

Revenue Law
ISBN: 1 85836 569 4

For further information or to place an order, please contact:

Customer Services
Old Bailey Press at Holborn College
Woolwich Road, Charlton
London, SE7 8LN
Telephone: 020 8317 6039
Fax: 020 8317 6004
Website: www.oldbaileypress.co.uk
E-Mail: customerservices@oldbaileypress.co.uk

Old Bailey Press

The Old Bailey Press Integrated Student Law Library is tailor-made to help you at every stage of your studies, from the preliminaries of each subject through to the final examination. The series of Textbooks, Revision WorkBooks, 150 Leading Cases and Cracknell's Statutes are interrelated to provide you with a comprehensive set of study materials.

You can buy Old Bailey Press books from your University Bookshop, your local Bookshop, directly using this form, or you can order a free catalogue of our titles from the address shown overleaf.

The following subjects each have a Textbook, 150 Leading Cases, Revision WorkBook and Cracknell's Statutes unless otherwise stated.

Administrative Law
Commercial Law
Company Law
Conflict of Laws
Constitutional Law
Conveyancing (Textbook and 150 Leading Cases)
Criminal Law
Criminology (Textbook and Sourcebook)
Employment Law (Textbook and Cracknell's Statutes)
English and European Legal Systems
Equity and Trusts
Evidence
Family Law
Jurisprudence: The Philosophy of Law (Textbook, Sourcebook and
    Revision WorkBook)
Land: The Law of Real Property
Law of International Trade
Law of the European Union
Legal Skills and System
    (Textbook)
Obligations: Contract Law
Obligations: The Law of Tort
Public International Law
Revenue Law (Textbook,
    Revision WorkBook and
    Cracknell's Statutes)
Succession (Textbook, Revision
    WorkBook and Cracknell's
    Statutes)

Mail order prices:	
Textbook	£15.95
150 Leading Cases	£12.95
Revision WorkBook	£10.95
Cracknell's Statutes	£11.95
Suggested Solutions 1999–2000	£6.95
Suggested Solutions 2000–2001	£6.95
Suggested Solutions 2001–2002	£6.95
101 Questions and Answers	£7.95
Law Update 2004	£10.95
Law Update 2005	£10.95

Please note details and prices are subject to alteration.

To complete your order, please fill in the form below:

Module	Books required	Quantity	Price	Cost
		Postage		
		TOTAL		

For the UK and Europe, add £4.95 for the first book ordered, then add £1.00 for each subsequent book ordered for postage and packing.
For the rest of the world, add 50% for airmail.

ORDERING

By telephone to Customer Services at 020 8317 6039, with your credit card to hand.

By fax to 020 8317 6004 (giving your credit card details).

Website: www.oldbaileypress.co.uk
E-Mail: customerservices@oldbaileypress.co.uk

By post to: Customer Services, Old Bailey Press at Holborn College, Woolwich Road, Charlton, London, SE7 8LN.

When ordering by post, please enclose full payment by cheque or banker's draft, or complete the credit card details below. You may also order a free catalogue of our complete range of titles from this address.

We aim to despatch your books within 3 working days of receiving your order. All parts of the form must be completed.

Name

Address

Postcode   E-Mail
                                                      Telephone

Total value of order, including postage: £

I enclose a cheque/banker's draft for the above sum, or

charge my   ☐ Access/Mastercard   ☐ Visa   ☐ American Express

Cardholder: ....

Card number

☐☐☐☐ ☐☐☐☐ ☐☐☐☐ ☐☐☐☐

Expiry date   ☐☐☐☐

Signature: ....Date: ....